THE ORIGINS OF

Thomas Moore

THE ORIGINS OF

Thomas Moore

ADVENTURER, FUR TRADER, NAVIGATOR
1654–C.1724

A Theory from a
Genetic and Historic Perspective

VICKY MOORE JACOBS

PFISTER | CALHOUN PRESS

The Origins of Thomas Moore

Adventurer, Fur Trader, Navigator | 1654–c.1724

A Theory from a Genetic and Historic Perspective

DESIGN | Curt Carpenter

ISBN 978-1-7376436-5-4

Printed in the United States of America

PFISTER | CALHOUN PRESS
1342 Raindrop Lane | Golden, Colorado 80401

Dedicated to my father

NORMAN EMILE MOORE, SR.

(1933 – 2020)

TABLE OF CONTENTS

LIST OF FIGURES

PREFACE

MUCH RESEARCH AND THOUSANDS OF HOURS have been spent by hundreds of people in search of more information regarding the background of Thomas Moore. The Thomas Moore I speak of was born, presumably in London, about 1654. His father's name was Edward Moore who was a Master Cannoneer in Dover Castle. Thomas Moore worked for Hudson's Bay Company from 1671 to 1678. It is also known that Thomas Moore married Jeanne Lemelin in Quebec City in 1690. By now, many of you recognize this Thomas Moore I depict as that elusive ancestor of yours for whom there is hardly any further information to be found other than what you already have known for years.

There have been posts, blogs and searches for others who may be related to this Thomas Moore in hopes of garnering more insight as to what Thomas Moore's origins were. Many of you have written up your genealogies, all in nice order, but have been unable to delve past the brick wall of Thomas Moore's ancestry. However, you, as well as I, frustratingly continued searching.

Indeed, I share your passion for wanting to know further about the history of this Moore family. I am an historian and have spent several years studying the historical events surrounding Thomas Moore, his father Edward Moore and the politics of their day. Luckily, we do have a small number of informative documented facts which will enable and guide us to establish our common ancestor's history.

Within this book, I explain concrete historical facts and how they may relate to coincidental events along our Moore's travels. The decades between 1600 and 1660 were a period of huge political turmoil for Scotland, England, Ireland and France. These turbulent times led to mass migration with the Plantation of Ulster in Northern Ireland and simultaneously to America's Virginia plantation and even further afield to Australia. Examining these historic events can lead us down a path which reveal details of human interaction and circumstances which can help uncover our family history.

Like you, I also have written up my extensive Moore genealogy of French-Canadian ancestors back to Thomas Moore in the 17th century. Of course, the most frustrating aspect has been the lack of specific details for Thomas Moore. In fact, there are conflicting details written about him.

He was Irish as stated by Pierre Georges Roy in his book *The Isle of Orleans*. He was English, as written by the nun's at L'Hotel Dieu in Quebec in 1690. His origins have been elusive.

For years, either Ireland or England were the two country choices in which to search for any further details regarding the origins of Thomas Moore. Search as I may, I was no further ahead with any new material in 2017 than I was in 1973 when I initially began my research! Determination was my calling to solve this mystery.

It wasn't until genetic DNA tests and more specifically Genetic Genealogy studies came into existence that I was pointed in the right direction as to where to look for answers to my questions. The introduction of DNA testing and Genetic Genealogy have become game changers for solving the mystery of one's ancestry. Once there was a specific location to look towards, the answers seemed to all fall into place.

The reader will be taken back in time to proceed along a path that the ancestors of Thomas Moore would have taken. My sound and reasonable theory will illuminate the history which was taking place throughout the years and, with the help of genetic genealogy, show the evolution of this Moore family who ended up as French Canadians along the St. Lawrence River Valley of Canada. ⚜

NOTE TO READER: *When I am referring to an ancestor of those people who are directly descended from Thomas Moore, I will be using the terms "our", "we" or "this study's Moore" to designate it. For example: Thomas Moore, born 1654, can also be referred to as "our" Thomas Moore. I will write similarly regarding Edward Moore (Thomas's father), born @1612, as "our" Edward Moore. Speaking in more general terms in referring to this family, I will refer to it as "this study's Moore" or "this Moore study."*

My voice will be heard to help with explanations in all **DISCUSSION** *sections located in various chapters. These sections will piece together the historic information in relationship with "this Moore study's" movements through time.*

DISCLAIMER: *The genealogies listed in this theory should in no way be added to Ancestry, Family Tree or any other genealogy website as there is no solid, conclusive proof for it to be added on such sites.*

ACKNOWLEDGMENTS

DNA STUDIES AND GENETIC GENEALOGY CHANGED MY LIFE. The knowledge of my ancestor's journey through life would not have been possible without these two scientific breakthroughs in my lifetime. What's more, the serendipitous chances of meeting distant cousins, Maurice Moore and Eric Moore, were highlights of my life, each of whom have written wonderful genealogies of their own. Having the chance to converse and get to know fellow genealogist, Langley Muir, during my book's discovery process brought further clarity for me. I greatly appreciate these men, including my father, Norman Moore, Sr., for taking the Y-DNA tests needed for my research. Without each of them, I would have no theory.

I extend gratitude to Dr. Tyrone Bowes for his ingenious work in the realm of genetic genealogy. He examined these Y-DNA tests, which explore only the male direct paternal line. He then detailed two Autosomal DNA studies, which look at both the male and female sides of the DNA picture. In linking the surnames of common ancestors retrieved from these specific tests with his *Surname Map* of the exact place families lived in the early censuses of Ireland and Scotland, he is able to correlate the location from where our ancestors hailed. The worldwide database of Y-DNA tests associated with surnames, as well as their locations in the world, are extensively detailed and growing more each year! DNA databases have allowed genetic scientists to capture specific information about the human race and their migration over the millennia.

I want to thank by brother, Norman Moore, Jr., for gifting me some important relevant books and for our many phone discussions theorizing possibilities of our ancestor's whereabouts. He was also insightful in helping me clarify my goal and to hone in on an appropriate title.

A big thank you goes to my sister, Christine Moore Skrocki, for her help in researching many details over several years, including many trips to Quebec City and even to Ireland. Thank you for being on this journey with me. Thank you to my sister, Michele Moore, for helping to motivate me throughout the process with her positive words of encouragement.

My deep appreciation to my husband, Scott, for his immeasurable patience through all the hours, dare I say years, of my reading endless history books and finally sitting at my computer to write this book at the expense of time that could have been spent with him.

To my forever friend, Jodi Buchan, for her encouragement and sharing her expertise in writing. Kudos to Curt Carpenter for strongly suggesting producing this book instead of leaving it obscurely on the internet nowhere to be found.

I was fortunate to share genealogy interests with my mother, Gloria Gunther Moore, who has worked extensively on her own sides' ancestors. It provided us endless conversations and memorable times digging for information together, side by side, in our trips to the Family History Library in Salt Lake City, Utah. We shared excitement over the smallest new details that would come to light.

Finally, and most importantly, to my father, Norman E. Moore, Sr., whose unending encouragement and excitement at finding out more information about his "Irish side" prompted me to try and solve its mystery.

INTRODUCTION

THIS BOOK WILL GIVE THE READER an in-depth insight into the origin of Thomas Moore's ancestors like none other available. It explores the details from the years of the Vikings into Scotland, to the Ulster Plantation, to the Irish Rebellion, the English Civil wars, and more. The information will give the reader a complete understanding of what Thomas Moore's ancestors lived through and the choices they made to survive and thrive. His history and ancestry have been elusive; until now.

Although there are no known documents which directly indicate the particulars of Thomas Moore's origins, it can be determined through four diverse aspects; DNA tests, Genetic Genealogy studies, documented facts broadly known about Thomas Moore and the sequences of historical events. All this information combined can come together to form an educated theory as to the origin of Thomas Moore, why they migrated to various places and, more importantly, why a man, born in London with a Scotch-Irish father, ended up living in French Canada.

Who is Thomas Moore?

Thomas Moore was born in the city of London, England in 1654 amidst a population of just below two hundred thousand. London was a bustling port town with an international presence.

Thomas led a varied and fascinating life. In October 1671, at the age of seventeen, he was hired by the nascent Hudson's Bay Company (HBC) which was headquartered in London. His first duty was to help unload the vast cache of furs which had just arrived in London from Hudson Bay aboard the ships *Wivenhoe* and *Prince Rupert*. The furs were to be sold at auction. The sale would fetch a large sum of money for the company.

Moore's first actual voyage expedition into Hudson Bay came in the spring of 1672. His immediate boss was Charles Bayly. He worked closely with many of the great navigators and fur traders of his time during his tenure with HBC, including Pierre-Esprit Radisson and Medard Chouart des Groseilliers. He was valuable to the company because he could speak Cree. He continued his work for the Hudson's Bay Company until 1678 as a fur trader and explorer. However, even though Thomas re-applied in 1678, he was not further engaged. In that same year, from his previous exploratory notes, Moore drew up his map of the *Western Shore of*

James Bay. Thomas Moore was one of only two HBC employees to have plotted a map for the company.

Eight years later in 1686, Moore was hired by the Compagnie du Nord, which was headquartered out of Quebec City with further investors in France. He was one of seventy adventurers, along with thirty soldiers, who was hired for an overland expedition from Montreal to the southern tip of James Bay. Their mission, which was led by Pierre Chevalier de Troyes, was to completely rid the English fur trading presence in Hudson Bay.

For the Quebec based company, Moore was again contracted by Pierre Le Moyne d'Iberville in 1688–89 as a ship's pilot. This time, the expedition into Hudson Bay was by water. The Compagnie du Nord had finally received the full backing of the French and Quebec provincial governments and were supplied the provisions and munitions needed to continue to go against English established forts.

In 1706, Moore was commander of *La Maria*. He was commissioned by the Governor of Quebec to sail to New England and to exchange forty-three English prisoners held by Quebec in exchange for fifty-seven French prisoners held in New England.

Thomas Moore became the pilot for Guillaume Gaillard in 1707 *"to go privateering aboard 'La-Nostre-Dame-de-Victoire' against the enemies of the state, in the vicinity of Cape Breton, Newfoundland, the Grand Banks, and elsewhere."* Sadly, he and his investors came up empty handed.

In 1713, Thomas Moore was master pilot on a ship sailing to Labrador. He died before 1724 as the marriage certificate of that year for his son, Pierre, states that his father was dead.

Most of the above information has been gleaned from the *Dictionary of Canadian Biography* for Thomas Moore (Thorman, Thomas Moore 1969, revised 1982) and *The Isle of Orleans* by Pierre Georges Roy's chapter entitled *"An Irish Seaman in 1690"* (P. G. Roy 1928, 345).

Additional sources describe what nationality Thomas Moore was, albeit in opposition. One is titled *"An Irish Seaman in 1690"* (P. G. Roy 1928, 345–6). Here, the author Pierre Georges Roy firmly declares that Thomas Moore was an Irish Catholic from Dover, England who settled at Saint-Laurent on the Island of Orleans in 1690 [Appendix 1].

One source explains that Thomas Moore is an Englishman and a native of London (Talbot 1971–1978, 206). Another source relates that Thomas Moore was of St. Mary's parish in Dover, Kent County, England (Jette 1983, 826) . Yet another source skirts the issue altogether by simply stating that his parents resided in Dover, England, parish of St. Mary the Virgin (Denissen 1987, 862), [Appendix 2].

Further information documented about Thomas Moore is that he was the son of Edward Moore, a master cannoneer at Dover Castle in England, and Cecilia Richardson, a native of Dover. In 1690, Thomas adjured his Anglican faith at L'Hotel Dieu and became Catholic. In the same year, he married Jeanne Lemelin, daughter of Jean Lemelin dit Tourangeau and Marguerite Brassard. The couple bought property and lived in the village of Saint-Laurent on the Ile d'Orleans which is across the St. Laurence River from the capital of Quebec City.

Thomas and Jeanne gave birth to six children in total but only two lived to adulthood; Pierre, who was the fourth son and was born 10 September 1704, and Marie-Lousie, the only daughter, who was born 19 November 1708. Unfortunately, Marie-Louise and her husband, Louis Mallet, were convicted of counterfeiting money by imitating "Card Money"; the currency being used in New France at the time due to the lack of hard cash from France. Husband and wife, who were only twenty-eight at the time, were both hanged in the public square of the lower town of Quebec that very same day.

Thomas Moore's son, Pierre Moore, lived to become the son who carried on Thomas Moore's family name and DNA.

Thomas Moore has been imprinted in history through the documents he left behind. However, in a more tangible way, he has also been kept alive by the thousands of descendants who still roam this earth. All serious family historians in search of information on Thomas Moore have come across this same printed material easily accessed through simple Google searches these days. What used to be cavernous library detective work has been transformed by the internet's vast resources easily available to all. ⚜

DIRECT LINEAGE OF THOMAS MOORE TO THE AUTHOR

I

Edward Moore m. *Cecilia Richardson*[1]

II

Thomas Moore m. 6 Apr 1690 Jeanne Lemelin

III

Pierre Moore m. 26 Nov 1724 Genevieve-Louisa Gendron

IV

Francois Moore[2] m. 26 Nov 1753 Marie-Louise Demeules

V

Laurence Moore m. 3 Mar 1794 Susanne Pineau dit Laperle

VI

Paul Moore m. abt. 1828 Felicity Robitaille

VII

Francis Moore m. 31 May 1859 Euphrosine Jeanne Boyer

VIII

Alexander Moore m. 13 Apr 1896 Katherine Mabel Benoit

IX

Oscar Paul Moore m. 17 Apr 1933 Marie Beulah Nellett

X

Norman Emile Moore, Sr. m. 9 May 1953 Gloria Joan Gunther

XI

Vicky Cecelia Moore m. 21 Jul 1990 R. Scott Jacobs

---

[1] This study researches the possibility of Cecilia Richardson being Edward Moore's second marriage.

[2] Three direct descendants from three of Thomas Moore's great-grandsons (Francois Moore's sons) are the DNA studies for this book.

But what does the DNA of the descendants of Thomas Moore tell us of the origin of his ancestors?

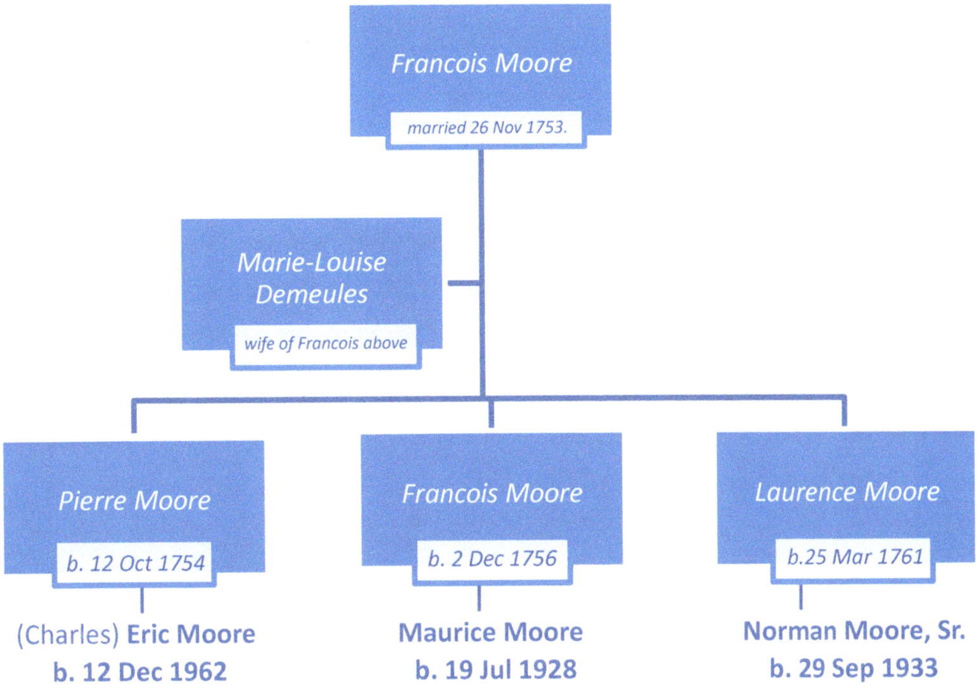

Figure 1. Diagram of those tested

Three of Francois Moore and Marie-Louise Demeules' sons' direct descendants were tested as studies for this book.

(Charles) Eric Moore, Maurice Moore and Norman Moore, Sr. are all descendants from one common ancestor named Francois Moore-IV (Pierre-III, Thomas-II, Edward-I). Francois is Thomas Moore's grandson. Francois Moore married 26 Nov 1753 in St. Jean, Ile d'Orleans, Quebec, Canada, to Marie-Louise Demeules (Desmeules) and they had six sons.

–**Eric Moore** descends from their oldest son named Pierre, b. 12 Oct 1754, Saint Laurent, I.O.

–**Maurice Moore** descends from their second oldest son named Francois, b. 2 Dec 1756, St. Charles, Bellechasse.

–**Norman Moore, Sr.** descends from the 4th oldest son named Laurence (Laurent), b. 25 Mar 1761, St. Charles, Bellechasse, Quebec.

All three men took Y-DNA tests. Y-DNA tests ONLY explore the straight paternal line. mtDNA ONLY tests directly through the female line.

DNA Tests

DNA testing for family historians became available on a commercial basis in the year 2000 through FamilyTree DNA (FTdna). Autosomal DNA tests through Family Tree were available in 2010. The data bases of those submitting their DNA for testing across the spectrum of commercial sites have continued to grow exponentially since then.

FamilyTree DNA is the only company to offer dedicated Y-DNA and mtDNA testing. They also offer Surname and Haplogroup projects. It is the company that is the best for figuring out distant ancestry. It is great for those who already have their genealogy tree and want to go beyond the paper trail. They had 1.4 million customers as of November 2021 (McDermott 2021). Neither Family Tree DNA, MyHeritage nor GEDmatch sell, lease or otherwise share their customers' DNA (Estes, 2019: The Year and Decade of Change 2019).

The FamilyTree Y-DNA test for Norman Moore, Sr. was completed on 7 Feb 2007. His autosomal test results were 30 May 2017.

The Family Tree Y-DNA test for Eric Moore was March of 2007.

I received each admixture result in percentages which divvied out the various geographical regions from where our ancestors were suspected to hail. [fig. 2] An admixture test's timeline equals roughly 500 years ago. The following figure has been updated to the most recent results.

FamilyTree DNA results as of 17 April 2019		Updated as of September 2021	
Norman Moore, Sr. | Y-DNA test shows Haplogroup R-M512/R1a			
European	98%	European	100%
*West & Central Europe	88%	**Western Europe**	**92%**
*SE Europe	10%	*England, Wales, Scots	57%
Trace Results		*Central Europe	26%
*North Africa	<2%	*Ireland	9%
		Southern Europe	**8%**
Eric Moore | Y-DNA test shows Haplogroup R-M512/R1a			
European	100%	European	100%
*West & Central Europe	94%	**Western Europe**	**92%**
*British Isles	6%	*England, Wales, Scots	57%
		*Central Europe	26%
		*Ireland	9%
		Southern Europe	**8%**

**NOTE: Both Norman and Eric had both parents of French-Canadian descent. West Europe includes UK (which is England, Scotland, Wales and Northern Ireland), Ireland, France, Belgium, etc. Central Europe includes Germany, Austria, Hungary, etc. SE Europe includes Austria, Albania, Bosnia, Bulgaria, Croatia, Greece, parts of Italy and Ukraine, etc. These countries all show the migration pattern of the R1a Haplogroup.*

Figure 2. FamilyTree DNA test results for Norman Moore, Sr. and Eric Moore

Searching for evidence of an English or an Irish heritage with this DNA test still left me in limbo. So, in 2013, I tried again only this time with AncestryDNA. The results were still vague and not specific enough to reveal whether the ancestors were either English or Irish.

AncestryDNA testing began in 2012. It is the best choice for beginning genealogy and family history research. They have the most extensive database, so one will find the most DNA matches with this site. It is great for starting your genealogy tree. You do not need a subscription to build your own family tree. A subscription is primarily for the research side of Ancestry and allows you to view billions of genealogical records. They had 20 million customers as of November 2021 (McDermott 2021). Ancestry and 23andMe sell consumer's DNA to both known and unknown partners if customers opt-in to additional research. Furthermore, Ancestry, as of September 2, 2021 stated that they can do anything they want with every image in your tree. With that, one should consider the cost of your privacy by creating a tree on Ancestry vs. the ease of accessing other people's trees and all of the other information available on their site (Estes 2021).[3]

The original AncestryDNA test date for Norman Moore, Sr. was 2013. The original AncestryDNA test date for Maurice Moore was July of 2016.

The following statistics are the results of these admixture tests:

Norman Moore, Sr. | Y-DNA tests show him belonging in Haplogroup R1a

AncestryDNA as of 17 April 2019		Updated as of July 2020		Updated - September 2021	
France	94%	France	91%	France	91%
Norway	5%	Norway	3%	Norway	3%
Native American	1%	Indigenous Amer North	1%	Indigenous Amer North	<1%
Additional Communities stated:		England & NW Europe	5%	England & NW Europe	3%
St. Laurence River French Settlers				Ireland	3%
Montreal & Detroit French Settlers					

NOTE: Both of Norman Moore's parents were of French-Canadian descent

Maurice Moore | Y-DNA tests show him belonging in Haplogroup R1a

AncestryDNA as of 17 April 2019		Updated as of July 2020		Updated - September 2021	
France	60%	France	69%	France	77%
Great Britain	26%	Eng and NW Europe	10%	------------------	-----
Ireland/Scotland/Wales	7%	Scotland, N. Ireland	8%	Scotland	6%
Germanic Europe	6%	Sweden	8%	Sweden & Denmark	8%
East Europe & Russia	1%	Ireland	3%	Ireland	3%
		Wales	2%	Wales	6%

Additional Communities stated for Maurice Moore:

St. Laurence River French Settlers, Beauce, Quebec French Settlers

NOTE: Maurice's father was French Canadian and his mother was English

Figure 3. AncestryDNA results for Norman Moore, Sr. and Maurice Moore

---

3 My personal tree is within my computer on a purchased software program from Family Tree.

In comparing the admixture results[4] from both Family Tree and Ancestry, of course one can see the French percentages as very high. There are further indications of a high percentage of British Isles/West Europe which would include Northern Ireland/Scotland/Wales as well as England. Further, there is also an indication of Norway and Sweden, showing Viking heritage.

These tests were interesting but not specific enough for my research. I was left longing for more details.

Genetic Genealogy Study

Through an online genealogy blog, I came across information regarding a compelling technique discovered by Dr. Tyrone Bowes which made complete sense to me. Being that he only specializes in genetic genealogy studies from Ireland, Scotland, England and Wales, his information was just what I needed. Per his request, I uploaded the FamilyTree DNA information I had for Norman Moore, Sr. to Ysearch, a site that captured any and all brand's DNA tests for their data base. Having completed this upload, Dr. Bowes set out to perform his first Case Study to decipher Norman Moore's *Paternal Ancestral Genetic Homeland* which was completed on 27 May 2017 [See Appendix 3 for the full report].

Within this vast data base of hundreds of thousands of DNA samples, many specific surnames showed up as being "genetically related" to Norman Moore. With this information in hand, Dr. Bowes went to work searching his tedious individualized country *Surname Maps*[5] which indicate the location of farmer's lands from early 1800 censuses. These farmers had remained on their lands for generations, interacting and intermarrying with surrounding neighbors and neighbor's relatives. Neighbors lived in clustered groups for generations, not moving around as subsequent generations do these days.

Taking a close look at the eighteen surnames which were identified as Norman Moore's "genetic cousins," Dr. Bowes searched on his *Ireland Surname Map*. None of those eighteen names were clustered together. Dr. Bowes then searched on his *England Surname Map*. Again, nothing was found as a cluster for those specific eighteen "genetic cousin" names.

Finally, to my ultimate surprise, he found the group of "genetic cousin" names clustered together in the southwest of Scotland around the Isles of Argyll, specifically with the town of Rothesay on the Isle of Bute at its center. According to Dr. Tyrone Bowes, ". . . if the surnames revealed in a Y-DNA test did not arise from a group of related males living when surnames first appeared [around 1000 years ago], then what is the alternative explanation? Where else would these surnames have come from?"

---

[4] Admixture analysis is a method of inferring someone's geographical origins based on an analysis of their ancestry. It is one of the components of an autosomal DNA test.

[5] Bowes has prepared individual *Surname Maps* for England, Scotland, Wales and Ireland. They are for purchase on his website.

Scotland being the origin of Thomas Moore's ancestors was never on my radar and it had never been mentioned in any of the material written about Thomas Moore! Furthermore, Dr. Bowes was able to identify Mr. Norman Moore's DNA as being typical DNA from Viking Heritage [Appendix 3].

However, we need not take Dr. Bowes' word for it solely. The *FamilyTree Big Y 700* genetic DNA test for Norman Moore, Sr. verified the empirical data of the Bowes report and proved the descent from Norwegian Vikings. [fig. 4, 5]

In the beginning, DNA studies were dismissed by "*peers who regarded archives as paramount*" (Khatchadourian 2021). As time has marched on, the methods of DNA tests and genetic genealogy have become more science-based and more mainstream; an addition to archives as part of the whole picture of one's ancestral background.

The three following genetic studies by Dr. Tyrone Bowes may be explored in full detail within their respective Appendices.

• *Pinpointing the Moore Scottish Paternal Ancestral Genetic Homeland:*
A Scottish Case Study
The person tested was Norman Moore, Sr. It was completed on 27 May 2017 [Appendix 3]. This study explores the specific details of Dr. Bowes technique in deciphering the origins of Norman Moore's ancestry, which was explained above.

• *An Autosomal DNA Case Study*
The person tested was Eric Moore. It was completed on 25 July 2019 [Appendix 4]. This study will be discussed in full in Chapter Five. It reveals the secondary and tertiary locations for the migration of the Moore family.

• *Reconstruction the Moore Ancient Paternal Ancestral Journey*
The person tested was Norman Moore, Sr. It was completed on 19 June 2017 [Appendix 5]. With this report, Dr. Bowes details the location of this Moore study's Viking journey.

But First Some DNA Terms and DNA background

The study of DNA has a language all its own. In order to understand the following information, it is necessary to understand some of the basic terms.

DNA (deoxyribonucleic acid) is a molecule composed of two polynucleotide chains that coil around each other to form a double helix carrying genetic instructions for the development, function, growth and reproduction of all known organisms. It is a self-replication material that is present in nearly all living organisms. It is the carrier of genetic information. It strings together some three billion pairs of nucleotides, each represented by an initial; A, C, G, and T; the programming language of genetic code.

These thread-like structures, are divided into twenty-three coiled strands and are called chromosomes. Stranded chromosome pairs numbered 1–22 are called autosomes. Each parent contributes one chromosome to each pair so that offspring get half of their chromosomes from their mother and half from their father.

The 23rd stranded pair is labelled either the X or Y chromosome and it determines one's biological sex. Females (XX) inherit an X-chromosome from each of their parents, while males (XY) inherit an X-chromosome from their mother and a Y-chromosome from their father.

To simplify the definition of a chromosome, it is a strand of DNA that is encoded with genes. Humans have twenty-two pairs of these chromosomes plus the two sex chromosomes for a total of forty-six. Chromosomes help ensure that DNA is replicated and distributed appropriately during cell division (generic Google and Wikipedia sites).

There are three major types of genealogical DNA tests:
Autosomal (atDNA), mitochondrial (mtDNA), and Y-DNA.

As the science continued to evolve, it became possible to analyze bits of information from the Y-chromosome known as Y-DNA. Y-chromosomes are passed on from father to son with little mutation, and because surnames historically were passed down the same way, the confluence is useful to genealogists.

Researchers could use Y-DNA to establish the pedigree of a man with an unknown identity. This is similar for mtDNA, which is passed down on the maternal line. In this way, Y-DNA and mt-DNA have genuine applications for tracing ancestry.

Autosomal DNA tests look at chromosome pairs 1–22 and the X part of the 23rd chromosome. Autosomal DNA tests track tiny genetic mutations. These mutations, called single-nucleotide polymorphisms, or SNP(s), combine in unique patterns that are passed from one generation to the next: a child will share 50% of them with each parent, about 25% with each grandparent, 12.5% with each great-grandparent, and so on. The unit for measuring these DNA segments are called centimorgans (Hay 2021).

The more shared DNA or centimorgans, the closer in relation one is to another. Conversely, the smaller amount of shared DNA with someone shows relationships much further back in time; even up to 1000 years ago. These are the "genetic relatives" used by Dr. Tyrone Bowes' studies.

Ancestral societies which share SNP patterns are called haplogroups. Most haplogroups can be further subdivided multiple times into sub-clades. The sub-clade group for those who tested for this book's study is within the R1a Haplogroup.

In 2010, a couple of men named Curtis Rogers and John Olson created a web site called GEDmatch. Their original intent was to support software that could compare family trees. Anyone who had taken any brand of commercial DNA tests, ie: Family Tree DNA, AncestryDNA, 23 and Me,

My Heritage DNA, etc., were encouraged to upload their DNA Kits or profiles for free to the GEDmatch platform which continued to capture a huge data base of participants. Soon the site allowed segment-by segment comparisons of autosomal DNA. GEDmatch was an open site. It was a non-profit, commercially free site for serious genealogists (Khatchadourian 2021).

Two very similar sites to GEDmatch were opened by FamilyTree DNA (FTdna). They were called Ysearch.org and Mitosearch.org and were started in 2010 as well. They also encouraged people from any other testing company to download their kit information for comparison purposes. The vast majority of DNA results on these two sites were contributed to by FTdna customers, but they also managed Y-DNA and mtDNA results from customers of other testing companies.

Ysearch was the site that Dr. Tyrone Bowes accessed to utilize the largest data base possible to find the matches for his genetic genealogy studies. It was from this data base that the genetic study of Norman Moore, Sr. took place in May of 2017. Luckily, I had hired Norman Moore's test while all that information was still available!

By 24 May 2018, only one year later, Ysearch and Mitosearch both were no longer accessible due to privacy laws set by EU General Data Protection (GDPR). Unfortunately, many of the results uploaded to Ysearch and Mitosearch have been lost forever because the participant has either passed away or is no longer active.

It was a huge loss to Bowes's research and genetic genealogy in general. However, over time, the data base of the FamilyTree DNA site grew substantially. Because of the huge influx of new data and with the aid of his extensive *Surname Maps*, Bowes is still able to clearly indicate a person's origin using their DNA information.

By 2018, GEDmatch was closed to the general public due to privacy laws as well. In December of 2019, GEDmatch was acquired by a forensic firm named Verogen and is only open to crime genealogy in homicides and sexual assault to help identify perpetrators through DNA. It has helped to solve thousands of cold cases (Khatchadourian 2021).

FamilyTree Big Y 700

To substantiate Dr. Bowes's information, I sought the *Big Y 700* test from Family Tree. 700 individual SNPs were tested to confirm Norman Moore, Sr.'s haplogroup. I wasn't disappointed.

The *FamilyTree Big Y 700* test results for Norman Moore, Sr. were confirmed on 22 November 2021. He belongs to Haplogroup R-BY71057. In studying the information, Norman Moore, Sr. was once again confirmed as being from Viking Heritage as well as having links to Scotland. For specific information's sake, his SNPs are listed here below in full [fig. 4].

Phylogenetic Tree for Norman E. Moore, Sr.
from FTdna Big Y 700 testing as of 22 Nov 2021 *(to be read from the bottom up)*

SNP	***Estimated* Date /years ago[6]**	**Notes** (Hay 2021)
R-BY71057	1100 +/- 600	b. @ the year 952 CE
R-YP4241	1200 +/- 300	Norway
R-S6821		Norway
R-CTS4179	2,400 +/- 400	Scandinavia, Scotland & Ireland (Viking Heritage)
R-L448	2,800 +/- 500	
R-S5153		
R-S5301		
R-S4458		
R-Z284	4000 +/- 600	Scandinavian subclade with an epicenter in central Norway. It is found also in places colonized by Norwegian Vikings in Scotland, Eng. & Ireland. Copper to Early Bronze Age.
R-Y2395		Scandinavian branch
R-Z282	4,900 +/- 700	
R-Z283		R1a1a1b1 - Main Central & East European Branch
R-PF6162		
R-M417	5,600 +/- 800	R1a1a1 - 99% of modern R1a descends from this branch. Bronze Age onwards.
R-M198/R-M512		R1a1a
R-M459		R1a1
R-M420	18,000 +/- 3000	R1a – Paleolithic Northeast Europe & Siberia
R-M173	23,000 +/- 3000 R1	
R-M207	27,000 +/- 4000	**R Haplogroup** - Originated in North Asia just before the Last Glacial Maximum (26,000-19,000 ybp[7])

Figure 4. Phylogenetic Tree for Norman Moore, Sr.

[6] At this time, 2022, there are *no official* dates for this Haplogroup. FamilyTree DNA is working diligently on this at the present time. These dates are only their *estimated* dates.

[7] Ybp stands for "years before present." Present is signified as 1965.

Official Scientific Phylogenetic Tree Haplogroup for R1a (Abbreviated)

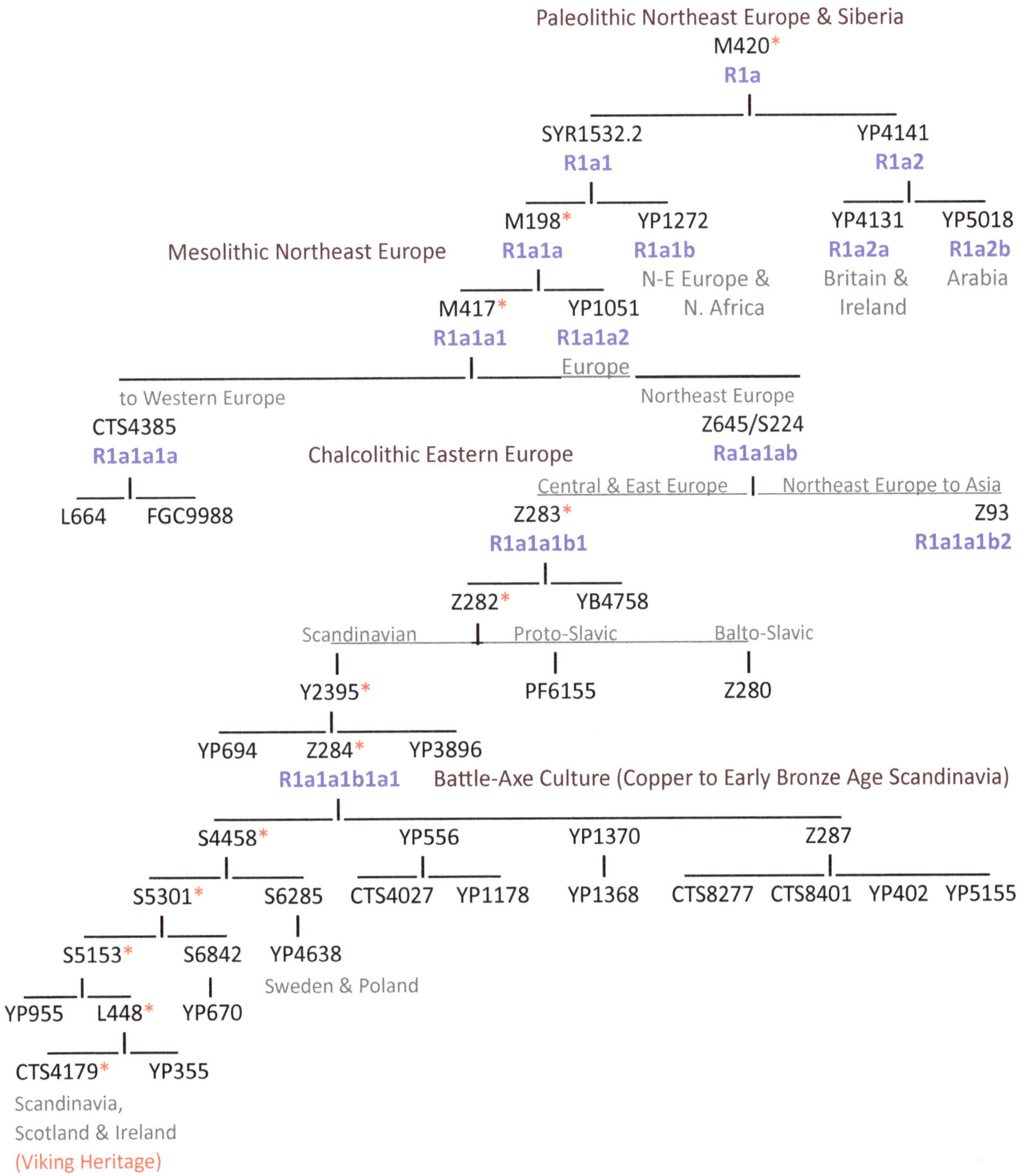

***Figure 5. Official Scientific Phylogenetic Tree of Haplogroup R1a** (as of February 2017)*

Source: Adapted from https://www.eupedia.com/europe/haplogroup_R1a_Y_DNA.shtml (Hay 2021).

Those SNPs which match Norman E. Moore, Sr.'s SNPs are marked with a red asterisk*.

Arrival of the major Y-chromosome haplogroups to Scotland (Beaty 2009, 33)

10,000 BCE[8]	Evidence that small groups of foraging peoples had reached the Scottish coast: **R1b**
4,000 BCE	Brought to Scotland during Neolithic times or Roman occupation being 43–410 A.D. Evidence of agriculture appears in Scotland: **? E1b1b, J1, G1?**
400-900 CE	Anglo-Saxon invasions: R1
500-1000 CE	DalRaida Kingdom. Influx of Irish immigrants to Scotland: **R1b & I1a**
800-1100 CE	The Viking Age in Scotland. Occupation of the Isles and coastal region: **I1a & R1a**

An allele is one of two, or more, versions of the same gene at the same place on a chromosome. A haplogroup is a combination of alleles at different chromosomal regions that are closely linked and that tend to be inherited together.

Haplogroups such as **R1a**, G, D, E, J2 and K are often shared by individuals of the same surname supporting the concept that surname sharing is often due to common ancestry. Y-chromosome data, typically less diverse and more locally distributed within Europe, is suited for an investigation of Scottish ancestry. (Beaty 2009, 95, 102)

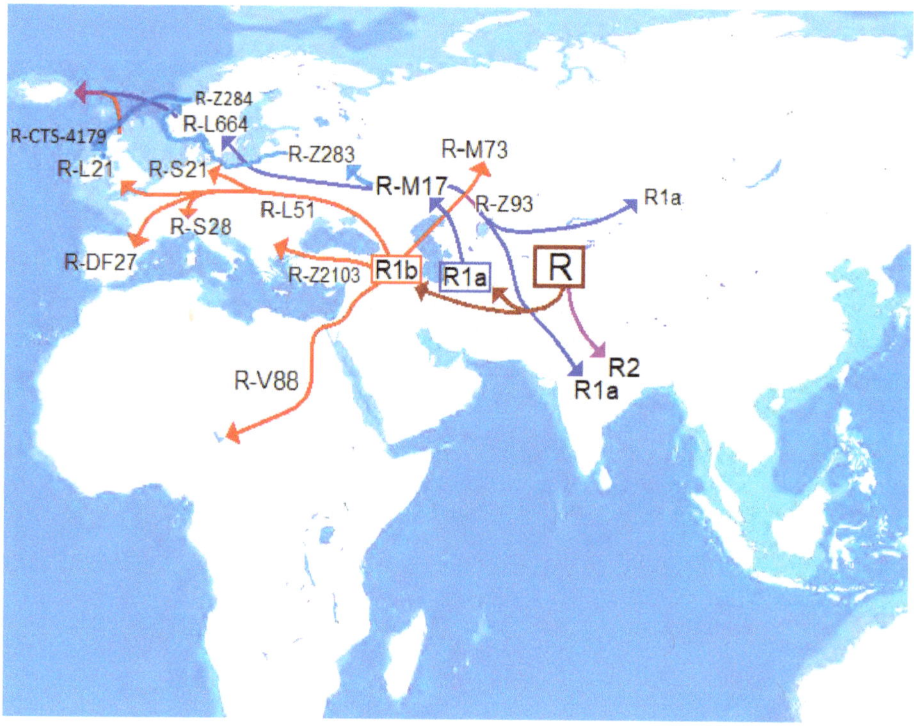

Figure 6. Haplogroup R with subclades R1a and R1b

Source: https://www.commons.wikimedia.org/wiki/File:Haplogroup_R_(T-DNA).png

[8] BCE stands for Before Common Era. CE stands for Common Era. These are secular terms replacing BC and AD.

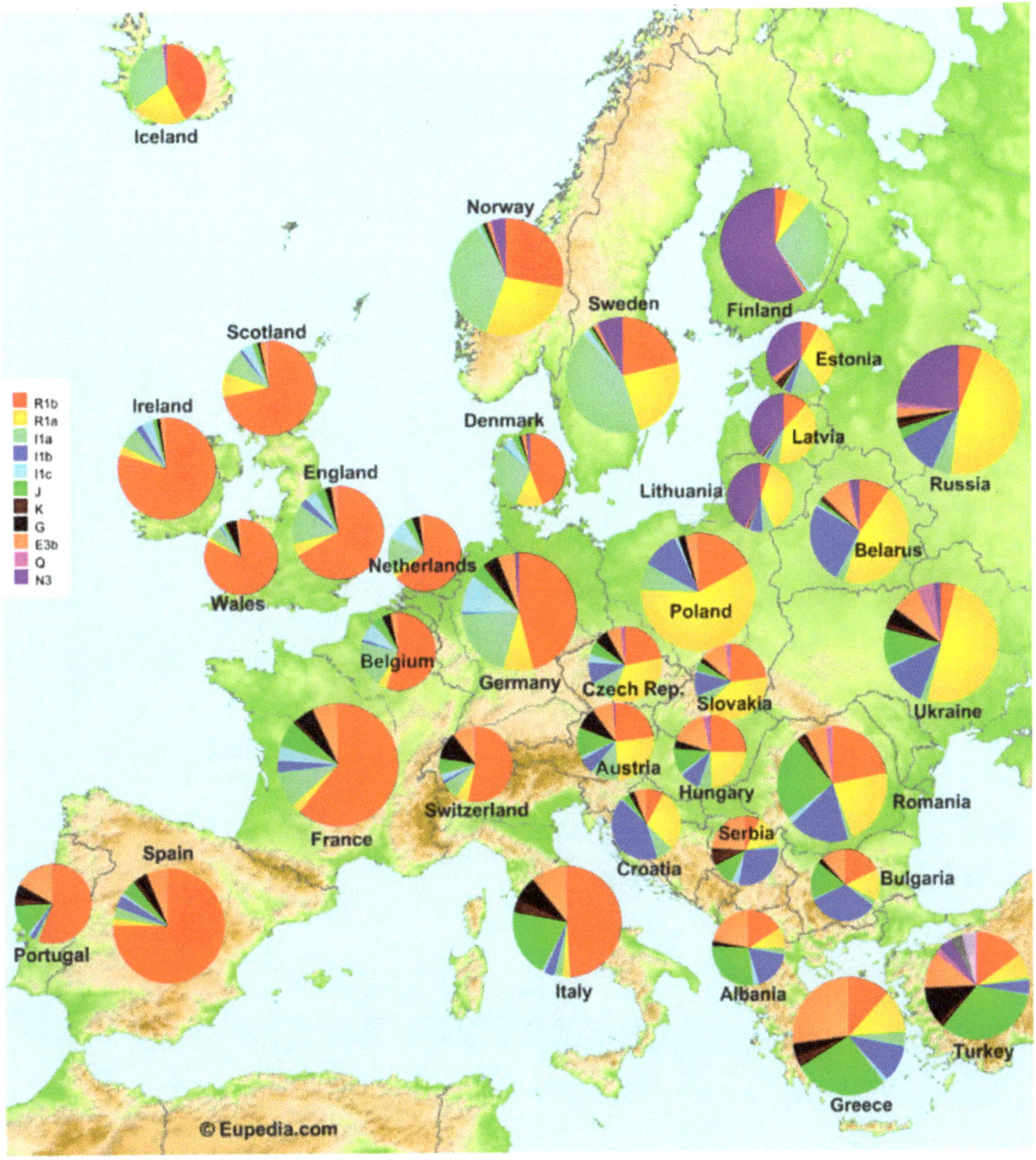

Figure 7. Genetic Map of Europe

Source: https://www.brilliantmaps.com/the-genetic-map-of-Europe (Eupedia contributors 2015)

Now, this was a whole new world for me to look for answers! Research into this avenue of study commenced at once. Forget my dead-ends of the past. All at once, the historic information started falling into place. The history of Rothesay, Isle of Bute, does indeed show Vikings on the island as early as the 9th century. The Isle of Bute was part of the Lordship of the Isles. Chapter ONE will begin with this history. ⚜

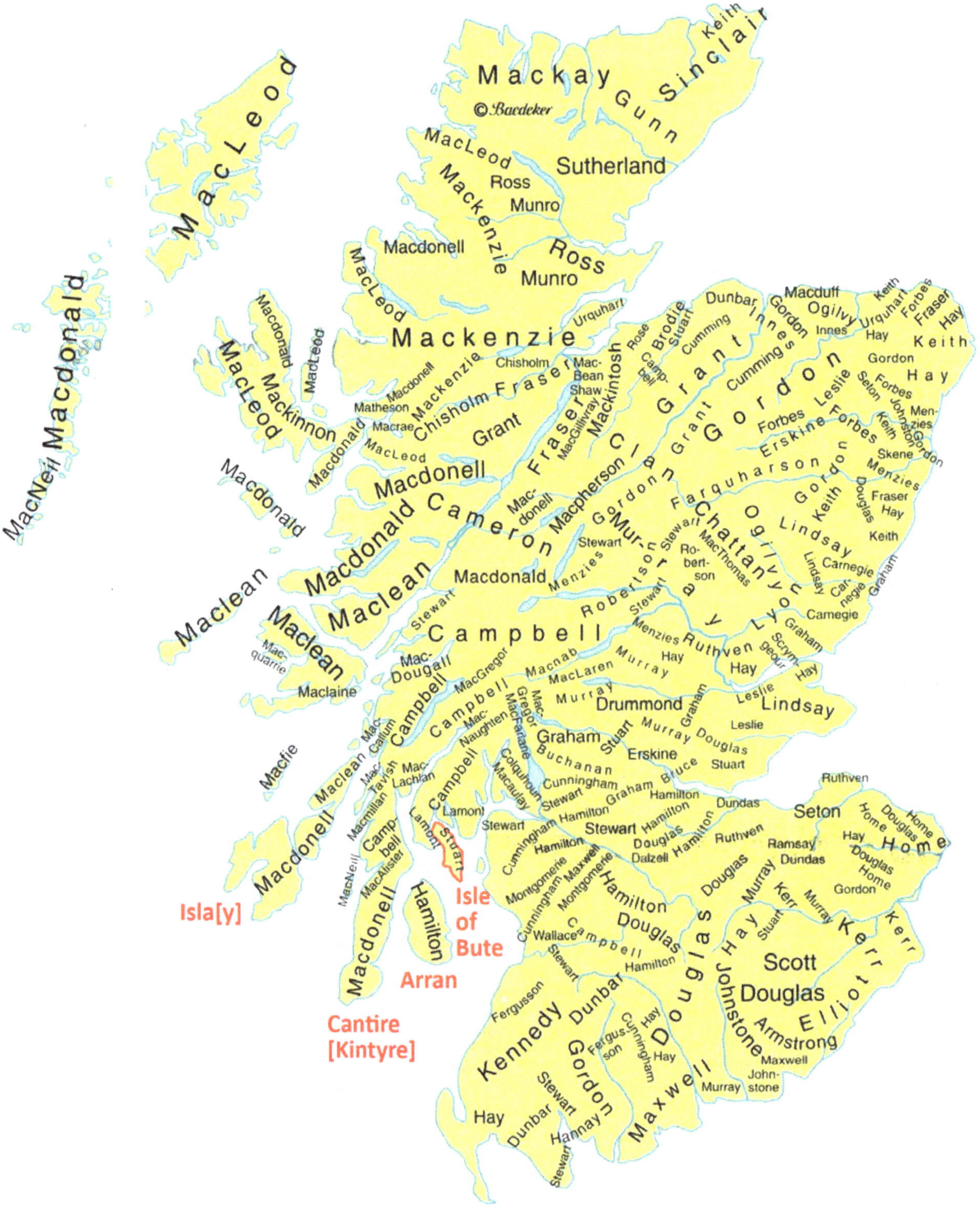

Figure 8. The Clans of Scotland

Source: Map with permission from https://www.planetware.com/map/scotland-clans-of-the-Scottish-highlands-and-lowlands-map-sco-sco32.htm.!

Figure 9. County and Province Map of Ireland and Northern Ireland

Source: Map courtesy of Family History Center, Salt Lake City, Utah.

"Genetic Genealogy is a Lead Generator."

—CECE MOORE
Genetic Genealogist

1

Clans MacDonnell & Stewart Intersect with Muir

THE MACDONNELL AND STEWART FAMILIES were integral to the development of the Isle of Bute in the territory of the Lordship of the Isles. Having transplanted to the Isle of Bute from Norway in the Viking age, Thomas Moore's ancestors would have become vassals and adherents of these powerful families.

Intermarriages

Robert the Bruce (1274–1329) united the Scottish clans and became the first King of Scotland in 1306. His daughter, Marjorie Bruce, married Walter Stewart, High Steward of Scotland.[9] Their son was Robert Stewart. In 1346/7, Robert married Elizabeth Muir, (Mure, More) of the house of Rowallan in Ayrshire, Scotland. Robert succeeded his childless uncle, David II of Scotland in 1371 as King Robert II, continuing the succession of the Royal House of Stewart (Stuart).[10] Their eldest son, John Stewart, became King Robert III in 1390. Two of Robert III's sons were the elder David Stewart, Duke of Rothesay, and James Stewart who became King James I in 1406 after Robert III's death at Rothesay Castle on Isle of Bute.

The daughter of Robert II and Elizabeth Muir, Margaret Stewart, married John MacDonnell, Lord of Isla and Cantire (Kintyre) in 1350. Their second son was John Mor MacDonnell who married Margery Byset in 1399 (R. G. Hill 1873, 30 #32). Margery was the sole heir of her father's extensive Antrim lands in Ulster, Northern Ireland.

Therefore, both King James Stewart I of Scotland and John Mor MacDonnell, Lord of the Isles, were grandsons of King Robert II and thus closely related as first cousins.

---

9 High Steward of Scotland is a heredity title.

10 The present Queen Elizabeth II descends from the Royal House of Stewart on both sides of her family.

Figure 10. Territory of the Lordship of the Isles

Source: Map from https://www.wikitree.com/photo/png/Ragnaldsson-1.

The MacDonnell Clan | The Earls of Antrim

The MacDonnell clan of Scotland were known as Lords of the Isles (R. G. Hill 1873, 1). From the date of the marriage alliance between the families of Byset and MacDonnell in about the year 1399, several members of the latter began to settle on the Antrim coast in Ulster (R. G. Hill 1873, 35). The Bysets had purchased extensive lands on the Antrim coast from the Norman, Richard de Burgh, Earl of Ulster. Before the close of the thirteenth century, the Bysets held the seven lordships of the Glynns; and a century later, the sole heir was Margery Byset. As mentioned above, Margery Byset married John Mor MacDonnell.

Years earlier, the head of Clann Domnaill, Alexander Og Mac Domnaill, King of Argyll, as well as his first cousin, Donald of Isla[y], were killed with Edward Bruce (Robert's brother) in 1318 at the Battle of Fochart during the end of the Edward's disastrous invasion of Ireland (1315–1318.) The death of the head of the related Clann Ruaidri, King of the Hebrides, in the same conflict, proves the strong support from the Clan Domnaill (Clan MacDonnell) for Edward the Bruce's attempt at conquering Ireland (Duffy 1991, 312). Continuous fighting over domination of the Scottish Isles continued over many years.

Finally, having had enough of these on-going power struggles, King of Scotland James III[11] and his council deemed there should be *"but one King in Scotland"* (R. G. Hill 1873, 29) and the formal surrender of the title "Kingdom of the Isles" took place in 1476. James III and the Scottish Parliament passed a law which prohibited Alexander of Isla and Cantire from *"ever setting foot on Scottish soil again or ever owning an acre of land in that kingdom"* (R. G. Hill 1873, 36).

Subsequently, Alexander MacDonnell, former Lord of Isla and Cantire and son of John Cahanagh MacDonnell, had to leave Scotland in about the year 1493 (R. G. Hill 1873, 78 #106). Following along with Alexander, leader of the Clan Ian Vohr (descendants of John Mor MacDonnell), into their new lands of Antrim, Ulster, were not only a large number of his own broken clan, but also many soldiers from several smaller clans (R. G. Hill 1873, 35–36).

Alexander MacDonnell is traditionally said to have occupied the fortress of Dunanynie overlooking Ballycastle Bay, Barony of Cary in Antrim (R. G. Hill 1873, 38). Alexander, who died in 1540, had a famous son named Sorley Boy, d. 1589, who had a son named Randal Arranagh MacDonnell. In 1586, a ceremony was held in Dublin Castle in front of a portrait of Queen Elizabeth I which granted Sorley Boy, who was now in his eighties, all his conquests from the MacQuillans. These lands consisted of the "tuogh"[12] from the Bush River to the Bann River, which included Dunluce, as well as the three further "tuoghs" of Dunseverick, Loughghile and Ballymoney. In return, he received an English patent giving him the legal title to his territories. He was also made the queen's constable of Dunluce Castle (McDonnell 2004, 14–16). These territories are presently within the area referred to as "The Route" [fig. 11].

Although the MacDonnells had held lands in northern Antrim since around the year 1555 (R. G. Hill 1873, 123–4) which they had acquired through continuous fighting with the MacQuillans, they weren't granted formal lands for Plantation from James VI and I until the year 1603 through Randal Arranagh MacDonnell (R. G. Hill 1873, 196).

Randal Arranagh MacDonnell was fully named Randal Arranagh mac Sorley MacDonnell indicating that he had been fostered out to the Stewart family of Arran, and that he was the famous Sorley Boy's son. No sooner had Randal moved into Dunluce Castle in 1601 than the rebel leader, Hugh O'Neill, Earl of Tyrone, requested Clan MacDonnell's help in fighting the English, with the aid of the Spanish, at Kinsale, County Cork [fig. 9]. Randal Arranagh set out from Dunluce in November 1601 (McDonnell 2004, 19) with about 800 of Clandonnell to come

---

[11] King of Scotland 1460–1488

[12] Tuogh was an English transliteration of the Irish word "tuath" meaning a tribal territory.

to O'Neill's aid. Having marched the full length of Ireland from the north to the south in severe winter weather conditions, Tyrone's Irish army was devastatingly defeated at Kinsale with most of Randal's men perishing at the disastrous battle (R. G. Hill 1873, 194 #2,5).[13]

It was at this point that Randal MacDonnell decided that it would be in his best interest to switch sides and surrender to the English. In the Fall of 1602, MacDonnell offered to fight against Tyrone on the side of Sir Arthur Chichester, the English Governor garrisoned at Carrickfergus Castle (R. G. Hill 1873, 196). As a result, by letters patent dated May 28, 1603, the new King James VI and I confirmed the grant first given by Queen Elizabeth I in 1602 to Randal Arranagh of his Antrim lands back in what was technically known as surrender and regrant[14] (R. G. Hill 1873, 196).

The entire clan territory in the Route and the Glynns, covering 333,907 acres between Larne and Coleraine, was granted to MacDonnell in return for a promise of good behavior, and to transform the old clan territory into an English-style estate (McDonnell 2004, 19) [fig. 11].

Randal Arranagh received the honor of knighthood in 1603, that of Viscount of Dunluce in 1618 and he became the 1st Earl of Antrim in 1620 (R. G. Hill 1873, 231). So, in 1603, Antrim's Plantation of his extensive lands with native Irish and both English and Scottish settlers began. The Viscount's three baronies in Antrim were regarded as three different kinds of areas for plantation of new settlers. Cary barony was described in the *1630 Muster Rolls* as Native Lands, an area set aside mainly for Highland Scots who were loyal to the MacDonnells. Dunluce Barony was an area set aside mainly for English and Lowland Scots who had been encouraged to settle there by the Earl of Antrim. Kilconway barony was an area set aside for the servitors and the Irish (Macafee 2018, 2). Rev. George Hill, an authority on the history of the MacDonnells of Antrim, states:

> *Soon after 1603, he began to let out to the natives on the coast, and also to the Scottish settlers, such arable portions of his lands as had been depopulated by the war, for terms varying from twenty-one to 301 years. Among the most respectable of his native tenantry were O'Neills, O'Hara's, O'Dowds, O'Cahans, O'Murrays, O'Hagans, Magees, Macormacks, Macduffys, Macphetricks, and Machenrys. Among the Scottish settlers on his lands may be specially mentioned the Boyds, Kennedys, Hamiltons, Stewarts,*

[13] See more on the Battle of Kinsale in Chapter 2.

[14] Surrender and regrant was a process which began in Henry VIII's times in which Gaelic leaders submitted their land and traditional titles over to the English authority and, in return, they were given a royal charter to hold their lands for the crown as loyal subjects. In exchange for the title and land grant, the newly made lord was required to provide the king of England with rent and military service and to ensure that his kin were also loyal to the crown (Havranek 2014, 32).

Macnaghtens, Macsulays, Dunlops, Dicks, Hutchins, Mackays, Browns, Shaws, and Moores. (R. G. Hill 1873, 229)

However, there did exist, previous to these settlements, an old medieval town of Dunluce at the base of Dunluce Castle. An on-going archaeological dig headed by the Northern Ireland Environment Agency in conjunction with Queen's University Belfast revealed a seal dated 1550 depicting the Dunluce Castle with flags flying. They also uncovered a metal buckle and a silver Queen Mary groat (coin) minted in the 1550's proving that a phase of settlement existed on that site far earlier than that of the 1603 Plantation (M. O'Neill 2014).

Figure 11. Villages and Towns in North Antrim

Source: Map adapted from http://www.placenamesni.org/map

(See Figure 9 for the location of Antrim in Ulster, Northern Ireland.)

The Stewarts of Isle of Bute and Ballintoy

In specifically looking at the History of the Isle of Bute, Scotland, regarding its kirks (churches) and the Vikings, according to Gilbert Markus in his *Place Names of Bute*,

> *The parish of Kingarth was in the medieval diocese of Sodor of the Isles. In the twelfth century, the parish of Kingarth embraced the entire island of Bute. The center of the parish was the church of St. Blane, known for a time as Kilblaan, at the south end of the parish. This was the site of the old monastery of Kingarth, apparently founded in the sixth century, and continuing as a church site until the Viking raids—and perhaps even during the Viking raids—and thereafter, as findings of Scandinavian artefacts in the vicinity of the church suggest that Christianized Norse, or Gall-Ghaidheil, were there.*
>
> *Though the whole island of Bute had formerly been a single parish centered on the church of St. Blane at Kingarth, Rothesay increased in importance during the thirteenth century as Stewart control of the island grew and as Rothesay castle became a strategic key to lordship of the Clyde firth area. Its erection as the seat of a Sheriffdom and as a Burgh in 1401 can be seen as both reflecting and enhancing its importance. With the comparatively large numbers of people involved in manning and servicing this new Stewart stronghold, a new church was needed and the parish of Rothesay was therefore carved out of the old parish of Kingarth before 1286, and its kirk was built on the hill overlooking the town.* (Markus 2012, ppgs. 139, 476)

Robert Bruce's daughter, Marjorie Bruce, became the wife of Walter, the Steward of Scotland and their son became Robert II of Scotland, the first of the Stewart line of kings. During young Robert's minority, his grandfather, King Robert Bruce, granted him the Island of Bute. During the existence of the island kingdom, the Lords of the Isles (MacDonnell) invariably spent a portion of the season on Bute, known as *Buda*, or the royal residence. At an early period, Bute was held alternately, and sometimes as a joint possession, by the families of Stewart and MacDonnell. The last MacDonnell who owned Bute was Angus MacDonnell of Isla who married, in the late 13th century, Agnes O'Cahan, a daughter of the chieftain of Dunseveric Castle in Antrim (R. G. Hill 1865, 2–3).

Subsequently, after a period of time, Robert II's third great grandson, Archibald Stewart, became "*embroiled in Henry VIII's intrigues*" and in 1544 organized the opposition to the Regency of Arran, during the minority of Mary Queen of Scots. His side lost and Archibald was made to forfeit his lands which were then granted by Queen Mary to the Campbells of Ardkinglas. Archibald Stewart was allowed to retain a small shred of his estates in Scotland but, in 1559, the last of his property was sold and soon afterwards, his sons relocated to Antrim's north shore as early as 1560. Their first place of settlement was Dunseverick in the parish of Billy, Barony of Cary. From there the family moved to a town called Ballinstraid (now Straidh) in the parish of Ballintoy (R. G. Hill 1865, 4) [fig. 11].

In 1625, Archibald Stewart's great grandson, also named Archibald, received a grant from Randal MacDonnell, first Earl of Antrim, of the two districts known as Ballylough and Ballintoy for the yearly rent of nine pounds sterling. Stewart was allowed to sublet his lands only to Scotch tenants. In addition, upon the death of the Lord Antrim's agent, Archibald Stewart was appointed to become the Lord's new agent in 1630 (R. G. Hill 1865, 5). As one can see, the two families of MacDonnell and Stewart, being cousins, had long histories together both in Bute and in Antrim.

Muirs/Moores of Bute

Given that Sorley Boy MacDonnell had formally received the lands in Dunluce, Ballymoney, Loughguile and Dunseverick way back in 1586, it is conceivable that Muirs/Moores from Bute could have settled on Antrim lands way before the Lord of Antrim's Plantation in 1603 or James VI and I's official Plantation scheme of 1610. Early records simply do not exist for lists of tenant farmers on their lands for these times. Although, given that there were already known Scotch settlements on their lands at the time (Perceval-Maxwell 1990, 229), the MacDonnell's Antrim lands from the 1550s or the Stewart of Ballintoy area lands from the 1560s would have been very enticing to younger sons of Isle of Bute Muir farmers who were not going to inherit anything from their fathers in Scotland [fig. 11, 14].

DISCUSSION | *Pre-Plantation 1590*

It is highly likely that a family Muir (anglicized to Moore) was established from Bute, Scotland onto Antrim lands prior to the official Plantation of Ulster in 1610. This Moore settled with his family in the area of Dunluce; Earl of Antrim lands. They could have arrived as early as 1585/90. If 1590 is taken as the date, Moore, age about thirty-six at the time of his migration, would have been born c. 1554 in Bute, Scotland. He reasonably could have had a couple of sons who were about the ages of eighteen (born c. 1572) and fifteen (born c. 1575) who also would have been born in Bute, Scotland immigrating to County Antrim with their father. ⚜

2

Irish Wars and the Flight of the Earls

IRELAND HAD BEEN CLAIMED AS A LORDSHIP by the English Crown since 1175, but this Lordship was only in theory and the reality was quite different. By the 1350's, the area under English control had shrunk to only the Pale; an area around Dublin. The rest of the country was controlled by Irish Gaelic lordships (Lenihan 2008, 1).

The people, according to an eye witness account written in 1548 by Italian Paolo Giovio, an historian at the time, were:

> *... in truth uncultivated, unfamiliar with luxury, and uncorrupted by foreign allurements, absolutely spurn the plough; they reject the mattock*[15] *and refuse to sweat for anything but war, in which they think almost nothing worth pursuing except honour. Since they are content with livestock, milk, cheese and honeycombs, as well as fish, bird-catching and hunting, they do not envy the gifts of 'Ceres'* (agriculture) *and 'Bacchus'* (wine) *brought to the tables of their princes, since commonly they prefer oatcakes and beer in cups, and they feast greatly on beans* (f. 34v). *The people live here and there, and in choosing locations in which to settle they look for the advantages afforded by marshes and mountains* (f. 35v). Giovio goes on to say; *All Irish, even in harsh and wooded places, observe the Christian liturgy and are educated by bishops through qualified teachers of Latin literature and the art of music* (f. 36v). *They set a higher value on military pursuits than on profits from trade. The custom is not to sustain disputes for long* (f.37v) *and quarrels are settled either by arms or by a speedy judgement. Soldiers are held in the highest honour-Knights above all, then heavily armed foot-soldiers, called galloglass... who are like veterans brought up in the camps and bringing forth wars from wars. A Laird* (Clan lord) *divides all his lands and fortunes*

---

[15] similar to a pickaxe

with the gallowglas, since, lacking riches, he pays their wage with these basics of life, and also with clothes, arms and horses (f. 38r). (Harris May 2007, 285–6)

In 1542, King Henry VIII first began the process of conquering Ireland for the English Crown, declaring himself King of Ireland which was to be a Kingdom rather than a Lordship. He initiated a policy of conquest and colonization. One such policy was that of surrender and regrant; the head of an Irish Clan, the Laird, would give all of his land to the Crown and pledge fealty and homage to the King in exchange for an English title, such as an Earl, and the use of his land back. They further agreed to reject papal jurisdiction, perform military service and pay rent as specified, adopt English customs and language and generally structure their territory in an English manner (Lenihan 2008, 3). If a Gaelic lord submitted in person to Henry VIII, he would be made an Earl. If he submitted via proxy, he would only be made a Baron or Viscount. In this way, if the Earl did not do what the King wanted, the King could confiscate all of his lands (Havranek 2014). In 1541, due to the defections of many of their under lords, a great many Gaelic lords participated in this new policy which included Conn O'Neill being created the Earl of Tyrone, Murrough O'Brien becoming the Earl of Thomond and Ulick Burke the Earl of Clanricard (Lenihan 2008, 3).

The laws set forth, first by King Henry VIII and then his predecessors, King Edward VI, Queen Mary and then Queen Elizabeth I, became stricter against the Gaelic Irish people as the years went by. It became unlawful for the mere Irish to own land, intermarry with the English, hold public office in government, be in a position of rank in the army or even continue with their Catholic religion. During these times, the various Gaelic Irish Lords continued their rebellion against such strict laws. Gaelic lands were systematically becoming acquired by the English government with some technicality or other in which the Gaelic lords had to acquiesce. For instance, from 1556 to 1562, the O'More and O'Connor clansmen of Laois and Offaly received only one third of their territory following surrender, with the rest of their lands to be assigned to frontier garrisons and to deserving Englishmen born in England or Ireland (Lenihan 2008, 4).

As religious differences grew deeper in Europe with Elizabeth I's excommunication by Pope Pius V in February of 1570, there was a greater urgency in advancing the policy of anglicizing Ireland (McCavitt 2002, 9). The main goal of this anglicization was to unite the three kingdoms into the same religion; that being Anglican with the English Monarch as its head. This goal became more and more of the central issue and the foremost reason for the divisiveness and ultimately control of the land and privileges for the English and the Crown. Securing the conversion of the Irish population to Protestantism was a fundamental objective (McCavitt 2002, 10).

Following the failure of the Spanish Armada in 1588, which was a national catastrophe for Spain (Ronald 2007, 314), the Catholic Spanish King Phillip II decided to take advantage of the Irish rebels in order to create a new front in the war against England. Spanish aid was offered to the Irish rebels in the expectation that tying the English down in Ireland might draw even more English resources away from the English allies in the Netherlands, the Dutch Estates, which were engaged in a long rebellion against Spanish rule (Ronald 2007, 291–2). In addition, Phillip II had enough of the losses of his ships to the English queen's pirate merchant adventurers (Ronald 2007, 278–9).

The constant threat of Spanish intervention to help the Irish rebels continued to frustrate the English crown's advancements in Ireland. Hugh O'Neill, the Earl of Tyrone, was determined that the Spanish would honor their word. The ousting of the Protestant English from Ireland became his goal and he committed himself to the international Catholic cause and declared "*faith and fatherland*" as his new rhetoric to gain a broader appeal in Ireland (McCavitt 2002, 14–16). For O'Neill, what had started out as simply trying to protect his inheritance had changed into that of a religious warrior (McCavitt 2002, 26).

Nine Years War | 1594 to 1603

The Nine Year's War was basically the conflict between a Catholic Confederacy of Gaelic lords created and led by Hugh O'Neill, Earl of Tyrone, and his Ulster ally, Red Hugh O'Donnell, Earl of Tyrconnell[16] on the one side and Elizabeth I and her government on the other. The Confederacy was strongest among the Gaelic lords of Ulster at first and then it took over much of Ireland (D. E. O'Neill 2009, 4). The Nine Year's War was a military, political, ideological and religious struggle that engulfed the whole island (E. O'Neill 2009, 241).

At a battle near Armagh in 1598, O'Neill took a government force unaware killing hundreds, including their general. He sent to Spain for reinforcements which never came (Cavendish 2007). Elizabeth I's forces and O'Neill had many similar skirmishes on and off, ending mostly in stalemate. While the queen wanted Ireland under English control, she did not want to deplete her coffers in doing so. Between trying to enforce her English laws and then, with the threat of eminent Spanish involvement in Ulster, giving in to Hugh O'Neill and the Confederacy with official pardons, the conflicts continued. As the conflicts grew from O'Neill's initial desires being only to prevent encroachment of government officials and soldiers on his lands and privileges and so to preserve his own province-wide power, O'Neill was ultimately unsuccessful in gaining the support of the important Old English lords or the various cities and corporate towns in the country (D. E. O'Neill 2009, 4). The war spread and large parts of Leinster and Connaught were

[16] The lands of Tyrconnell are basically the area of the present-day County Donegal.

overrun with fighting. The rebel's Confederate force raided Munster and led to the collapse of the English plantation there (D. E. O'Neill 2009, 6).

In 1599, Elizabeth was forced to send 16,000 troops, the largest army ever to leave England during Elizabeth I's reign, with Robert Devereux, the Earl of Essex, in command (McCavitt 2002, 29). With Essex's abject failure to bring O'Neill and his Confederates to terms, Charles Blount, Lord Mountjoy, was sent to succeed him (Lenihan 2008, 15). Mountjoy was only able to bring Tyrone to terms after some three years of grueling campaigns when Tyrone was forced to fight on unknown turf at Kinsale (McCavitt 2002, 27).

Battle of Kinsale | 2 Oct 1601 to 3 Jan 1602

With the continued pleading of Hugh O'Neill and the Irish Confederate rebels, on 21 September 1601, a Spanish force of over 3000 men landed at Kinsale, County Cork (McCavitt 2002, 37). The Spaniards rushed to fortify the town and the surrounding area to withstand the approaching English armies. The English laid siege to Kinsale with a force of 12,000 men. The Gaelic Irish Lords of Ulster, Hugh O'Neill and his ally Red Hugh O'Donnell, were forced to leave Ulster to go to the Irish Rebel forces' aid. O'Neill had also convinced Randal MacDonnell, Earl of Antrim, to join them with about 800 of the Clandonnell (R. G. Hill 1873, 194). They joined with Captain Richard Tyrell of Westmeath and their combined forces came to 6,180 men. On their 300-mile winter march from Ulster in the north to Kinsale in the south of Ireland [fig. 9], they were successful in cutting off much of the opposing English army's supply lines across the island. But, in the end, the English scouts were aware of the Irish troop movements and the English led their forces to meet the enemy (McCavitt 2002, 38, 41).

Tyrone did not have the advantage of choosing his own ground. When Tyrone deployed his troops to march to battle in the early hours of 3 Jan 1602, he did so in a conventional manner; that of the three-battle formation of musket, pike and cavalry (McGurk 2002, 64). As Tyrone's army proceeded in their fight, they became spread out. Furthermore, the Spanish had not engaged the English army simultaneously with the Irish Rebels as planned. O'Neill ordered a retreat into the marshes hoping to mire the English cavalry in the soft land. The Irish became overpowered by the English cavalry showing that the tactics of the Irish infantry were much inferior to that of the well drilled professional army of the English (McCavitt 2002, 42). The English calvary pursued the fleeing Irish *"who butchered them without mercy for a mile and a half as they raced from the battlefield"* (McGurk 2002, 65).

The Spanish, who had held the town of Kinsale for more than three months and had lost many men in the siege, surrendered the town to the English and were allowed to sail back to Spain. This loss put an end to Spanish help in Ireland and much of the Irish resistance. Tyrone's

Irish forces suffered huge losses and the balance of the Irish fled back to Ulster (McGurk 2002, 65–66). Hundreds of Clandonnell's men and their supports had perished (R. G. Hill 1873, 194). Many of the Irish survivors also fled Ireland to fight for the Spanish King Phillip III in the Spanish Netherlands (Mesa 2014, 14).

The result of the war was the extension of English rule to the whole island of Ireland for the first time and the beginning of the end of the autonomous Gaelic and Old English lordships, representing a key turning point in Irish History (E. O'Neill 2009, 241).

Flight of the Earls | 1607

After the defeat of the Irish at Kinsale, the English kept up their relentless and systematic attacks on the rebel Irish. Having enjoyed a prolonged period of successes, Hugh O'Neill's decision-making had become questionable, and his influence over other chieftains in the rebel confederacy correspondingly weakened. Red Hugh O'Donnell travelled to the Spanish Court to lobby for a new invasion force. While there, he was struck down by a sudden illness and died, allegedly poisoned at the hands of an English assassin (McCavitt 2002, 43). The rebel confederacy was irreversibly weakened but the rebellion had not been suppressed.

The English were more than frustrated in their search for a quick end to the war. English General, Lord Mountjoy, was now following Lord Deputy Sir Arthur Chichesters' all-out policy of "*spoliation and extermination.*" The degree of devastation wrought by this scorched-earth tactic was to eventually claim 60,000 lives perishing from famine. According to Fynes Moryson, Mountjoy's secretary, "*no spectacle was more frequent in the ditches of towns and especially in wasted countries, than to see multitudes of these poor people dead with their mouths all colored green by eating nettles*" (McCavitt 2002, 46).

With the desertion of many of his leading commanders, Tyrone became severely weakened and was forced to submit to Queen Elizabeth's representative, Lord Mountjoy, at Mellifont on 30 March 1603, only 6 days after the death of the queen, 24 March 1603, with Tyrone having not yet heard of the news (McCavitt 2002, 50). Despite a generous settlement in which he retained his earldom, O'Neill still found English rule unacceptable (Flight of the Earls n.d.). Furthermore, due to the ravishing English military campaign, large areas of Tyrone's lands in Ulster were laid waste (McCavitt 2002, 51).

On the death of Elizabeth I, James VI of Scotland acceded to the English throne as James I and took the title of James VI and I. Though a Protestant, as the son of the Catholic Mary Queen of Scots, King James VI and I was generally considered in Ireland to be sympathetic to the Catholics. However, the ongoing English laws oppressing the Irish continued. Tyrone was now claiming that he was championing the Catholic cause (McCavitt 2002, 52). Not only were the Gaelic Irish rebelling, but the Old English, most of whom were Catholics, were being discriminated against as well. Traditional rivals of the Gaelic Irish since the twelfth century, the Old English, descendants of the original Anglo-Norman settlers, had become "*more Irish than the Irish themselves*" (The Coming of the Normans n.d., 2).

Plots to overthrow English rule continued and in November of 1605, the Gunpowder Plot was uncovered. Guy Fawkes and his fellow Catholic conspirators had attempted to assassinate the king and his ministers in parliament. As a result, the plot solicited strict new laws, named Mandates, from Chichester, now the Lord Deputy of Ireland. All priests were to be banned from Ireland and individuals were to attend Protestant worship or else be fined up to 100 pounds while they were also imprisoned *"till they conform themselves"* (McCavitt 2002, 57–59). Both Gaelic Irish and Old English recusants, those who refused to attend the services of the Protestant established church, began to realign themselves away from the English crown and towards Catholic Spain (McCavitt 2002, 53).

Hugh O'Neill, Earl of Tyrone, became afraid that his plotting with Spain about a Catholic revolt in Ireland was to be found out by the king (McCavitt 2002, 87). Furthermore, the Mandates campaign and his perceived complicity in the Gunpowder Plot all played a part in convincing Tyrone to flee Ireland (Lenihan 2008, 14). This would eventually become known as the *Flight of the Earls*.

On 4 September 1607, the earls of Tyrone and Tyrconnell, along with some ninety-nine friends, relatives and followers, boarded ship to sail away from Lough Swilly into perpetual exile (McCavitt 2002, 93) (Perceval-Maxwell 1990, 71). They were accompanied by Cuconnaught Maquire, owner of half the county of Fermanagh. Thus, much of Fermanagh as well as the counties of Tyrone and Donegal were now open lands for plantation once the fugitives were convicted of treason (Perceval-Maxwell 1990, 76). After the April 1608 rebellion of Sir Cahir O'Dogherty, the English extended the area available for plantation to County Coleraine. In short, for one reason or another, the crown claimed to have at its disposal either the whole or a large portion of the counties of Tyrone, Donegal, Coleraine[17], Armagh, Cavan and Fermanagh (Perceval-Maxwell 1990, 79–80) [fig. 14]. ⚜

[17] County Londonderry was initially known as County Coleraine before it took on its present name in 1613.

Figure 12. Scotland and Northern Ireland

Source: Map adapted from: https://commons.wikimedia.org/wiki/File:Scotland_map-en.jpg

The green line indicates the Highlands boundary. From this map, one can see how close the two countries of Scotland and Ireland are and how easy it would have been to consider the Argyll Isles of Scotland one with Ulster's Antrim Coast and the Glynns of Northern Ireland.

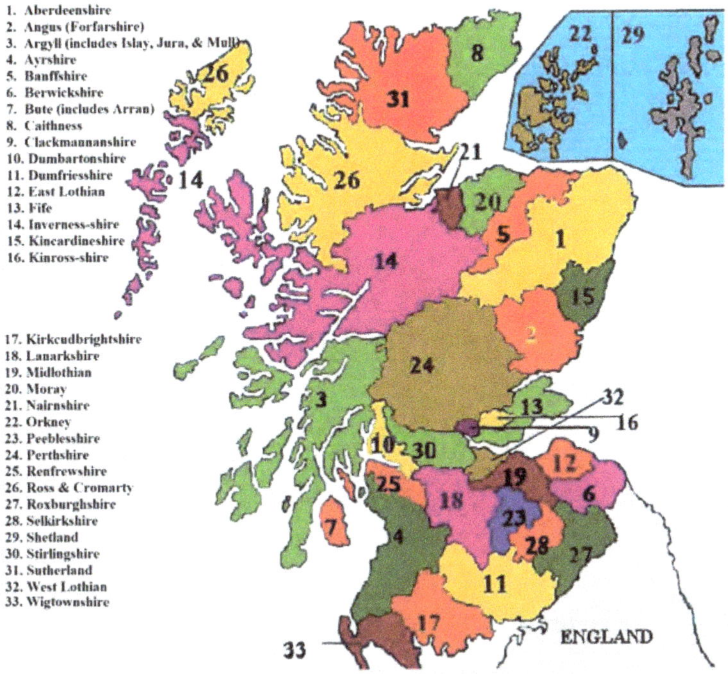

Figure 13. County Map of Scotland

Source: Map with permission from http://www.genuki.org.uk/big/sct/sct_cmap

Figure 14. The Plantation of Ulster Surname Map 1610–1630

Source: Map taken from Ulster-Scots Agency at https://www.ulsterscotsagency.com.

The light grey areas of Antrim and Down show the area of private settlement pre-1610 and the dark grey area shows the official Plantation lands.

3

The Plantation and the plantation

MANY HISTORIANS USE PLANTATION with a capital "P" to designate the official one started by the King in 1609/10 and plantation with a small "p" to identify the earlier private plantations of Antrim and Down.

The mainland of Scotland is divided into four main regions: Highlands, Lowlands, Borders-Southwest and the Inner and Outer Hebrides Islands. The Lowlands and the Borders-Southwest counties were the areas from where most of the planters (settlers) originated [fig. 12].

The anglicized Lowlands are made up of the counties of Haddington, Edinburgh, Linlithgow, Selkirk, Peebles, North Lanark, Stirling, Clackmannan, Fife, Kinross, Angus, Kincardine, and even parts of Perth and Aberdeen. The Celtic[18] Borders-Southwest regions are broken down into the Border counties consisting of Berwick, Roxburgh, Dumfries, South Lanark and the Southwest counties listed as Kirkcudbright, Wigton, Ayr and Renfrew (J. M. Hill 1993, 25) (Perceval-Maxwell 1990, 104) [fig. 13].

The Isle of Bute is part of Argyllshire, divided into highland and lowland areas by the Highland Boundary Fault [fig. 12]. Rothesay, the capital of Isle of Bute, is located in the Lowland area. However, historically, it was part of the Territory of the Lordship (Kingdom) of the Isles [fig. 10].

Montgomery, Hamilton & Con O'Neill and the plantations of Down and Lower Antrim

The Irish lands of Lower Clandeboye, Upper Clandeboye[19] and the Great Ards were disputed territories. They had been claimed by a branch of the O'Neill's in the 1300's but were also

[18] This Celtic term is primarily a linguistic one.

[19] Clandeboye was a kingdom of Gaelic Ireland, comprising of what is now south County Antrim, north County Down, and the barony of Loughinsholin in south County Londonderry.

regarded as a major part of the ancient Anglo-Norman Earldom of Ulster which had been established by the English Crown in 1205.

There was a degree of co-operation between the Crown and the O'Neill's of Clandeboye. Sir Brian O'Neill was knighted for his service to the Crown, but fell out of favor with Queen Elizabeth I. So, in 1572, Sir Brian adopted a scorched earth policy, burning the major buildings and priories to prevent the incoming English army from using them as garrisons.

Sir Brian O'Neill's claim to the lands passed to Niall O'Neill, and then to Niall's son, Con O'Neill. Con lived in the grand Norman castle known as Castle Reagh, situated on Castlereagh Hill overlooking the then small village of Belfast. By this stage, Lower Clandeboye, Upper Clandeboye and the Great Ards were *"waste and uninhabited"* (S. J. Hamilton 1867, General Appendix lxxvi).

Around Christmas 1602, Con O'Neill was imprisoned in Carrickfergus Castle for *"levying war against the queen"* and was destined to be executed. Sir Arthur Chichester, the queen's Lord Deputy in Ireland, offered to hang Con O'Neill without a trial, feasibly to secure the lands for himself. Fortunately for O'Neill, Queen Elizabeth I died in March 1603 before he could be executed. She was childless and so her nearest relative, King James VI of Scotland, succeeded her and became King James VI and I of England, Scotland, Ireland and Wales in July of 1603. The new Scottish Monarch had many long-term Scot associates, including James Hamilton and Hugh Montgomery (Ulster-Scots Agency 2006).

Sir Hugh Montgomery | 1560–1636
First Viscount of the Great Ards | Aristocrat and Soldier

Montgomery was the son of the Fifth Laird of Braidstane near Beith in Ayrshire, and a soldier. He spent time at the French court and became Captain of Foot of a Scottish Regiment in Holland, under the then Prince of Orange.[20] When Hugh Montgomery's father died, he returned to Braidstane to become the Sixth Laird.

Montgomery planned Con O'Neill's escape from Carrickfergus castle and secured O'Neill's pardon from King James VI and I. Montgomery's reward was to be half of Con O'Neill's lands. However, James Hamilton intervened and secured one third of the lands for himself. Hamilton and Montgomery became bitter rivals.

Montgomery founded Newtownards (Newton), restoring the Priory and built the town's Market Cross, which was based on the design of the Market Cross in Edinburgh. He formalized the sea trading route between Donaghadee in County Down, Northern Ireland and Portpatrick in County Wigtownshire, Scotland, and was granted a number of former church lands in South

[20] King William (of Orange) III of England's great grandfather.

Antrim. Newtownards prospered under Montgomery, so much so that by 1613 the town could send two members to Parliament. He was buried in Newtownards Priory in May 1636 (Ulster-Scots Agency 2006).

Sir James Hamilton | 1559 – 1644
First Viscount Clandeboye | Minister's Son and Academic

Hamilton was a minister's son from Dunlop in Ayrshire and an academic. In 1591 he was appointed a Fellow of Trinity College in Dublin, and was made Bursar in 1598. He was an agent for King James VI of Scotland in Ireland, and was also appointed as Scottish agent at the English court of Elizabeth I. In March 1603, Hamilton brought official news of Elizabeth's death to Scotland—an event which made James VI of Scotland also James I of England, known as The Union of the Crowns.

Consequently, Hamilton had great influence with James VI and I, which he shrewdly used to gain a foothold in Ulster by intervening in the negotiations between Hugh Montgomery and Con O'Neill to secure one third of O'Neill's lands in County Down.

In addition, Hamilton was granted fishing rights to the River Bann and the area of Coleraine both in County Antrim. In April 1606, he sold off his Antrim interests to concentrate on County Down, founding Bangor and Killyleagh, and establishing churches for his settlers in Dundonald, Killinchy, Ballyhalbert and Holywood. By the time of his death, he had acquired lands in County Cavan, Roscommon, Meath, Westmeath and Wexford. He was buried in Bangor Abbey in 1644 (Ulster-Scots Agency 2006).

The plantations of Antrim (1603–4) and Down (1603–10)

In order to make the expense of importing settlers worthwhile, grants had to be made on a huge scale. Yet the Crown possessed little land in Ulster to grant to those willing to establish settlements. Servitors, those who had served in Elizabeth I and then James VI and I's army in the Nine Years' War, quickly snapped up scattered Abbey lands. Until the Flight of the Earls in 1607, such grants could be made only in Antrim and Down from Con O'Neill's lands, and as these two counties had the additional advantage of being situated closest to Scotland, it was in this region that the first concentration of Lowland Scots occurred (Perceval-Maxwell 1990, 47).

"*The whole region of the county Antrim was wasted by rebellion*" (Erck 1851, 137). The first Scot who was officially (re)granted land in North Antrim by the new King James was Sir Randal MacDonnell on 11 May 1603 who received all of the Route and the Glynns, well over 300,000 acres[21] (Perceval-Maxwell 1990, 48). The grant was again reassigned 6 July 1604 and for the

---

[21] The Antrim estate was a landed estate which at one time included the whole of the four northern baronies of County Antrim, an area of more than 330,000 acres; Glenarm, Dunluce, Kilconway and Cary [fig. 18].

first time it stated specific terms for the division of the MacDonnell lands. Sir Randal MacDonnell was to,

> *... divide the said territories into several precincts, each to contain 2000 a [cres] at least, and to give different names to each division, that so they may become different manors—to set apart 500 a [cres] in each for demesne-lands, and to build a castle or mansion-house upon each, within seven years-to hold courts baron, and appoint seneschals.* (Erck 1851, 137) (Irish Record Commissioner 1830, 58)

There was no mention of importing settlers from either England or Scotland during that time.

James Hamilton became the first Scot to acquire a legal title to territory in Down. According to a letter from the king dated 16 April 1605, initially all of the O'Neill estate was to be granted to Hamilton, who promised *"to inhabit the said territory and lands with English or Scotchmen."* By the agreement of 30 April, Hamilton received a grant of the land, but he also agreed to pass at some future date one-third of it to Montgomery and another third to Con O'Neill. O'Neill was to receive half of Upper or Southern Clandeboye, with the center of his estate at Castlereagh, while the two Scots were to divide equally the other half of Upper Clandeboye and the whole of the Great Ards between them. Montgomery and Hamilton would supply English and Scottish tenants to populate one-third of Con's estate (Perceval-Maxwell 1990, 52). The complicated method used for dividing the O'Neill lands was necessary in order that *"the sea coasts might be possessed by Scottish men, who would be traders as proper for his Majestie's future advantage"* (Montgomery 1869, 32–3). In addition, it was divided in order to secure a safe beachhead in Ulster from which expeditions might be launched quickly to control rebellions that broke out elsewhere in the province (Perceval-Maxwell 1990, 53).

The Down scheme (schematic) was one of the first moves in the process that led to an attempt to repopulate the whole of Ulster with British (Scotch or English) inhabitants. For the first time in King James VI and I's reign, a grant of Irish land had been made conditional upon the introduction of Scotch or English tenants (Perceval-Maxwell 1990, 53). James Hamilton's brothers, Gavin and John, became denizens in May of 1605 and followed James to Ireland. By 1606, among those settling on the Hamilton estates were families with such names as Maxwell, Rose, Barclay, More and Baylie (Perceval-Maxwell 1990, 56–7).

The *Montgomery Manuscripts* contain much more detailed information about the Ulster settlements than what is available from the *Hamilton Manuscripts*. Among those Montgomery persuaded to come over to Ulster were a number of lairds from his own district, often of his own or his wife's family who were given freehold estates of up to 1,000 acres. Besides such gentry, artisans such as smiths, masons and carpenters came over to construct the necessary buildings, while another group, described as *"healthy able men"* became small landholders with from two to four acres apiece (Montgomery 1869, 55, 59).

When the settlers began to arrive in May 1606, they found that the countryside was devastated from years of war. Their first priority was to find shelter. Some materials, such as timber, they found locally. Other necessities they received from Portpatrick or Stranraer, Scotland. With favorable winds, the voyage between Scotland and Down took less than three hours. During the summer, ships arrived two to three times a week bringing supplies and a constant stream of immigrants (Perceval-Maxwell 1990, 59–60).

Figure 15. Close proximity of Montgomery, Hamilton, Mure of Rowallan and Muir/Moore on Bute

Source: Map adapted from http://www.google.com/maps

One well known Muir/Mure family from the same Barony of Ayrshire was the Mures of Rowallan in Kilmaurs, who's residence was within just a few miles of Sir Hugh Montgomery (1560–1636), Sixth Laird of Braidstane near Beith and Sir James Hamilton (1559–1644), from Dunlop. The distance from Kilmaurs to Dunlop is 5.7 miles and the distance from Kilmaurs to Beith is 12.9 miles. The Mures of Rowallan family, and all its junior branches, would have heard of the opportunities which were acclaimed by the early settlements of Down and Antrim.

While County Down developed as strongholds of Scots clustered together, the grant of the entire Route and the Glynns to Sir Randal MacDonnell of Antrim estates developed differently. The Scots who entered Antrim from 1606 onwards could not all settle in one spot. There remained in County Antrim numerous Irish and Islanders. Therefore, the Lowland settlers tended to be mixed with the former inhabitants. Down accepted the idea of saturation of an area with new inhabitants from either England or Scotland, whereas Antrim preferred to leave the bulk of the land in Irish and Islander hands while establishing a series of fortified posts as an ever-present reminder of English power (Perceval-Maxwell 1990, 66–7).

Once settlers moved to either Antrim or Down, they did not necessarily stay there as other opportunities presented themselves further westward.

The Official Plantation of Ulster | 1610

It should be noted that even before the formal beginning of the Plantation of Ulster, some Scots already lived in the area. At Strabane, County Tyrone, a Scottish settlement had remained ever since Agnes Campbell had brought over with her some thousand men at the time of her marriage to Tirlough Luineach O'Neill in 1569. At the beginning of the 17th century, this settlement consisted of some 60–80 families and still retained a distinctly Scottish identity (Perceval-Maxwell 1990, 68).

With the Flight of the Earls and the Scotch King James VI coming to the throne of England, the timing of huge tracts of available land could not have been better for a major migration to Northern Ireland to begin. Furthermore, the Plantation of Ulster coincided with the English plantations of many other locations including Jamestown, Virginia in America, Bermuda and Guiana. The English found themselves in need of planters and the Scots found the cooperation with the English to plant in Ulster very accommodating (Perceval-Maxwell 1990, 14).

Ulster had become desolate due to the devastating campaigns and scorched earth policies of the English. In addition, the loss of the Battle of Kinsale and widespread famine left a population of Irish and Old English which only needed to use one third of the lands in Ulster, while the British (English and Scots) could occupy the other two-thirds and would be able to support 40,000 additional people (Perceval-Maxwell 1990, 18).

Meanwhile, overcrowding of the lands in Scotland, especially in the Borders, led to civil unrest. Stern laws passed by James VI and I in 1605 began to force idle men to either enter some legal trade or leave their homes to serve in the army or navy of either their own or some foreign monarch. This surplus of men led to either enforced or voluntary migration (Perceval-Maxwell 1990, 23–28). Even so, the first formal invitation to the Scots from the king to participate in the Plantation was made only in 1609, but by this year, numerous Lowland Scots, on their own initiative, had already established themselves along the coasts of Antrim and Down in the previous plantations (Perceval-Maxwell 1990, 45).

King James VI and I's reasons for a Plantation in Ulster were three-fold: 1) To curtail the cost of keeping order in Ulster by planting it with civil people. 2) To strategically control the north of Ireland and its coastline to extend England's power. 3) To establish Ireland as a part of protestant Europe.

> *The idea of replacing what he regarded as barbarity with civilization struck his imagination as a thoroughly worthwhile object for a king to pursue . . . by which he might be remembered.* (Perceval-Maxwell 1990, 74–75)

The Irish still received a considerable portion of the land. About 79,000 acres were assigned to them, compared with 53,000 given to the servitors[22] and 155,000 acres to be divided between the English and the Scotch settlers. These lands excluded bogs and mountains. Precincts (baronies) were divided into proportions (estates). The Undertakers'[23] proportions were to be divided into three sizes: 1,000, 1,500 and 2,000 acres and the Chief Undertakers could have estates of 3,000 acres each. Each man was to be assigned his land by lot, and the crown was to grant it in fee-farm, with the first four year's rent free. All proportions were to have their buildings completed within three and a half years: the large sized lands had to have a castle with a bawn (court) surrounding it; the middle-sized lands only had to have a stone or brick house with a bawn; and on the small lands only a bawn was required. Every 1,000 acres were to consist of twenty-four able bodied Scots or English men over the age of eighteen, and these were to come from at least ten different families. Two of the families were to be made freeholders, three more were to receive leases for three lives or twenty-one years for every 100 acres, while the remainder were to consist of cottagers. It was the duty of the undertaker to provide houses for all of these families close to the fortifications on his proportion. Most importantly of all, both undertakers and their tenants were required to take the Oath of Supremacy (Perceval-Maxwell 1990, 82–83). This oath was to acknowledge that the King had royal ecclesiastical supremacy. In other words, that he was the supreme head of the church (Lenihan, Consolidating Conquest - Ireland 1603–1727 2008, 15)

The escheated (confiscated) districts assigned to the Scots were territories in the counties of Armagh, Cavan, Donegal, Tyrone and Fermanagh. In 1610, the precincts assigned to the Scots within those counties were: the northern half of the Fews in Armagh; Strabane and Mountjoy in

[22] Fighting soldiers given land in lieu of back pay owed to them.

[23] So named because they were to "undertake" the project of settling the lands.

Tyrone; Bolagh, Banagh and Portlough in Donegal; Magheraboy and Knockninny in Fermanagh and Clankee and Tullyhunco in Cavan (Perceval-Maxwell 1990, 87–89). Ulster's inland regions were scarcely documented while its coastline was erratically charted by even the best of maps (Harris May 2007, 271).

The Scots received in all some 81,000 acres distributed among nine precincts but the reality was, due to poor surveying and the absence of existing maps, the Undertakers held between two and three times as much land as was stated in their patents (Perceval-Maxwell 1990, 82–89). In all, there were sixty-one Scots who were *initially* granted, as ordinary undertakers, proportions equally divided between the east and the west of the Lowlands and Southwest Scotland. These men had influence at court or family connections with a chief undertaker and enough money to be able to afford the huge costs of settling the lands in Ulster by providing housing, men, cattle, and provisions needed for a four-year period of free rents (Perceval-Maxwell 1990, 102). Conspicuous by their absence were the lairds (lords) from the unruly Border areas (Perceval-Maxwell 1990, 104–105).

Hugh amounts of Scots took advantage of land and low rents in the Ulster Plantation:

> *The 14,000 adult Scots who populated Ulster during the official Jacobean Plantation came largely from the eight counties which lie either along the border with England, or up the west coast to* [but not including] *Argyllshire. These immigrants consisted of a cross-section of Lowland society, though the less well-off and less stable elements probably predominated.* (Perceval-Maxwell 1990, 289)

The terms Denizens and Britishness

For Scots to become English subjects in Ireland, it was necessary to obtain Letters of Denization. To acquire these letters patent, one was made to pay a fee and take the Oath of Allegiance to the British Crown.

Becoming a legal denizen secured a Scotsman in Ireland an intermediate position between an alien and a native-born English subject. He had the privilege of purchasing land, but heirs born before the date of denization could not inherit the land on the denizen's death. A denizen could use the law courts, but was not qualified to hold any office of trust, civil or military (The Plantation of Ulster n.d.).

Naturalization, which could only be applied for after seven years of denization, would allow all of the English laws and rights of citizenship as if he had been born an English subject. All Scots settling in Ireland were required to be denizens (R. G. Hill 1873, 153).

The sense of Britishness soon came to the foreground with the crowning of King James VI & I who styled himself "King of Great Britain, France and Ireland" in 1603. The king wanted to make Scottish subjects in Ireland an extension of England in all manners political and religious.

The idea that Great Britain was synonymous with strictly English identity was prevalent from 1642 to 1660 (Bates 2014, 6, 9).

The term British gained further hold in printed material in 1610 with the Ulster Plantation. Soon it was embraced by many Scots and some English alike, mostly for trading purposes. Scots in London were viewed with no problem or malice. They were accepted figures in London due to their Britishness (Murdoch 2008, 259).

In early population counts for Ulster in 1613, 1619 & 1622, census takers only labeled men as either Native Irish or British. It is impossible to decern the percentage of actual Scots versus English through their methods (Hunter, Plantations in Ulster, 1600–41 2018). The *1630 Muster of Ulster* used the term British tenants for the Earl of Antrim estates, also not defining its citizens as either Scots or Englishmen (Hunter, 'Men and arms' The Ulster settlers, c. 1630 2012). By the 1640's to early 1650's, the term British was usually used to show support for the Stuart-Royalist cause during the British Civil Wars (Murdoch 2008, 258).

In 1603, the Scots King James VI succeeded to the English throne after the death of Elizabeth I and became King James VI and I. His main goal was to unify the countries of England, Scotland, Ireland and Wales by introducing the concept of "Britishness" among his citizens.

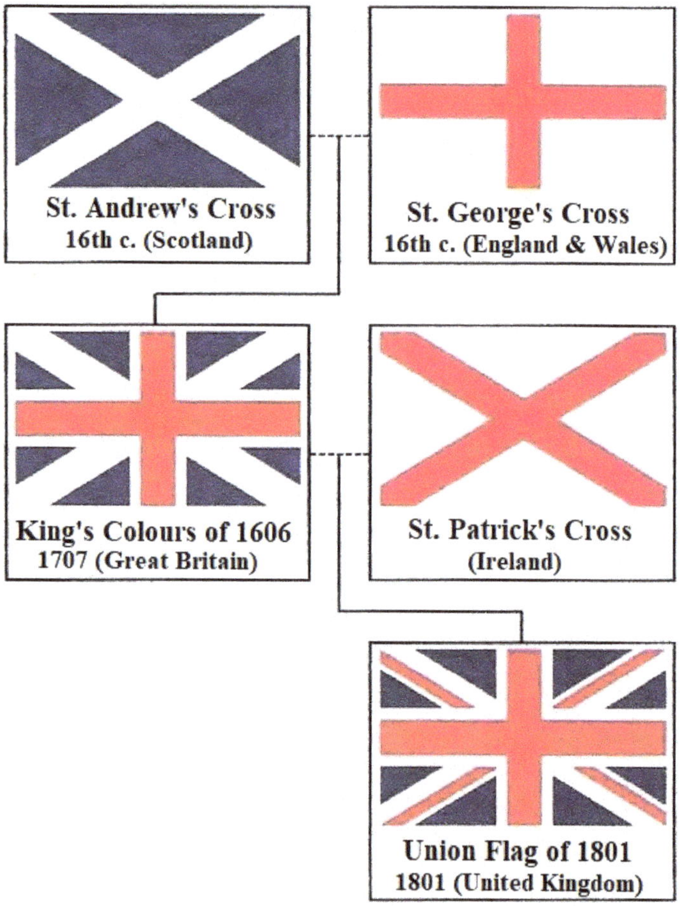

Figure 16. Evolution of the Union Flag

Source: https://en.wikipedia.org/w/index.php?title=Flag_of_the_United_Kingdom&oldid=1044532295

Difference Between the UK, Great Britain and England

England is a country that is part of the (UK) United Kingdom. The United Kingdom includes the countries of England, Scotland, Wales and Northern Ireland. Great Britain consists of only England, Scotland and Wales as well as several offshore islands including the Hebrides in Scotland.

4
Muir/Moore Families

THE HISTORIC TRADITION OF NAMING PATTERNS in British and Irish families from around the 16th and 17th centuries were as follows: The first son was named after the father's father, the second son was named after the mother's father, the third son was named after the father, the fourth son was named after the father's eldest brother, the first daughter after the mother's mother, the second daughter after the father's mother, the third daughter after the mother and the forth daughter after the mother's eldest sister. If this tradition was not strictly adhered to, one would still see names of parents and grandparents, siblings, aunts and uncles repeated, but not necessarily in any order. While over half of the names in a family will appear to be repeats, there always seems to be a few totally different ones (Baxter 4th Edition 1999). As Scot Muir or Mure families moved to Ireland, their names became anglicized to More or Moore.

This tradition of naming patterns compels one to search for the first names of Edward and Thomas when looking for the ancestors of Edward Moore (b. *c.*1612), Master gunner at Dover Castle, and his son Thomas Moore (b. 1654 in London), Hudson's Bay Company employee. The names of Robert or John, Thomas's brothers from Dover, or even the name William, due to the high number of Williams associated with the name Edward throughout the early 17th century, are also important.

Bute Muirs

The History of the County of Bute and Certain Families Connected Therewith by John Eaton Reid, published in Glasgow 1864, page 242, states:

> *The Muirs or Moores, as the name was one time spelled, have long held an influential position in Bute. They are said to have been a branch of the Ayrshire family of Rowallan, but it is uncertain when they settled in Bute. They are, however, first traced in the Bush*

Farm, near Rothesay, during the time of the first Earl of Bute, and afterwards at Parkhouse or Barone Park, where John Muir resided during the early part of last century [1700's]. (Reid 1864, 242)

There are three separate Muir family genealogies located at the Bute Museum in Rothesay on the Isle of Bute, Scotland all of which have been written up by Isabel Sharp, head of the Bute Genealogical Society. The earliest date entered is contained in the *Muir 2 Tree* of a John Muir, born 6 Jul 1692, written by Ms. Sharp along with the help of Langley Muir, a genealogist from Ottawa, Canada who had visited her in September of 2018. Both the *Muir 2 Tree* and the *Muir 3 Tree* include the first name of Thomas but the earliest date in which it is mentioned is not until the mid-1700's, with only the *Muir 3 Tree* naming a Thomas consistently throughout the generations. The *Muir 3 Tree* also contains the names of many Johns and Roberts. Within the three Muir genealogies held at the Bute Museum, the first name of Edward does not exist in any of their earlier dates.

DISCUSSION

Since it is Rothesay on the Isle of Bute that Dr. Tyrone Bowes' report claims that this study's Moore/Muir comes from in Scotland, a closer investigation of the Muirs from this area is required.

On May 19, 2020, I had the pleasure and luck to make contact with Langley Muir who descends from the *Muir 2 Tree* on Bute. He agreed to take a DNA test to see if we were related. The results showed that we were not. Langley descends from Brythonic Celts and our Moores come from Vikings. This study's Moore family was on Bute long before Langley Muir's family arrived in the late 17th century.[24] We were from completely different families. Furthermore, Mr. L. Muir informed me that there does not exist any Muir families presently on the Isle of Bute who were original to Bute as far as existing records show. In other words, there is no chance of a DNA test of any of the farmers living on Bute named Muir to be related to our Moores. Even so, there could be an outside chance of someday finding and testing a descendant of the *Muir 1 Tree* or the *Muir 3 Tree*.

Viking Moores

However, there is another possibility of Moores on Bute other than Reid's assertion above and it is that the Moores of Viking descent started settling on the Isle of Bute in the mid 9th century. According to the *History of the County of Bute* by Reid, the Vikings arrived on Bute in the 9th

---

24 Mr. L. Muir's tree begins with the birth of his ancestor in 1696 and, as early as 1654, our ancestor Thomas Moore was born in London. However, the actual date of Mr. L. Muir's families' arrival on Bute has not been established.

century. People started taking surnames around the 11th century. Norway claimed, by right of conquest, the possession of Bute, Arran, and the Cumbrays as far back as 870AD. Shortly after, the Isles were governed by a succession of local chiefs until the period of the invasion of Magnus Barefoot, in 1093, 1098 and 1102 when he established the Dominion of Norway (Reid 1864, 35). This study's Viking Moores arrived on Bute between 800AD and 1100AD; which was the age of the Vikings.

The Norwegian, King Magnus Barefoot [Appendex 6], was killed in battle in 1103 and the local chiefs again asserted their claims. Olave the Red, King of Man (1112–1152), ascended the throne of the Isles and reigned for forty years. He was succeeded by his son, Godred the Black. In 1140, one of Olave's daughters, Ragnhildis, married Somerled, Prince of Argyle. Somerled became one of the most powerful chieftains in the western Isles. In the year 1156, Somerled joined in a rebellion against his bother-in-law, Godred the Black, and with a fleet of eighty galleys engaged in the Battle of Epiphany that resulted in a treaty which ceded Bute, Arran, the Cumbrays, Islay, Jura, Mull and Kintyre along with several small islands to his sons. After Somerled's death in 1164, his son Dugald received Mull, Coll, Tiree, and Jura; Ranald (or Reginald) possessed Islay and Kintyre; and Angus obtained Bute. In 1210, Angus and his three sons were killed in a battle at Skye. Ranald then claimed both Bute and Arran which was then bestowed to his son Ruari, whose descendants were called Macruari. (Reid 1864, 35–7) Ranald endowed Islay and Kintyre to his other son Donnell, from whom all the Macdonnells derive their surname (R. G. Hill 1873, 10).

Meanwhile, Walter the High Steward of Scotland, having helped with the defeat of Somerled at Renfrew in 1164, had seized the Island of Bute by order of the King of Scotland, Malcom IV (R. G. Hill 1873, 10) (Reid 1864, 46). The right of the Stewarts was further strengthened by the marriage of Allan, son and heir of Walter the High Steward to Jane, the daughter and heiress of one of Angus's sons named James[25] who was killed with him in 1210. These rights of the Stewarts were disputed by both Ranald, the son of Somerled, and Ranald's eldest son Ruari (Reid 1864, 38).

The many descendants of Somerled maintained the title of Kings of the Isles and rendered minimal service to either the King of Norway from those residing in the Isles or to the King of Scotland from those living on the mainland (R. G. Hill 1873, 10). In 1230 (Manuscript of Flatey 1784, 34), King Haakon IV[26] of Norway declared the King of the [South] Isles to be Uspac (Ospakr-Hakon), son of Dugald (Dugall), one of the sons of Somerled, and sent with him a powerful fleet to maintain his dominions. A major conflict happened on Bute where the Stewarts

[25] Through this marriage, the MacDonnells, MacRories and MacDougalls, all descendants of Somerled, became cousins to the Stewarts.

[26] Also referred to as *Haakon the Old* or just *Haco*.

held Rothesay castle[27]. It took three days for the castle to fall to the Norwegians; the Steward was shot dead. The Rothesay garrison capitulated and accepted the terms of the Norwegians, who had lost about three hundred men. The Norwegians departed with much wealth but only got close to the south coast off Kintyre where they met a great storm and lost three ships with the men and all that was on board. Uspac died on his way back to Norway near Kintyre. After his death, in the spring of 1231, the Norwegians, along with the King of the (south) Isles which was Olave the Red, gathered on the Isle of Man (Reid 1864, 37–9). From there, King Olave remaining behind, the Norwegians fought with the Scots on Kintyre and then proceeded north to the Orkney Islands and on to Norway (Manuscript of Flatey 1784, 39–40).

The strength of the King of Scotland was increasing and it became difficult for the chiefs in Bute and Arran to refuse him their allegiances. King Haakon IV was demanding the possession of all the islands off the mainland of Scotland. The King of Scotland, now Alexander III[28], would not relinquish Bute, Arran, and the two Cumbraes. These lands, along with the large territory of Kintyre (Cantire) became a source of fierce contention between the Scots and Norwegians. The Stewarts were rapidly dispossessing the descendants of Somerled of their lands in Bute. Ruari went directly to King Haakon IV in Norway and returned from Bergen with him and his large fleets' expedition to establish his claims to the Hebrides (Reid 1864, 40–1).

This led to the famous Battle of Largs on 3 October 1263 (Reid 1864, 43). The result of the battle was that Haco's expedition was repelled from Largs on the mainland of Scotland and they eventually retreated back to Norway. Haakon IV, the last Norwegian king to rule over the Southern Isles (Sudreyjar), died at Kirkwall on the Island of Orkney 15 December 1263 on his voyage home (R. G. Hill 1873, 11–12). Later, Haakon IV's son, King Magnus VI, negotiated a Treaty of Peace in 1266 with Alexander III that Scotland would pay *"four thousand Merks (Roman Standard), payable in four equal instalments, with a quitrent of one hundred merks forever."* The Norwegians *"renounced all claim to the Western Isles, including those in the Firth of Clyde."* Furthermore, Alexander's four-year-old daughter, Margaret, was betrothed to the son of the King of Norway and the sons of Ruari were forced to leave Bute and Arran (Reid 1864, 44).

Robert the Bruce and the Isle of Bute

In 1305, Walter the High Steward of Scotland entered into a contract with Robert the Bruce to undermine the power of England in Scotland. Bruce was crowned King of Scotland at Scone 27 March 1306 which he then declared independence from England although he would still have to fight the English King Edward I for it. King Edward I died in 1307 on his way to battle with

[27] 1228~1230, the date of this conflict, was the first mention of Rothesay Castle in history.

[28] Alexander II died in 1249.

Bruce. In 1313, Bruce took the Isle of Man and Rothesay Castle. In 1314, Bute was held for King Robert Bruce by Angus of Isle, of the family of Somerled. It was afterwards held by Robert, the son and heir of Walter the High Steward. The Battle of Bannockburn on 24 June 1314 secured the defeat of King Edward II of England and established the Scotch royal succession of King Robert II. Both Walter High Steward of Scotland and Angus of Isle fought at the battle of Bannockburn with Robert the Bruce (Reid 1864, 48–51).

> *As long as only one hundred of us remain alive we will never on any conditions be brought under English rule.*
>
> —The Declaration of Arbroath[29], 6 April 1320

DISCUSSION

Regarding the Muir/Moore of this study's interest, it seems reasonable that, having lived on Bute anywhere from 800 to 1100 A.D., the family would have assimilated with the ever-changing climate of political, military, economic, and social dynamics on the island. At times, they may have fought for the Norwegians, other times they may have fought for the Scottish crown, depending on who their feudal lord was and what benefits they could gain. By the time of Bruce's rise to becoming King Robert I, the Muir/Moore's of Bute would have fought on the same side as other Scots on Bute as vassals or adherents of the Stewarts. They would have been embroiled in the same history as the Stewarts and hence eventually able to take advantage of what the Stewart or the MacDonnell migration to Ulster had to offer.

The Ayrshire family of the Mures of Rowallan

A genealogy entitled, *The Historie and Descent of the House of Rowallane, written by Sir William Mure, Knight of Rowallan, written in, or prior to, 1657* was published in Glasgow in 1825. According to the author, Sir Gilchrist Mure was granted the lands of Rowallan in reward for his service to Alexander III, King of Scotland, at the Battle of Largs [fig. 15] in 1263 (Mac Giolla-Domhnaigh 1923). According to Clan Muir Society, Gilchrist Mure "*led the offensive that drove the Norwegians back to the sea.*"

In 1346, Elizabeth Mure (Muir) of Rowallan, the great-great granddaughter of Gilchrist Mure, the patriarch of Mure's of Rowallan (d. 1280), married Robert the Bruce's grandson, Robert, who was to become the future King Robert II. Robert was the son of Robert the Bruce's only daughter, Marjorie Bruce and her husband, Walter the High Steward of Scotland. The surname

29 From the "Letter of the Barons of Scotland" to Pope John XXII. It was a declaration in the name of the "*whole community of the Realm*" of their determination to maintain the independence of Scotland and to support King Robert Bruce.

appears to have been spelled More at first and then changed over time to the spelling of Muir or Mure due to accents and spelling by the way the word sounded (Clan Muir Society 1999).

Sir William Mure distinctly states that the Mures originally came from *"the Ancient Tribe of O'More in Ireland."*[30] Mr. Mure enumerates the following Junior Branches of the Mures of Rowallan's extended families copied word for word thusly:

> *Thence it is that the house of Caldwell, The progenie of Robert Mure of Camb-Ceskane, of which Glanerstone, Thorntone. And the house of Achindraine, the progenie of Andro Mure of Monyhagen of which CloneCard, Held ordinarlie from one age to another, Sonnes of this familie........In like manner also the house of Pokellie, with the severall branches thereof, The house of Parke, Of which Midltone, & Altoneburne, Of which Spitleside, Brownehill, and the Mures of Tarboltone The House of Skeldone, of which the Mures of woodland, Knockmarlioch & Killikie, The houses of Skemore & Annestone with their branches The Mures of duglasedale, Carses & Calder, The house of bogside, of which the Mures of Arrathill, Mures of Irwing & Polmadie of which the most of the Mures of Glasgow: The houses of Baldochat in golloway, of Sanquhare, of drwmskieoch, of Achinneill, of Arioland, with the Mures of the Chappell, of which the Mures of Edinburgh for the most part. The house of Ormishugh, The houses of CassenCarie & fferrie, of blacklaw & skirnalland, of Well, ffinnickhill, & Clarkland, of Litle-Cesnock and little finnick, Houses of the latest descent, some whereof falling to Airs female some perishing throw oppression of the greater, some throw proper Misgoverment Or siding with parties with whom they wer broken, few of all being standing families at the present, at the surname of Mure, All of them I say diversified their Armes from other, And from the Paternall Coat, except in the stars & mullets, by additionall Nottes of distinction as the maisters of Herauldrie to the most considerable did appoint, or as best pleased the fansie of other to make choyce of for themselves.*
> (Mure 1825, 24–27)

Considering the above list, one can begin to understand the multitude of Mure/Muir families that can all claim as being a descendant from the Mures of Rowallan.[31]

---

[30] However, this has not been proven.

[31] As for the castle itself, Rowallan was bought by Niall Campbell in 1989 and thirteen years later received consent for its renovation. It opened as an AirB&B in 2019.

DISCUSSION

If the *Muir 2 Tree* on Bute were a junior branch of the Rowallan family as claimed, they could have migrated to Bute at the end of the 17th century, but they also may have migrated to Bute many years earlier. Or, indeed, it is quite possible that the *Muir 2 Tree* of Bute may not be affiliated with the Mures of Rowallan at all. It will be left to either Mr. L. Muir of the *Muir 2 Tree* or future genealogists to figure that out.

Various Muir families in Scotland

The Scottish Muir farming community's early census data from 1841 reveals at least **nine** distinct groups of Scottish Muir farmers in Scotland (Bowes 2017) [Appendix 4]. Other than the family of Muir/Moore on Bute, there are several Muir families found in the Lowlands. Many Scottish Moores are also found on the *Ancestry.com* website as being from around Lanarkshire, Ayrshire and Renfrewshire.

In addition, Muirs/Mures resided in the Midlothian areas around Edinburgh. For instance, in the Exchequer Rolls of Scotland Vol IX A.D. 1480–1487 Addenda 1437–1487, assigned feudal lands show that a William Mure is tenant with his son Edward of Newtoungrange, Midlothian, Scotland. Fast forward to the early 1600's in the *Ancestry.com* records, a junior branch of that family is found just 5 miles (E. by S.) in the parish of Inveresk, Musselburgh. There is an Edward Muir who is born 22 Jul 1610 to a father named Edward Muir in Inveresk with Musselburgh, Midlothian. Also, a William Moore married Marion Knycht of the same parish on 26 Jan 1608 as well as also having a child named William who was born on 21 Oct 1610 in the same parish. In the parish of Leith South near Edinburgh, there is a Thomas Muir who was born on 14 Jul 1610 to an Edward Muir and Margrat Bredie (ScotlandsPeople.gov.uk).

DISCUSSION

Another example of Muirs in different areas of Scotland would be that of the Muirs hailing from Lanarkshire. On the *Ancestry.com* web site, Norman Moore, Sr. is depicted as being related in the FamilyFinder DNA Matches section to four separate families with a link to the surname of Muir. Two families do not know from where in Scotland they came, but the other two Muir families state Lanarkshire as the County in Scotland from which their ancestors lived in the 18th century. The closest family in proven relation to Norman Moore, Sr., according to the Ancestry DNA, is from the Carstairs/Carluke[32] area of Lanarkshire as follows: Thomas-1 (b. 1700) married in 1724 Carluke, Lanarkshire to Marion Hart (b. 1704). Their son was James

---

32 St. Andrew's Church in Carluke, now a Church of Scotland, dates from 1296. It is reputed to be the place where William Wallace was declared Guardian of Scotland in 1297 (Martin 1999).

Mure-2 (b. 1729) in Carstairs, Lanarkshire and married in 1757 Carluke to Janet Harvie[33] (b. 1733) Lesmanagow, Lanarkshire. Their son Thomas Muir-3 (b. 1760) in Carluke and married in 1790 Carluke to Jean Clark. As is the case with the three Muir genealogies from the Isle of Bute, this family's written genealogy only dates back to the early 1700's, which is still about 100 years later than the date needed to connect any Muir/Moore family to the Ulster Plantation of the early 1600's, and who knows from whence they came. However, they do appear to be very distant cousins.

Clan Muir (Clan Muir Society 1999) (Clan Muir n.d.)

Anyone hailing from Scotland would be connected to a family tartan. Clan Muir is a Scottish clan that is armigerous, meaning that it has no chief recognized by the Court of the Lord Lyon. Clan membership is determined by surname. There are other clans which recognize some Moore's as part of their septs.

Clan affiliation by spelling variation

- Muir/Mure/Moore | most common in Clan Campbell.
- Moir/Moire | most common in Clan Gordon.
- Moore | most common in Clan Leslie.
- More | most common in Clan Grant.
- Langmoore/Longmuir | most common in Clan Boyd.

Members of Clan Muir who do not give their allegiance to any of the clans that list their surname as a sept or who do not have a family history of belonging to any of the aforementioned clans wear the Muir tartan. (Clan Muir membership guide)

Clan Muir does not have any septs, though common variations of the name *Muir* or *Moore* are associated with the clan.

- Muir/More/Moore/Mure | most common in Ayrshire and areas southwest Scotland.
- Moar/Moare/Moer | most common in Orkney and Shetland.
- Moir/Moire | most common in Aberdeenshire and areas in the Southeast lowlands.
- Mohr/Mor | most common in the Central Lowlands.
- O'More/O'Morhda/O'Moore | most common in Ireland.

---

33 Janet's mother was Helen Hamilton, daughter of Alexander Hamilton b. 1675

Muir/Moore has the three variations of meaning: (K. Moore 2010)

- Large or big in Gaelic
- A moor or heath in middle English
- By the sea in Pictish

Clan Motto | Durum Patientia Frango: *By patience I break what is hard* (Clan Muir n.d.).

Figure 17. The Clansman's Strap and Buckle Badge and the Muir Tartan

Source: The Clan Muir Society (Clan Muir Society 1999)

5

Moores of Ballymoney, Antrim, and Northern Ireland

AS WAS THE CASE WITH DR. TYRONE BOWES' STUDIES of those surnames related as "genetic cousins" to Norman Moore, Sr.'s pointing to his Scottish origin being on Isle of Bute, the location of their Ulster transplantation can be garnered in much the same way. Families who lived clustered together in Scotland tended to stay together when transplanting to Ulster. This initial study tested only the male line using the Y-DNA test results.

Autosomal test of ones DNA is a different kind of study and it is used to examine both males *and* females which will make up one's ancestral lines. With this test, one will typically match a high percentage of individuals within the total data base. FTDNA's FamilyFinderDNA was used for this test. *"The more DNA that two people share, the more recent their shared ancestor once lived,"* states Dr. Tyrone Bowes.

Eric Moore: An Autosomal DNA Case Study, which was completed by Bowes on 25 July 2019, illustrates this in detail [Appendix 4]. Bowes found that Eric Moore matched 3,077 people. Out of that number, 1,203 people stated the ancestral origins of their oldest known ancestor, which indicates almost 40% of the total people genetically related; a pretty good percentage. In looking at this 40% for where these genetic relatives were from, Counties Antrim and Donegal in Ulster, Northern Ireland were revealed. Furthermore, most of these genetically related ancestral surnames were dominant in 16th and 17th century Scottish Plantation origins in Antrim.

An examination of Eric Moore's Autosomal DNA results showed strongest links to County Antrim where Bowes' study reveals two groups of Plantation Moores on his *Surname Map for Ulster*. One group of Moores were from the Belfast area. There were no other Isle of Bute surnames associated with that area. The other Moore group was from the area around Ballymoney, County Antrim. Family surnames from the Isle of Bute were all found living in very close vicinity of one another around the town of Ballymoney. Families tended to have generally remained in their areas of settlement for generations (Bowes, Eric Moore; An Autosomal DNA Case Study 2019).

Surnames of the families who eventually traveled together from Isle of Bute, Scotland to the area around Ballymoney, Antrim, Ulster, Northern Ireland: Lamont, Stewart, McAfee, Black, Barr, Jamison, McConaghy, McIntyre, Crawford and Duncan.

Some surnames who were shown to be "genetic cousins" of Norman Moore's study, were also shown to be clustered around the Ballymoney area of Antrim.

Surnames of Norman Moore, Sr.'s "Genetic Relatives." These are the surnames of families who are definitely related through a genetic connection using Y-DNA (Bowes 2017): Lamont, McCain, Jeffery, Livingston(e), Newton, MacEachern, MacDonald, McDaniel, McArthur, King, Alexander and McCunn. Those surnames which were found in the Ballymoney area were: Lamont, McKane (McCain/McCunn) and Alexander.

The last name of Moore seems to be still highly common in the area.

Most common surnames in Ballymoney in 1901: (Forebears.io 1901) Moore-15th, Lamont-19th, Kennedy-27th, Crawford-29th, Stewart-34th, Jamison-63rd, McAfee-67th, McConaghy-79th, McCann-88th, Barr-112th, McIntyre-121st, Black-196th

Figure 18. Baronies & Parishes of North Antrim

Source: Map adapted from http://www.billmacafee.com/ballintoy/admin/mapbarparishesnantrim.jpg

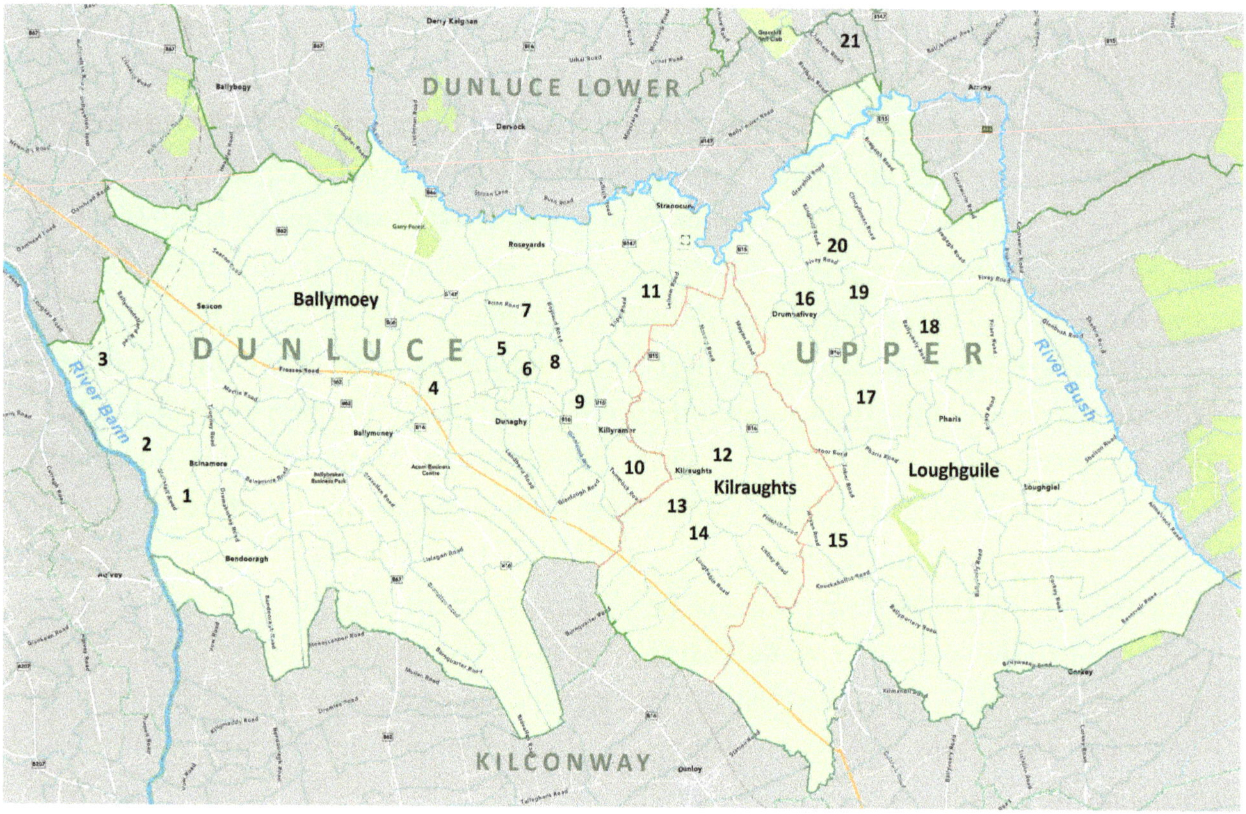

Figure 19. "Moore" Townlands, Barony of Dunluce Upper, between Rivers Bush & Bann

Source: Base map with the permission of the Northern Ireland Place-Name Project, QUB. http://www.placenamesni.org/map

Townland	Parish
1. Ballynacree More	Ballymoney
2. Drumaheglis	Ballymoney
3. Macfin	Ballymoney
4. Greenville	Ballymoney
5. Greenshields Lower	Ballymoney
6. Greenshields Upper	Ballymoney
7. Farranalessary	Ballymoney
8. Ballyboylands Lower	Ballymoney
9. Ballyboylands Upper	Ballymoney
10. Craigatempin	Ballymoney
11. Leitrim	Ballymoney
12. Kilraughts	Kilraughts
13. Magheraboy Upper	Kilraughts
14. Crosstagherty	Kilraughts
15. Lisnisk	Loughguile
16. Ballycregagh Lower	Loughguile
17. Turnagrove	Loughguile
18. Culbane	Loughguile
19. Drumdallagh (Ballinahone)	Loughguile
20. Ballycregagh Upper	Loughguile
21. Mullaghduff	Derrykeighan, Dunluce Lower Barony

Ballymoney was first referenced in the year 1305 as Balybony, in 1334 as Ballybony, in 1485 as Balleboni and in 1550 spelled both as Balebonad and Ballyvouny (Munn first published 1925, reprinted by Ballinascreen Historical Society 1985, 41). As mentioned in Chapter One, the MacDonnell clan, Earls of Antrim, *formally* received the toughs (tribal territory) which included Ballymoney and Loughguile in 1586. However, the clan had been in Antrim since around 1493 (R. G. Hill 1873, 78 #106).

Due to the lack of records from that time period, it is impossible to find the paper trail of the exact family, or even a date, for which this Moore study's ancestors transplanted into Ulster. Groups of families traveled together when settling on their new lands in Ulster and this study's Bute Moores were no exception. They settled in the Ballymoney area, according to the Bowes report, but of which three Moore families who settled in Ballymoney were they? This will take some further investigation.

Ballymoney Moores

Townlands of Moore families located in the Ballymoney, Co. Antrim, Ulster area in 1888 from *The Book of Antrim* written by George Henry Basset are as follows: (Bassett 1888)

1 | Stt Moore Crosstagherty, Kilraughts parish and William Moore, Magheraboy Upper, Kilraughts parish are right next to each other's lands and they were related.

2 | Farmers and Residents: People who were related with farmlands right next to each other: David Moore, Ballyboylands, Ballymoney parish, farmer; Thomas Moore, Ballyboylands; J.A. Moore, Farranlessary, Ballymoney parish; and Thomas Moore, Greenshields, Ballymoney parish, farmer.

3 | William and William Jr. Moore of Moorfort, Drumaheglis, Ballymoney parish, '*a new woolen factory has taken place of the old distillery at Drumaheglis*' whose ancestor was Sampson Moore d. 1775 of Moore Lodge, Ballynacree More, Ballymoney parish; both Quakers from Cumberland, England.

4 | There was also a James Moore of Leitrim listed in the 1888 directory.
Sub-post-offices are: Ballyboyland, Bendooragh, Drumaheglis, Finvoy, Garryduf, Killane, Killraughts, Pharis, Rosemount, Seacon. Many Lamonts also lived in this area at that time (Bassett 1888).

In the paper *North Antrim Families* by Thomas Bennett, the author states:

In Co. Antrim in the Ballymoney area there seem to have been three main groups of Moore families. I do not think they had a common origin.

First, there are our [meaning Bennett's] *Moores at Kilraghts.*

Then, the Moores of Ballyboyland, including the Moores of Fernalizery (Farranlessary) and their old line at Lisnisk and the Moores of Turnagrove.

Finally, the Moores of Moore Lodge, with their branches at Moore Fort, Moore's Grove, Cloves Hill and Lischeihan . . . There are quite a few other families in our area for whom I have been able to construct fragments of pedigree—Moore of Ballycraighagh & Ballinahone, Moore of Grigatempin, Moore of Lisnaglt & Mullaghduff—But without any idea of how they might be related, and only the slightest suggestions in that direction from names and places. As for the Moores at Lisnisk, it looks to me as though the original family there belonged to the Ballyboyland group. There is no correspondence between the known members of the Ballyboyland-Lisnisk group in the 17th Century and the Kilraghts group, or indeed those of Ballinacree. (Bennett 1974, 12)

It is reasonable that the Moores from the townlands of Ballycraighagh (Ballycregagh), Balinahone (now called Drumdallagh), Culbane & Turnagrove were part of the Ballyboyland-Lisnisk families because these townlands are clustered close together, if not next door to each other, in the parish of Loughguile.

Geographically, from left to right on a county Antrim parish map, one can locate the parish of Ballymoney, right next to the east lies Kilraghts and adjoining Kilraghts, to its east, is the parish of Loughguile [fig. 19].

Dorothy Arthur's *Graveyard* Books

Dorothy Arthur's years of work documenting the old graveyards in the Ballymoney area is a priceless gift to genealogists. She not only depicts what is said on the tombstone, along with a photo of it and provides a map of its location in the churchyards, but she also adds a genealogy of the deceased as well. Her books provide an insight into the intermarriage of the various Moore families in the area over many years. *Ballymoney Old Church Graveyard* was her first in 2008. She went on to complete two more books of interest; *Derrykeighan Old Church Graveyard* in 2012 and *Kilraughts Old Church Graveyard* in 2014 (Arthur, Ballymoney Old Church Graveyard 2008) (Arthur 2012) (Arthur 2014) .

In examining the Moores mentioned above, specifically in regards for the purpose of this research, there are no families that use the forename of Edward. There are many Williams and Johns. There is only one family that uses the forename of Thomas throughout the generations and they lived in the townlands of Ballyboylands and Greenshields, Ballymoney Parish, Dunluce Upper Barony (Arthur 2008, 240) (Bassett 1888).

DISCUSSION

This book's Moore study is not part of the Moores of Kilraghts due to the fact that Mr. Bennett claims be of the Moores of Kilraghts as well as claiming to being a part of the Mures of Rowallan family who were initially Irish back in the 500's. This study's DNA shows it is not part of that Irish group of people who settled in Scotland from the 6th to the 9th century (Snow 2001, 1-2). This study's Moore family were Vikings who settled in Bute, Scotland post 800 A.D. to 1100 A.D.

This Moore study is not part of the Moores of Ballinacree and Drumaheglis (Moore Lodge and Moore Fort) as they were Quakers originally from Cumberland, England.

If there are any relatives from this study's Moore family still in existence living in North Antrim, they are most likely part of the original Ballyboylands & Farranlessary, Ballymoney parish families which, over time, expanded into Loughguile parish into the townlands of Turnagrove, Ballinahone, and Ballycregagh. They also state that their original townland was Lisnisk, Loughguile Parish, noting that the date of 1642 is carved on a beam in one of their outhouses on that estate (Bennett 1974, 3).[34] It is noted in Mr. Bennett's paper that the Moores of Ballyboylands of the mid-17th century were Covenanters; members of the Reformed Presbyterian Church originating in Scotland (Bennett 1974, 13).

Many people in the north of Ireland signed the National Covenant in 1638 but the Scottish Solemn League and Covenant in Ulster was not officially formed until 1643 by Scottish Covenanters and English Parliamentarians (Ulster-Scots Agency 2007, #2, #3). These Moore study's ancestors were in Ulster prior to 1638. In fact, from the years of 1609 to 1631, due to Scottish Presbyterian ministers being established into Episcopalian Churches (Anglican Irish churches), the settlers worshiped as "Prescopalians", a term unique to Ireland (Kirkland 2018, 13).

From Ballymoney, Dunluce Barony, some families from these surrounding areas of the Earl of Antrim's estates, including these Moore study's ancestors, moved together further inland for land and opportunities of their own as native escheated Irish lands became available. ⚜

34 The date of 1642 on an outhouse beam means nothing as to the original date of settling. It was most likely rebuilt after its destruction from the Irish Rebellion.

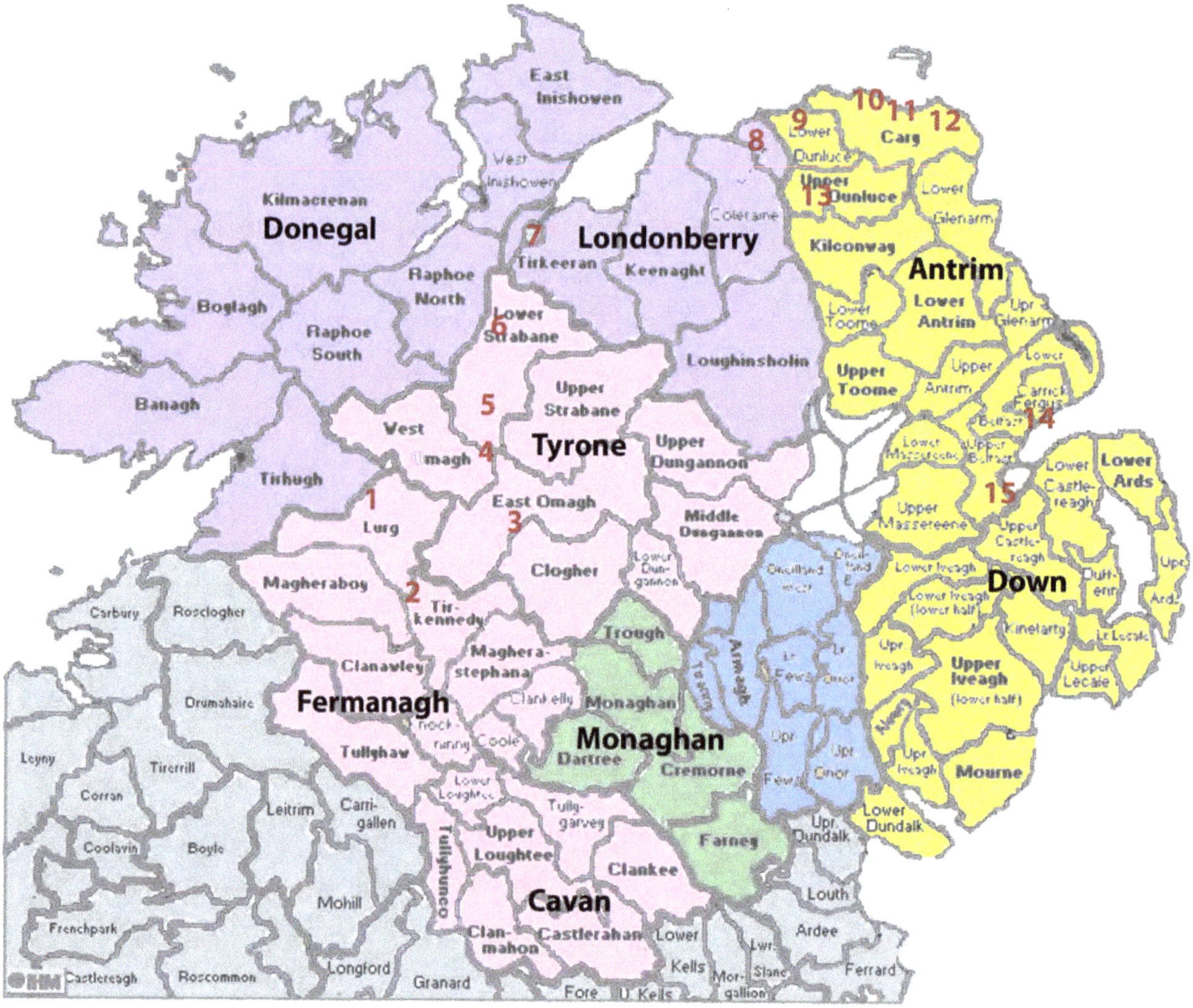

Figure 20. Baronies and Counties of Ulster with important towns referenced

Map adapted from an image by Dennis Walsh (Walsh 2003). https://www.sites.rootsweb.com/~irlkik/ihm/barony-map-ulster.htm
Donegal is not part of modern day Northern Ireland but it was part of the Plantation back then.

1. Bunaninver, Co. Fermanagh
2. Enniskillen, Co. Fermanagh
3. Edergoole, Co. Tyrone
4. Claraghmore, Co. Tyrone
5. Newtownstewart, Co. Tyrone
6. Strabane, Co. Tyrone
7. Londonderry, Co. Londonderry
8. Coleraine, Co. Londonderry
9. Dunluce, Co. Antrim
10. Dunseverick, Co. Antrim
11. Ballintoy, Co. Antrim
12. Ballycastle, Co. Antrim
13. Ballymoney, Co. Antrim
14. Carrickfergus, Co. Antrim
15. Belfast, Co. Antrim

Note for highlighted areas:[35]

- Yellow areas | privately settled
- Pink areas | Scots
- Green areas | Irish privately settled
- Blue areas | English
- Purple areas | English & Scots

[35] Over time, these restrictions were not strictly adhered to.

6
The Scottish Settlement of Fermanagh

AS MORE AND MORE LANDS OPENED UP in other Plantation counties of Ulster, younger sons took advantage of the opportunity to branch out on their own to secure lands for themselves. They left the original plantation sites and moved inland with their families to newer grounds (Johnston 2018). Movement like this would have been common during the early 1600's and was a factor in the expansion of British (English and Scots) landholdings as men took leases on townlands that had previously been let to native Irish tenants (Hunter, 'Men and arms' The Ulster settlers, c. 1630 2012, xviii). Furthermore, the practice of one landlord drawing tenants from another was much easier than when the alternative was to persuade settlers to cross the Irish Sea and even having to pay for their passage (Perceval-Maxwell 1990, 179). First English, then quickly after mostly Scots, settled in Fermanagh. Unfortunately, in Captain Nicholas Pynnar's *1622 Survey of Ulster*, there was no distinction between the designation of either English or Scot as he signified the settlers with the term "British" for all non-Irish settlers (Perceval-Maxwell 1990, 166–7).

Archdale Estate, Bunaninver, County Fermanagh

In 1615, John Archdale, an original English Undertaker from Darsham in Suffolk, was portioned 1000 acres in County Fermanagh (Perceval-Maxwell 1990, 362). He built a castle and bawn at Tallanagh (modern Bunaninver townland) in the parish of Derryvullan, Barony of Lurg, County Fermanagh. This townland is located 9 miles north of Enniskillen on the east side of the lake named Lower Lough Erne. The description of Archdale's castle was:

> *A simple rectangular bawn, with, originally, square towers flanking the entrance, and a three storye house opposite the gateway. It is built using coursed rubble masonry, had a parapet wall-walk supported by moulded corbels, and a gateway decorated with quirk-mouding. As these techniques of corbelling and decoration are of Scottish origin, this castle is the earliest dated example of Scotch workmanship in Fermanagh.* (Johnston 1978, 370)

Archdale had granted about a third of the estate at the same time, reasonably to pay the costs of the construction work (Johnston 1978, 370). The following information is found in the same inquisition which was noted at Enniskillen on the 27 April 1629:

> *The said John Archdall did grant 4 ½ tates unto William and Thomas Lawton, gentlemen, their heirs and assignes forever. The said John Archdall did grant 2 tates of ½ quarter of land to William Johnson and Owen Griffith, their heirs and assignes, forever. The said John Archdall, by coppie of court-rowle, at a court held for the manor of Tallanagh, did grant one and a half tate, or 3 parts of ½ a quarter unto William Johnson and Thomas Clarke, their heirs and assignes ; and half a quarter, being two tates, unto Thomas Moore and Edward Moore, and David Byas, their heirs and assignes.* (R. G. Hill 1877, 487)

The reason for the 1629 rework of the original 1615 grant was so that the grant could include the clause that the undertakers would be permitted to let one-quarter of their estates to the native Irish (Johnston 1978, 372).

DISCUSSION

Thomas Moore (b.*c.* 1609)and Edward Moore (b.*c.* 1592) were in all likelihood father and son and there is a good possibility that these two men are part of "our" Irish ancestry. They were from the Earl of Antrim estates in the Ballymoney area of the Barony of Dunluce Upper, Co. Antrim (Bowes, Eric Moore; An Autosomal DNA Case Study 2019). David Byas (Byers), the third person mentioned with Moores above, was also a Scotsman. It is possible that freeholders Thomas an Edward Moore were helping with the construction of the building for the Archdale estate in the Scottish manner as was in the case of Sir Thomas Ridgeway's tenants for his Clogher estates: *"Ten masons work upon the castle, and two smiths . . . and three of the said carpenters* are *to be made freeholders"* (R. G. Hill 1877, 538) .

Most of the Scotch settlers were nominally protestant in that they did not seem to have strong religious convictions. In addition, the settlers were often swayed by the beliefs of their landlords (Perceval-Maxwell 1990, 273). All of Archdale's freeholders were made to take the Oath of Supremacy (Perceval-Maxwell 1990, 88). By taking the Oath of Supremacy, Thomas and Edward Moore would have had to pledge that the English Monarch was the head of the Church, forsaking Presbyterianism or the Pope as the supreme head. This would make them part of the state Anglican Irish Church. From this specific event, our Moores would become part of the Church of Ireland, in other words, Anglican.

There is a high probability that "our" ancestors would have moved on from their initial rented lands in Antrim; as it was a common occurrence (Ulster-Scots Agency 2006) (Hunter, 'Men and arms' The Ulster settlers, c. 1630 2012, xviii). Further surname analysis depicts a movement from Ballymoney, County Antrim to the Omey (Omagh) area of County Tyrone [fig. 21].

Legend for lists below:
(R)=*Genetically Related per DNA;* ***(B)***=*Surnames from Bute;* ***(O)***=*Mustered in Omey (Omagh) Barony in 1630;* ***(S)***=*Mustered in Strabane Barony in 1630*

Surnames of people with whom Moores travelled from the Ballymoney area of County Antrim to the Omey area of County Tyrone depicting migration inland.
Sometime after the 1641–44 Rebellion, they settled back into the Newtownstewart area. (Using Bowes' *Ulster Surname Map* of 1841 farmers.)

Moore, Alexander-(R), [Mc]Arthur-(R), Stewart-(B), Duncan-(B), Crawford-(B), Brown, Huey, Pinkerton, Knox, Love, Hunter, Cunningham, Kerr, Anderson, Jack and Patrick.

The Four Baronies of County Tyrone in 1630:
O=*Omagh,* ***S***=*Strabane,* ***C***=*Clogher and* ***D***=*Dungannon*
Surnames from the above list of the 1841 farmers who were *ALSO* listed in the *1630 Ulster Muster* for County Tyrone showing the Baronies from which they mustered.

Alexander-(R) SCD, Stewart-(B) OC, Duncan-(B) C, Crawford-(B) CD, Brown-OSC, Knox-SC, Hunter-SC, Cunningham-CS and 11 Moores: 3 in Omey (Omagh) and 7 in Clogher.

Additional surnames[36] of Moore's Antrim neighbors listed in Co. Tyrone's *1630 Muster Rolls*, once again showing migration to inland properties.

Black-(B) O, Barr-(B) S, King-(R) S, Jamison-(B) CD, McCaen-(R) CS, McEachern-(R) S, Hill-SC, Cochrane-S, Patterson-S, White-S and Reid-C.

[36] But were not seen on Dr. Bowes' surname map from 1841.

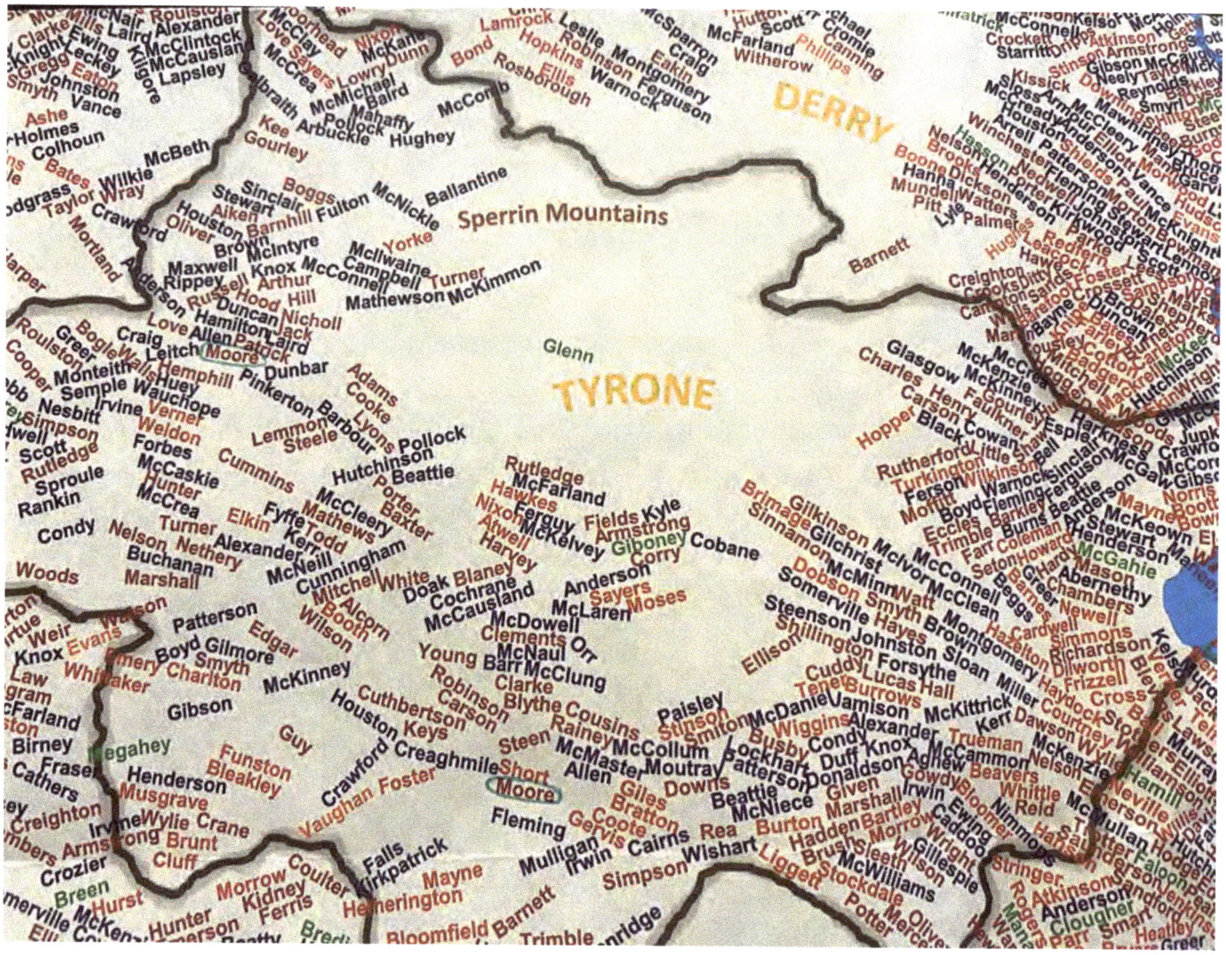

Figure 21. Irish Surname map showing location of "Moore" families in Co. Tyrone

Source: Map with permission from Dr. Tyrone Bowes at www.irishorigenes.com

This Ulster Surname Map of 1841 farmers shows a "Moore" family still living in the Omagh area of County Tyrone. Its second genetic-relative marker location would be in the northwestern area of Newtownstewart, Strabane Barony, County Tyrone[37] as this move would have taken place from Omagh sometime after the 1641 Irish Rebellion.

[37] The third area of concentration of Genetic-Relatives is in Donegal, but this Moore study's direct line would have been long gone by 1841.

7
1630 Muster Rolls of Ulster

LANDED ESTATES IN THE NEW PLANTATION SETTLEMENTS of Ulster were required to muster tenants for defense when areas were under threat from the native Irish. The *1630 Muster Rolls* for the Province of Ulster were carried out between the spring of 1629 and the spring of 1631. They contain the names of adult males on an estate bearing or capable of bearing arms and what they carried. These musters were important to show the strength of men readily available to fight for the English Monarch as needed. The *Muster rolls* are the most complete list of the settler population that is available and serves as a virtual census of men over eighteen for that period (Hunter, 'Men and arms' The Ulster settlers, c. 1630 2012, xv).

The requirement for undertakers to settle twenty-four men from ten families per 1000 acres meant that each family consisted of a father and one or more grown-up sons. Generally, if a family arrived in Ulster around 1615, the father would have been aged at least forty and the younger of the sons would have been at least eighteen years of age. By 1630, the father would have been in his late fifties or early sixties, the sons would have been in their thirties of forties, and some of the grandsons might have been old enough to muster (Hunter, 'Men and arms' The Ulster settlers, c. 1630 2012, xvii).

The *1630 Muster Rolls* are considered a linkage document in order to trace families across three or four generations. According to J.R. Hunter, the authority on the *1630 Ulster Muster*, a family connection is likely if a surname recurs two or three times in the muster list for an estate (Hunter, 'Men and arms' The Ulster settlers, c. 1630 2012, xvii). Figure 22 lists all the Earl of Antrim's British tenants with the surname of Moore who mustered on his Co. Antrim, Dunluce barony estates (where Ballymoney is located) [fig. 18, 20]. Unfortunately, the *Ulster muster* for Co. Antrim did not depict in which specific towns of Dunluce Barony his tenants lived. However, the list is divided into folios of those who mustered together and thus one can assume they are family members.

folio 148v	John	Moore	Dunluce	Sword only	Earl of Antrim's British tenants	Antrim
f. 149	Robert	Moore	Dunluce	Sword only	Earl of Antrim's British tenants	Antrim
	William	Moore	Dunluce	Sword only	Earl of Antrim's British tenants	Antrim
f. 150	John	Moore	Dunluce	Sword only	Earl of Antrim's British tenants	Antrim
	Gilbert	Moore	Dunluce	Sword only	Earl of Antrim's British tenants	Antrim
f. 150v	John	Moore	Dunluce	Sword only	Earl of Antrim's British tenants	Antrim
	John	Moore	Dunluce	Sword only	Earl of Antrim's British tenants	Antrim
f. 153	James	Moore	Dunluce	No Arms	Earl of Antrim's British tenants	Antrim
f. 154	James	Moore	Dunluce	No Arms	Earl of Antrim's British tenants	Antrim
	Thomas	Moore	Dunluce	No Arms	Earl of Antrim's British tenants	Antrim
	John	Moore	Dunluce	No Arms	Earl of Antrim's British tenants	Antrim
f. 155v	John	Moore	Dunluce	No Arms	Earl of Antrim's British tenants	Antrim
	Gilbert	Moore	Dunluce	No Arms	Earl of Antrim's British tenants	Antrim
f. 156	James	Moore	Dunluce	No Arms	Earl of Antrim's British tenants	Antrim
	Thomas	Moore	Dunluce	No Arms	Earl of Antrim's British tenants	Antrim
	James	Moore	Dunluce	No Arms	Earl of Antrim's British tenants	Antrim
f. 158	William	Moore	Dunluce	No Arms	Earl of Antrim's British tenants on his servitors	Antrim

Figure 22. Muster of the Earl of Antrim's British Moore tenants from Dunluce

The R. J. Hunter Collection of the *1630 Muster Rolls* for the Barony of Dunluce, Co. Antrim
Source: Information adapted from *Men and arms; the Ulster settlers, c. 1630* by R. J. Hunter and also
http://www.therjhuntercollection.com/resourcesmuster--rolls-c-1630/search-muster-rolls/.

Thomas and Edward are forenames one is primarily compelled to explore for this study's sake. There are two reasons one would search out these names. First, this Moore study's ancestor was Thomas (born 1654) and his father's name was Edward as stated in his Marriage Contract of 1690. Second, Thomas was affiliated with Edward in Co. Fermanagh in 1629. There are only two Thomas's in the entire Dunluce list; folio #154 listing James, Thomas and John and folio #156 listing James, Thomas and James. It is generally accepted that the first name listed would be the father followed by his grown-up sons.

Extrapolating this data from the muster describes this Moore family's three generations. Remaining in Ballymoney, Co. Antrim would be the immigrating family from Dunluce's folio #154 of James Moore, born in Bute, Scotland *c.*1554, and his son Thomas, born Bute *c.*1572, with his brother John, born Bute *c.*1575 [fig. 22].

Reviewing the historic tradition of naming patterns as described in Chapter 4, the first-born son was named after the father's father (FaFa), the 2nd born son was named after the mother's father (MoFa), the 3rd born son was named after the father (Fa) and the 4th born son was named after the father's eldest brother (FaBr). Interpreting that information, Thomas's (b. *c.*1572) first born would be named after his father, James. This James would have been born around 1588, maybe even still in Bute, Scotland, but travelling with his whole family group into the Ballymoney area around 1590. James (b. *c.*1588) would have named his first-born son after his father, Thomas, and his third born son after himself. These names correlate with folio #156 of a father named James (b. *c.*1588) mustering with his two grown-up sons of Thomas (b. *c.*1610) and James (b. *c.*1612) [Fig.22, 23]. All these people mustered in 1630 in the Ballymoney area of Dunluce on the Earl of Antrim's British tenants' estate.

Taking a look at the ages of the family members in folio #154 who first moved from Scotland to Ulster, one wonders if these men could have been that old and still muster in 1630. Consulting experts from the Ulster Historical Foundation confirmed that it would be quite possible for a man in his seventies with sons in their fifties to appear in the *muster roll.* Furthermore, settlers in North Antrim and County Down appear to have been about five to ten years older than those in other Ulster Counties [Appendix 5].

There are no Moore's with the first name of Edward recorded on any of the Antrim Estates, but that makes sense as Edward Moore had left Co. Antrim prior to the *1630 Muster* and was found mustering in Co. Tyrone instead.

The *1630 Muster* of the entirety of ULSTER lists ONLY two Edwards out of all the Moore surnames indexed. They are both named as mustering on the Hastings' Omey (Omagh, Co. Tyrone) estate and they were likely a father and his son. A William Moore is also listed in Omey (Omagh, Co. Tyrone) but on the estates of Captain Mervyn and it seems that he was somehow related.

If the father Edward was thirty-eight at the time, he would have been born c. 1592 and in Ballymoney, Co Antrim. Thomas, at around twenty-one years of age in 1630, was born c. 1609 and was an older son. Edward left Thomas his portion of land they farmed together in 1629 in Co. Fermanagh [Chapter Six]. He then moved on to Omey, Co. Tyrone with his younger son also named Edward, born c. 1612 and about eighteen years of age at the time. Both sons were born in Ballymoney, Co. Antrim. The father Edward (b. *c.* 1592) was doubtless a younger son himself since he migrated with his young family first to Fermanagh and next to Omagh leaving his family's original tenant lands in Antrim around the Ballymoney area in order to seek his own fortunes [fig. 23].

There was a movement of younger sons within the Ulster Province. The eldest son would stay on and take over the family farm and the younger sons had to move on. This was common in the 1620's and 1630's and a factor in the expansion of British landholding as younger sons took leases on townlands that had previously been let to native Irish tenants. (Hunter, 'Men and arms' The Ulster settlers, c. 1630 2012, xviii)

Edward seems to be an unusual name in this era for a Moore. The forename Edward does not exist for the earliest dates on any of the three Muir genealogies written up by Ms. Isabel Sharp in the Isle of Bute Genealogy center.[38] However, the names of Thomas, James and John do. In fact, the 'Muir 3 Tree' is the one tree that mentions the name Thomas most frequently as well as the names of James and John.

---

[38] Among these genealogies, the earliest date is that of 1692.

In reviewing Dorothy Arthur's *Graveyard* books from the Ballymoney area discussed in Chapter Five, there are no Edward Muirs/Moores mentioned in any of her four books of people buried in the area's graveyards. The earliest Moore detailed is a birth from 1678. This date is still not quite as early as that which would be needed to link our Moore study.

These facts make one think that the name Edward must have come from a *mother's* father's (MoFa) name, ie. a second born son. In looking at the first folio #154 of the father James (b. *c.*1554) having sons named Thomas and John, it has been already worked out that Thomas (b. *c.*1572) was father of folio #156. It is surely feasible that this same Thomas (b. *c.*1572) could have had a second son named after the *mother's* father (MoFa) with the name of Edward (born *c.*1592) in the Ballymoney area of Dunluce. The *mother's* father's name would have been 'Eamon' which is anglicized as either Edmund or Edward. Since Edward was a younger son, as he grew older, he would have moved on with his own family further west onto newly confiscated native Irish lands.

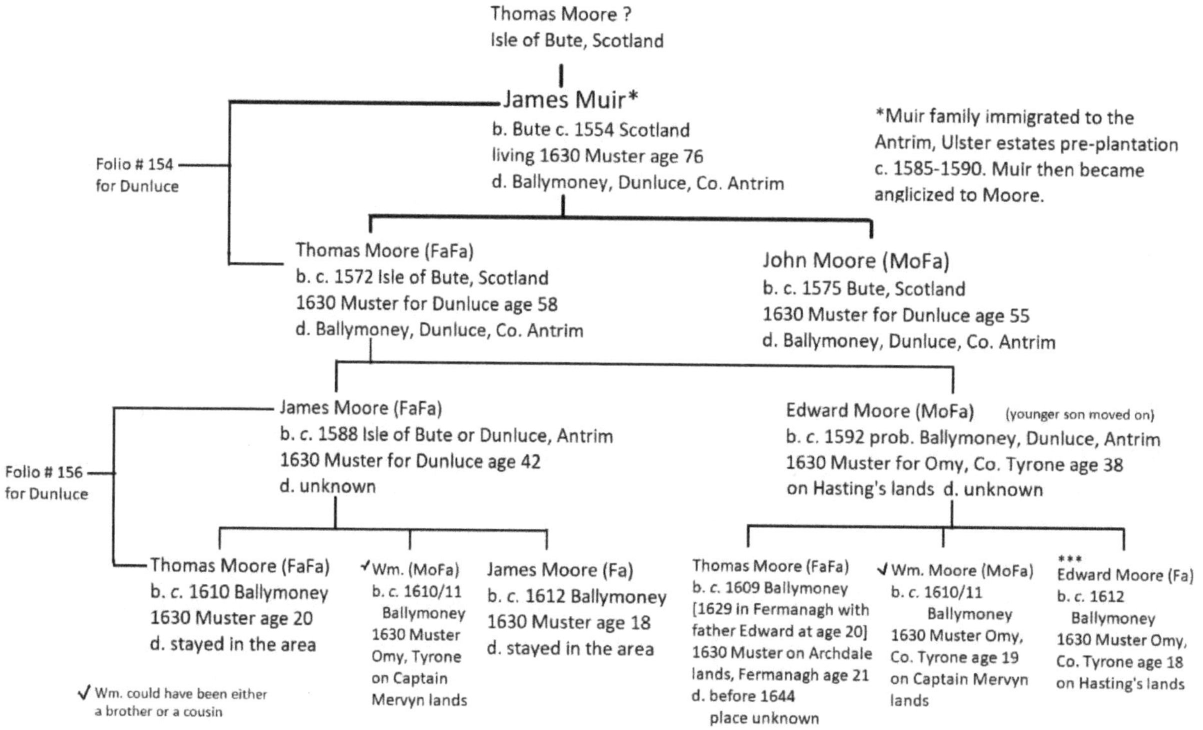

Figure 23. Genealogy chart detailing what the* 1630 Muster of Ulster *reveals

The illustrated diagram is garnered from the above discussion and also figure 22.
***Edward Moore continues in Figure 29. Chart by the author.

DISCUSSION | What the *1630 Muster of Ulster* reveals

• Thomas Moore (b. *c.*1609), now age twenty-one, mustered under the John Archdale estate in the barony of Lurg, Co. Fermanagh. There is no one named Edward Moore in the *1630 Fermanagh muster*. The *Muster* shows that his father, Edward (b. *c.* 1592), had left the balance of his Fermanagh lands and moved on to the next barony to the north with a younger son also named Edward (born *c.* 1612.)

• Edward Moore (b. c. 1592), now age thirty-eight, with a younger son Edward Moore (b. c. 1612), age eighteen, mustered under Lord Hastings (Protestant/Royalist) who held the townland of Claraghmore, Omey precinct, Co. Tyrone.

• William Moore (kin, b. *c.*1610/11, now around nineteen) mustered under Captain (James) Mervyn (Protestant/Royalist) who held the estate of Edergoole, Omey precinct, co. Tyrone.

In other words, Edward (b. *c.* 1592) first transplanted to Fermanagh in the 1620's, and was mentioned as a freeholder in 1629 on Archdale's land with his *first*-born son Thomas (b. *c.* 1609), named after Edward's father. He then moved on to the bordering land of Lord Hasting's Omey, Co. Tyrone estate and mustered in 1630 with his then 18-year-old *third*-born son Edward, named after himself, who would have been born *c.*1612 in the Ballymoney area.

Could the *second*-born son, who would have been named after the *mother's* father, been William, the same William who mustered on Captain Mervyn's Omey, Co. Tyrone estate? Or was he a cousin? One will never know, but it does seem that he was related somehow.

Figure 24. Archdale Castle in Bunaninver, Derryvullan, Lurg, County Fermanagh

Source: Map adapted from http://www.placenamesni.org/map

Thomas Moore (b.*c.* 1609) and Edward Moore (b.*c.* 1592) were found on the Archdale estates in 1629, as stated in Chapter Six. However, in the *1630 Muster Rolls*, only Thomas Moore mustered for John Archdale in the barony of Lurg, County Fermanagh, carrying no arms (Hunter, 'Men and arms' The Ulster settlers, c. 1630 2012, 41).

Lord Hastings, Omey, County Tyrone

In 1630, Edward Moore was found mustering with his son, also named Edward, in the next barony northeast from Lurg in the Barony of Omey (Omagh West) on the Lord Hastings estate of Cloghnamore (now Claraghmore), which was only about 23 miles away (Hunter, 'Men and arms' The Ulster settlers, c. 1630 2012, 68) [fig. 25].

Lord Henry Hastings, undertaker of 2000 acres, was the son and heir of Lord Francis Hastings, who succeeded in 1604 to become 7th Baron Hastings and 5th Earl of Huntingdon (Case on behalf of the Right Honourable Edith Maud, Countess of Loudoun...and Hastings, in the Peerage of England 1870, p. 61).

> *Soon afterwards, Lord Hastings disposed of these lands, as, on the 16th of April 1630, there was a grant thereof to William Unedale and Sir John Stanhope, of the small proportion of Cloghnamore* [Clonaghmore] *1000 acres, and 1627 acres and other parcels in the barony of Omey.* (R. G. Hill 1877, 538)

Figure 25. Hasting and Mervyn Estates at the time of the 1630 Muster

Source: Map adapted from http://www.placenamesni.org/map

This map shows the location of Lord Henry Hasting's Claraghmore Estate, Longfield East Parish, Omagh WestBarony, Co. Tyrone & Captain James Mervyn's Estate, Edergoole Townland, Drumragh Parish, Omagh East Barony, Co. Tyrone.

The historic townland of Clonaghmore is presently called Claraghmore, Parish of Longfield East in the Barony of Omagh West, Co. Tyrone.

Both Edward Moores were carrying snaphances (Hunter, 'Men and arms' The Ulster settlers, c. 1630 2012, 68). The weapons with which the tenants mustered were indications of their owners' wealth and social status. Firearms—in particular, *"the most advanced weapon, the snaphance"—were expensive, and so those who held them were probably wealthier than those who had "simple weapons such as a sword, pike, or halberd"* (Hunter, 'Men and arms' The Ulster settlers, c. 1630 2012, xviii).

Mervyn Estate, Omey, County Tyrone

The only other Moore listed as having mustered in the same Barony of Omey was William Moore who carried a sword, musket and bandoliers. He mustered under Captain James Mervyn, who was an undertaker of 6000 acres of land (Hunter, 'Men and arms' The Ulster settlers, c. 1630 2012, 69). Captain James Mervyn, the nephew of Lord George Audley, acquired his lands through his family. Lord George Audley had obtained a larger share than most other undertakers in the Plantation of Ulster.

> *By patent, dated 12th March, 1612, the King granted to George, Lord Audley, and Elizabeth, his wife, 2000 acres in the barony of Omagh, in the County of Tyrone, besides another 1000 acres in the same county, the lands in Omagh being erected at Lord Audley's request into the manor style of Stowbridge, those in Tyrone into the style of the manor of Heleigh.* (Prendergast 1874, 425)

Stowbridge and Heleigh were the family manors back in England. In addition, the family acquired 2000 acres called Fintona, 2000 acres called Edergoole (lower), 2000 acres called The Braid (Prendergast 1874, 543) and 3000 acres at Ravone (Lewis 1837).

Interestingly, the proportion of Lord Hastings' Claraghmore townland in the Parish of Longfield East, Omey precinct and the proportion of Mervyn's Edergoole townland in the parish of Drumragh, also in Omey precinct, were adjoining parishes [fig. 25]. William and Edward plausibly knew each other may have actually been kin. According to *Pynnar's Survey of 1622*, Captain James Mervyn's tenants *"totaled 41 families, able to make 48 men, which have taken the Oath of Supremacy"* (Prendergast 1874, 543). Captain James Mervyn's brother, Audley Mervyn, became his heir after his death. Audley Mervyn would eventually become an important figure during the 1641 Irish Rebellion and the subsequent English Civil Wars. ⚜

8

The 1641 Irish Rebellion

THE UNDERESTIMATION OF LAND AVAILABLE FOR SETTLEMENT in Ulster was eleven times greater than was initially thought. There were not enough settlers to work the land and, as a result, the Undertakers had to depend on a large body of native Irish to manage the land as rent-paying tenants. There were more native Irish than Scots or English settlers on the confiscated lands in 1613. Over the years, much of the native freeholds were lost through Crown confiscations (Gamble 2016, 24).

The Irish Rebellion of 1641 was a struggle on the part of the Irish chiefs, exiled nobles, clergy and the evicted Gaelic peasants to get possession of their estates and farms which had been occupied by the British settlers for nearly a generation. The most active amongst them was Rory O'Moore, an Irishman of *"high character, great ability, handsome person, and fascinating manners."* Associated with him were Connor Maguire, Costelloe M'Mahon, Thorlough O'Neill, Sir Phelim O'Neill, Sir Con Magennis, Colonel Hugh M'Mahon and the Rev. Dr. Heber M'Mahon. O'Moore visited the country going through the several provinces and, by communicating with the chiefs personally, organized the conspiracy to expel the British and recover the kingdom for Charles I and the Pope (Godkin n.d., 1). The establishment of 200 new towns (70% of the total) between 1603 and 1641 made a huge impact on the native Irish population and had exacerbated the situation (Smith 2013, 87). A concentrated look into the counties of Fermanagh, Tyrone, Antrim, Coleraine and Londonderry depict the specific struggles in those areas of Northern Ireland which would have concerned this Moore study's ancestors.

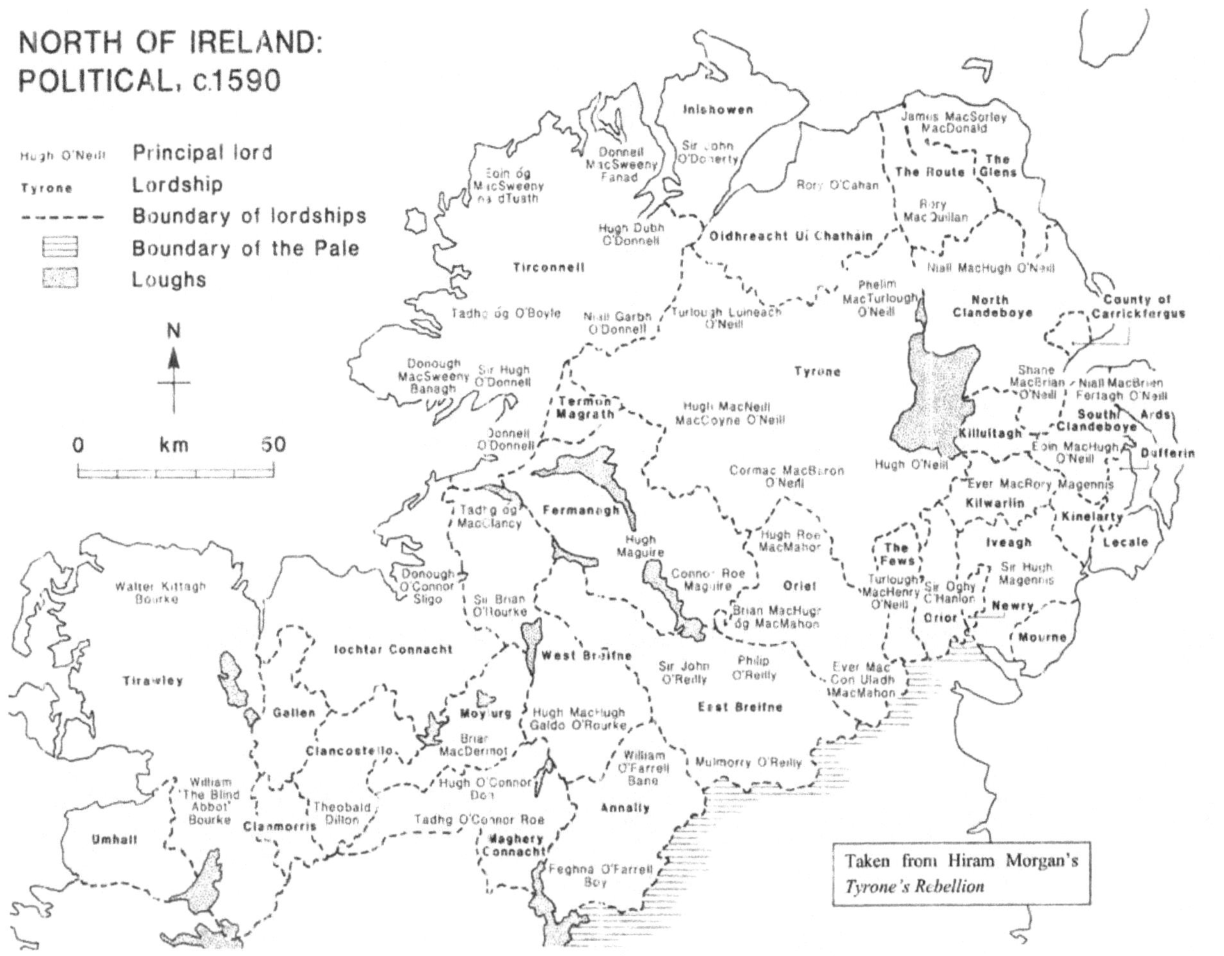

Figure 26. Location of the Major Irish Clans in Ulster c. 1590

Source: Map taken from Hiram Morgan's *Tyron's Rebellion* (Morgan 1999, xiv)

County Fermanagh

The Maguire clan were chiefs of Fermanagh since 1302. Around 1439, Clan Maguire moved their seat to Enniskillen Castle, sometimes known as Maguire Castle, which was on an island in Lough (Lake) Erne.

Connor Maguire, second Baron of Enniskillen, Co. Fernamagh, his brother Rory Maguire and Rory (Roger) O'Moore were some of the main figures at the start of the insurrection. Connor Maguire became overwhelmed with debts and, retaining only a fraction of his ancestral lands, longed for a revolution. Connor Maguire was the very first of the Ulster chiefs to join with Rory O'Moore, but when their plot of seizing Dublin Castle on the night of October 22, 1641 was betrayed by Owen O'Connolly to the lord justices, Connor became a prisoner of the Tower of London. Four years later he was hanged. His brother, Rory Maguire, took on the leadership of the sept of Fermanagh (O'Donovan 1861, 1, 3–4).

In 1612, James VI and I had granted to William Cole, Esq., one-third of the land on the island on condition that he build a town consisting of twenty British families. On the outbreak of the war in 1641, the town of Enniskillen was defended by its founder and governor, now Sir William Cole, who dispatched the first news of a rebellion to the English government. The inhabitants of Enniskillen were able to drive back the insurgents and to also secure its castle (Lewis 1840, 605).

Rory Maguire led the native's revolt and devised plans for the capturing of the planter's houses throughout Fermanagh. It became a ruthless and sometimes savage campaign as the peasantry sought revenge on their planter neighbors (Macauley n.d., 2).

County Tyrone

In County Tyrone, on the night of October 22, 1641, Sir Phelim O'Neill, along with the officers under his command, having a deep distrust of the Government in Dublin which was denouncing all the gentlemen of his creed and race, captured the forts of Charlemont and Mountjoy along with five of the surrounding towns, while the O'Reillys and the Maguires overran Cavan and Fermanagh. O'Neill set up his garrison at Dungannon, Co. Tyrone (Godkin n.d., 1).

Enniskillen, Derry (Londonderry), Coleraine, Belfast and Carrickfergus, along with some isolated castles, were still held by British garrisons, and the Protestant escapees fled to the protection of these strongholds. King Charles I, who was being held in Scotland, sent 1,500 men to Ulster which raised the Scottish Army to about 5,000 foot and calvary. The King also authorized the various Protestant landlords to raise regiments amongst their own tenants (Godkin n.d., 2). Originally local militias, they soon were incorporated into the East Ulster Army, which eventually became the Ulster British Army, and the West Ulster Army, all which became known as the Laggan Army (Ulster Ancestry n.d., 1).

The Irish, on the other hand, were ill equipped with armament. They had no time to even make pikes; Rory O'Moore had never seen military service and Sir Phelim O'Neill was only a civilian when he assumed the title of "the O'Neill" and also "Lord General of the Catholic army in Ulster." Terrible cruelties were used on both sides. The war took on a brutality of character foreign to the nature of O'Moore, O'Reilly, Maguire, Magennis and O'Neill (Godkin n.d., 2).

The same could be said of the English generals but they relied on the confidence that the power of England, along with the force of discipline, would make them victorious in the end and that their reward would be Irish estates (Godkin n.d., 2). In February 1642, the Long Parliament took the work of subjugation into their own hands and confiscated 2,500,000 acres of Irish lands. The lands were offered as security to "adventurers" who would advance money to meet the cost of the war in order to be repaid by the rebels' estates (Godkin n.d., 3).

County Antrim

By the time the Rebellion started, Randal MacDonnell, the 2nd Earl of Antrim had removed himself from Dunluce Castle and had taken up residence in Dublin.

The Irish army, led by the O'Cahans, advanced north through the Route burning towns and killing settlers. Early 1642, under the leadership of James McColl MacDonnell, they laid siege to the Presbyterians in Ballintoy Church.[39] When asked to surrender, the besieged called out "No Surrender!"[40] (Gamble 2016, 38).

In the same year, the Irish army, led by Turlough and Manus Roe O'Cahan, also burnt down Dunluce village, which lay 100 yards to the southwest of Dunluce Castle. The subsequent collapse of the walls and abandonment of the village left artifacts from that period which, only since 2011, are finally being excavated (Gamble 2016, 39).

On 11 February 1642, Archibald Stewart of Ballintoy, one of the captains of the citizens' militia, deployed from Coleraine with 300 English and 600 Scottish Protestant troops and marched towards Ballymoney with a plan to attack the Irish army. The Irish army, under the command of Alastar MacColl MacDonnell, a relative of the 2nd Earl of Antrim, attacked him first. The Coleraine forces were routed and 700 of their troops died in the battle. This day has become known as "Black Friday" (R. G. Hill 1873, 69, 70) (Gamble 2016, 41).

Coleraine

The 1st Siege of Coleraine, from 13 December 1641 to 16 May 1642, was led by Sir James MacDonnell, James McHenry and Alastar MacColl MacDonnell. The Irish rebels camped in the Ballyrashane area. Thousands of refugees flooded into Coleraine. The overcrowding, malnutrition and disease soon had the refugees dying at the rate of 150 people each day. One mass grave accommodated over 2,000 bodies. At least three mass graves were eventually used (Gamble 2016, 40).

Early May of 1642, the 2nd Earl of Antrim returned from Dublin to his territory and broke the siege not only of Ballintoy but also of Coleraine. At Coleraine, Antrim persuaded Alaster MacColl MacDonnell, who was chief in command of the siege, into relaxing the severity of the siege so that *"the inhabitants not only got ample space for themselves and their cattle, but were supplied with the best descriptions of food—beef and oatmeal."* Supplies were liberally provided and sent in from Antrim's own resources (R. G. Hill 1873, 72, f. 88). Antrim also helped rout the besieging Irish.

---

39 The same church that the Stewart family had originally built.

40 This motto is still being used today and can be seen on signs around Northern Ireland.

The Laggan Army slaughtered many Irish of the McGilligan sept in the northwest area of the Bann River and then relieved Coleraine on 16 May 1642. As Munro came with his forces into Ulster, Antrim *"ordered his tenants and followers, who had besieged Coleraine, and who had taken up arms in defense, to retire to the further parts of Ulster beyond the Bann"* (R. G. Hill 1873, 73–4). The Scottish Covenanting Army of Major-General George Munro took over Coleraine town in June. This Scottish Army became the unwelcome garrison troops in Coleraine town until 1649 (Gamble 2016, 40, 42).

In June 1642, Munro's Scottish Covenanting Army swept through Ballymoney to clear the area of the Irish rebels. One unit forced the surrender of a garrison of ninety MacDonnells at McNeghtens Fort near Ballybogey. Fifteen were taken to be interrogated and the remainder were massacred by the troops of Major O'Connolly. The troops involved in the massacre of the MacDonnells were the Campbells, the hereditary foes of the MacDonnells (Gamble 2016, 42).

Witnesses and Depositions

Audley Mervyn's firsthand account of what actually happened in Londonderry, Tyrone and Fermanagh during the Rebellion was provided in his speech to Parliament in 1642. Note here that the Rory Maguire of whom he speaks is actually Mervyn's own brother-in-law who became a leading insurgent.

Audley Mervyn was Lieutenant Colonel of the Protestant Ulster forces. He explained to the English Parliament, while there seeking further money for supplies, that in Fermanagh:

> *. . . where those that had escaped the fire and sward of Rory MaGuyre, the arch-rebel in that county, brother to the Lord of Enniskillen, drew themselves into Enniskillen castle... under the command of Sir William Cole, Colonel.* (Mervyn 1642, 6)

Archdale's tenants, including Thomas Moore (b. c. 1609), may have also tried to seek refuge in Enniskillen castle at the same time that *"MacGuire, having without any opposition in that Country, wasted, burnt, killed and pillaged"* (Mervyn 1642, 6) the surrounding areas.
Mervyn went on to explain that:

> *Most part of the British, of the Barony of Omagh, made their escaped towards Newtown, and Strabane, both places being of the Barony of Strabane, in the same county* [County Tyrone]. *The Barony of Clogher resorted to the Agher; the remaining Barony of Dongannon, were marcht up by Sir Thomas Staples and Lieutenant Colonell Saunderson forth of that Barony to Newtown, nigh twenty miles . . . to joyn with Sir William Stewarts forces there.* (Mervyn 1642, 7)

With the loss of Agher, *"the Towne of Agher being entred by the Rebells, and burnt immediately"*, and the *"loss of Strabane"*, the settlers sought refuge in the *"safety of the Citie of London-derry"* (Mervyn 1642, 11).

Sir William Stewart, who on 26 July 1629 was granted lands in the Barony of Strabane, had made his principal family residence in Newtownstewart, Co. Tyrone. His grandson, William Montgomery, had been residing there while attending school and depicted his hurried departure at the time of the outbreak in 1641:

> *I was kept at School in Newtoun Stewart house . . . and had a pike and musket made to my size; and on the 23rd of October, 1641, was in the Garden performing the postures of my Arms; my grandfather Sir William Stewart's foot company, himself viewing his soldiers and their Arms, and exercising them; when about four hours afternoon (to our amazement), a man half stript came with a letter, signifying the Insurrections, Murthers, and burnings on all sides, committed by the Irish. The messengers, one after another, came sweating and out of breath from divers quarters, with like consternation and haste as Job's escaped servants did to tell him of his losses; and they related the creull Massacres of divers Persons . . . Sir William, leaving a guard in his said house, went next morning with his Lady and Family to Strabane, and thence to Londonderry, ten miles further.*
> (Montgomery 1869, 407–8) (R. G. Hill 1877, 532/3 f.231)

The 1641 Depositions are firsthand reports taken by the British government of eye witnesses and people involved in the crimes of the Rebellion.[41] An example follows:

Deposition of Roger Markham taken 15 Feb 1642 in Dublin MS 839, fols 01r–023v

"Roger Markham was a servant of Sir Thomas Staples who owned Lissan House in Lissan, Parish of Drumragh, Barrony of Omagh East. Roger was with his son at the mills when several separate people started coming to Lissan to report confusing messages that the towns of Moneymore, Dungannon and Charlemount were taken but they did not know by whom. Staples was in Cookstown and upon hearing the news, sent for his wife and children to join him there for safety. But, before they received that message, '*there came divers of the Irish being most, or all of them his Tennants near Lissan the Cheife of which was Phillimie Modder O'Haghan, Patrick Mallon, Neale Oge O Quins son & the Prest . . . With 50 or 60*

[41] A complete account of all *1641 Depositions* can be found on Trinity College Dublin's website www.1641.tcd.ie.

more of the Irish' telling Mrs. Staples that they would *'secure her from all danger for that night . . . she being much astonished with feares.'* Markham rode out to James Steward's house, not far from Cookstown to find about 150 gentlemen of the county, both English and Scots, with Sir Thomas Staples in charge. *'Agayne these words passed that the Irish did not meane to Rob and spoile the Scots but only the English.'*

The 24th Day of October; News came that the house of a justice of the peace in those parts, Mr. Bradliff, was being pillaged by 100 or 200 of the Irish so, Sir Thomas Staples rode with Mr. Bradliff and 10 others to his house and saw many of the Irish there but they left as soon as they saw Staples riding up.

Staples wrote to his wife but the letter was *'interceipted by thos that was in his house soe that his Lady could not have a view of them and then they began to pillidge some of the Scots Soe that we understood that it would prove ill with us.'*

About the 30th of October, Sir Thomas Staples and company marched to a field near Augher where they met up with about 1600 men intent on going to Dungonnon and fight against Sir Phellim O'Neill, but many of their side *'went abroad and took much Cattell and our Randevoze was apoynted next morning at the Clogher.'* Sir William Stewart came there and told Sir Thomas Staples that *'it was best for him and his owne safeguard to goe along with Sir William Stewarte for he know non other way but that they must goe and mak the peace with the evemye if they could, soe my master went along to newtowne with Sir William Stewart which night after we Lodged on the Omie.'* They met up with Captain Mervyn in Omey who explained to them that he was intending *'to goe to newtown to get some 50 men from Sir William Stewart to fetch way his wife and children.'* So, Mervyn asked Stewart at the time of their meeting for the men and Stewart declined him help. Mervyn asked for 100 men to help to garrison Omey and Stewart again declined him. *'Soe my master with other few gentlemen went within a day or 2 to derry.'* Mervyn brought his wife and children back to Newtown and went to relieve the besieged town of Augher and was able to save about 1000 women and children. After departing Augher, *'they was not above a mile or 2 from the town before they saw the towne set on fire by the evemye, besides many wemen and children that perished they said William Stewart was turned Rebell. All* [towns] *within a mile of Colrane* [Coleraine] *and within a mile of derry was Burnt by the enemye.'* " (Trinitiy College Library Dublin n.d.)

According to the author William J. Smith in his book titled *Towards a Cultural Geography of the 1641 Rising/Rebellion,*

There became a revitalization of clan and lineage structures of overlapping and interwoven kinship networks, which link up the so-called septs. They no longer raided one another but they united in opposition to the settlers. (Smith 2013, 89)

The greatest settler impact in Ireland was in Ulster where it contained about 42% of the total settler population. At first, the typical attack involved an armed group of Irish descending upon a Protestant settler family and demanding, at knife point, that they leave their houses and farms and give up all of their possessions. Soon, the ethnic violence against the settlers left a number of places in Ireland littered with often mutilated dead bodies.

The British/Protestant settlers were killed/murdered in their homes, in the fields, in streets, on bridges, in woods, as prisoners, as well as convoys trying to get to safe places. Refugee men, women and children were hanged, drowned or otherwise so badly used by stripping and expulsions as to result in their death. Some died of exposure to the winter cold, others of hunger, thirst and exhaustion. (Smith 2013, 75–78)

It was believed by some of the Irish that the "*priests claimed that it was no sin to kill the protestants who are damned creatures*" (Walter 2013, 145). Insurgents in Fermanagh articulated a widely held belief that "*all that went to the* [Anglican] *church went to the devil*" and as allies of the devil, protestants were displeasing to God and posed a danger to the community (Cuarta 2007, 170). Anglican Bibles were not simply seized and destroyed but often subjected to public desecration and destruction (Walter 2013, 142). The beheading of victims in 1641 and the public display of their heads mimicked the terror tactics employed in the imposition of English rule over the Irish (Walter 2013, 140).

According to author John Prendergast's 1874 article on Audley Mervyn in Omey,

. . . and Colonel Mervyn gave notice to the Protestants about him to dispose of themselves towards Derry, and that he would adventure himself the last man. And so, by the blessing of God, many were saved, and himself, his wife, two sisters, and children, escaped in the night, saving nothing but their lives. (Prendergast 1874)

This Moore study's ancestors most certainly would have been displaced and sought refuge in the closest fort or castle town. ⚜

9
Transitioning from Ireland to England

ON 22 OCTOBER 1641, THE NATIVE IRISH, under Sir Phelim O'Neill, rose in rebellion in Counties Londonderry and Tyrone, and the walled city of Londonderry became a refuge for Protestant settlers from the surrounding areas. On 10 January 1642, the mayor wrote to the Lord Justices that *"the terror of the rebellion hath struck such a feare in the British of these partes that their harts are gone."* Local ships in Londonderry were employed to transport people to Scotland and England but there were not enough boats to meet demand. The mayor feared *"famines and infeccions and sicknes"* from the crowded city would decimate the colony (Forrest 2008, 33, 34).

Soon Derry (Londonderry) was besieged by O'Neill's Irish Army. A League of the Officers of Londonderry was set up as a militia to guard the city, with the raising of nine companies of foot soldiers, each assigned with a particular section of the walls of Derry to repair and to defend. It named 905 men in nine Foot Companies, consisting of ninety officers and 815 soldiers (Census Substitutes for Co. Derry 1637–47) (Forrest 2008, 34–39).

It is a fact that neither the *1628 Rent Roll* of Derry nor the *1630 Muster* of Derry listed any Edward Moore or William Moore in that town. However, by the 1642 *Garrison Muster Rolls* of [London] *Derry* they both showed up! In Sir Thomas Staples's Foot Company militia for the city of Derry, Edward Moore was ranked as Corporal and William Moore as a militia soldier. Staples, like both Edward and William Moore, was also from County Tyrone; Lissan House near Cookstown. Sir Audley Mervyn and Sir Thomas Staples evidently knew each other well from the letters written by Mervyn for the House of Commons (Mervyn 1642, 7) and also from Roger Markham's Deposition previously quoted.

In early 1642, Sir Ralph Gore's regiment was being moved north to around the city of Derry when he died. Sir Audley Mervyn took over the command and was allowed to raise the number of men to 1,000, many of the men being refugees from the devastated plantations of Tyrone (Forkan 2005, 51 f. 4). The Laggan Army consisted of four Regiments of Foot under Sir William and Sir Robert Steward, Sir Ralph Gore (later Audley Mervyn) and Sir William Gore (Ulster Ancestry n.d., 1). The regiment of Audley Mervyn and other locally recruited companies secured Derry city and its surrounding area as Sir William Stewart held the area known as the Laggan from Derry to Letterkenny and north towards Kilmacrennan. Sir William Cole held Enniskillen and the district there. Sir Robert Stewart had spent years in foreign service and, not having a base of his own, he also recruited from the many refugees and they were garrisoned at Raphoe, Co. Donegal (Forkan 2005, 51–2).

By April 1642 the city of Derry was close to starvation with the rebel siege, led by Sir Phelim O'Neill, camped at Strabane (Roots Ireland n.d., 20). On 3 September 1642, Sir John Vaughan wrote that *"Londonderry, with its garrison and a multitude of distressed people, was only able to feed a fourth of the people and since December 1641 they had buried 800 persons in the town"* (Forrest 2008, 40).

The siege of Derry was lifted on 17 May 1642 with the defeat of the Irish army, led by the O'Cahans (O'Kanes) near Dungiven, by an army consisting of east Donegal settlers (the Laggan army) and four companies of soldiers from Londonderry (Census Substitutes for Co. Derry 1637–47). The Laggan Army succeeded in preventing the capture of Londonderry by insurgent forces under Sir Phelim O'Neill (Ulster Ancestry n.d., 1).

The arrival at Carrickfergus of the Scottish Covenanter Army under Robert Munro in the spring of 1642 strengthened the position of the Ulster Army. By August, the Scots army was 10,000 men strong and were being paid for by the English Parliament. The Scottish forces, often with the severest techniques, helped not only to recapture territory but also to clear spaces for further Presbyterian Scottish colonization (Smith 2013, 80).

Eventually, the Irish joined forces with the Old Catholic English. They set up a secondary government in Kilkenny and became known as the Confederates (Lenihan 2001, 49). The Ulster British Army and Munro's Scottish Army[42] were the Confederates' main enemy (Forkan 2005, 53). In Ulster, by the end of April, there were up to 19,000 troops, regulars and volunteers, in the garrison or in the field (Godkin n.d., 3).

There were eventually six distinct armies that fought in Ireland during this time. In 1641, both King Charles I and the English Parliament raised their own armies to fight in Ireland. The Royalist Army of Charles I, under the Duke of Ormond, attacked the Irish Rebels while the Parliamentary Army initially defended Dublin. The Parliamentarians were Puritan in their devotions and sometimes derisively referred to as Roundheads. They were commanded by Cromwell and others, including Sir Charles Coote and George Monk.

---

[42] Commanded first by Robert Munro then later by his nephew George Munro.

The third army included the Scottish Covenanters who had, in Scotland, rebelled against Charles I in 1639. They were commanded by Major-General Robert Munro and his nephew, Sir George Munro. He took his army to Ulster in 1642 to defend the Ulster Scot Presbyterian settlers during the Irish Rebellion. The fourth army involved was the Scottish Royalist Army. They were Catholic and they supported both King Charles I and II (Gamble 2016, 29).

The fifth army was the Irish Army. The Ulster elements of the Irish Army were referred to as the Ulster army; a small confederation of native Irish that included the MacDonnells and the Old English.[43] They supported Charles I and were also referred to as Royalists. The Ulster army was composed of Irish Catholics under the command of Sir Phelim O'Neill, then Owen Roe O'Neill and after his death in 1649, the command passed on to Bishop MacMahon (Gamble 2016, 29). In June of 1642, a meeting of priests and prominent Catholic laymen at Kilkenny agreed on an Oath of Association binding the "Confederate Catholics of Ireland" with the advice and direction of the Supreme Council of the Confederate Catholics to be headquartered in Kilkenny (Lenihan 2001, 49). By October of 1642, Colonel Owen Roe O'Neill returned from Spanish service with 100 veteran officers and was immediately elected general-in-chief of the Catholic Irish forces. Catholics of the whole kingdom joined with the Kilkenny Confederates (Godkin n.d., 3).

The sixth army was known as the Laggan Army, a disciplined force of 8,000 Presbyterian volunteers raised by the brothers, Sir Robert and Sir William Stewart in east Donegal, Tyrone, Londonderry and Fermanagh. Contemporary documents often refer to this army as the British forces in Ulster (Ulster Ancestry n.d., 1). They were involved in an uneasy alliance with the Parliamentarians and the Scottish Covenanting army (Gamble 2016, 29).

September 14, 1643 marked the official cessation of hostilities in Ulster; however, the countryside was still very dangerous (Forrest 2008, 40).The following deposition will serve to illustrate this further:

The Deposition of Edward Moore and Margaret Moore dated 6 April 1644 taken in Dublin by Henry Brereton and Henry Jones
Reference: MS 839, fols 112r–112v

Edward Moore and Margar(et) Moore late of Londonderry sworne & examined before us his Majesties Commissioners thereunto appointed under the greate seale of Ireland this sixth day of April 1644 examined depose & say that about sixteene days since they, on theire way from Londonderry to Dublin, about six miles from Cavan were mett with about twenty of the Irish armed with swords, skeynes, & two firelocks who questioned them these

[43] Original Catholic Englishmen from the 1190's settlements.

deponents concerning theire quality, countey, place of aboad, & whither they were travailing: these Examinants answering, that they were British dwelling at Londonderry that they tooke theire way by Iniskillin hoping to meete a brother of his the deponents Edward Moore whom they found to have beene killed; and that now they were passing toward(s) Dublin & from thence to theire friends in England. Thereup(on) the said Irish laid hold on him the deponent Edward Moore stripping him out of all his clothes & shirt leaving him quite naked: & after stripped starke naked her the deponent Marga(ret) Moore in doing whereof they the said Irish did cast o(f) from her back a child of three quarters old, & thereby broke the skull thereof the braines appearing, so as it the next day died which child & one other about 5 yeares old were stripped out of theire clothes by a woman that was in that company. The Deponents futher say that they were at th(at) time robbed of foure pounds & ten shillings which the said Marg(arett) <4 li. 17 s 6 d.> Moore carried, & of seven shillings & six pence taken fro(m) the said Edward Moore. The said Irish also refused to leav(e) them a smale quantity of flowre which they reserved for theire two children upon the way so that they the deponents went four days, until they came to Drogheda, without any foode other then herbes gathered in the fieldes, & one twopenny loafe given by some troopers whom they mett. They further say that the said Irish who so robbed them tooke away and did teare their passe which the deponents had under the hand of Captain Henry Vaughan of Londonderry, & were no waies moved to spare them the Examinants in respect of the Cessation which they pleaded. But who they were that so robbed them these deponents cannot tell being strangers in the Country: only that the said Irish when then they had doned as aforesaid bade the deponents report, if they so pleased, that they were of the Realyes [O'Reillys] who had so used them.

Jurat ixo Aprilis 1644
Hen: Jones
Hen: Brereton (Trinitiy College Library Dublin n.d.)

The brother Edward Moore (b.c. 1612) was most likely searching for was Thomas Moore (b. *c.* 1609) who had mustered in 1630 on Sir John Archdale's lands. The O'Reillys and Maguires had overrun Cavan and Fermanagh (Godkin n.d., 1). As a matter of fact, the vast majority of Tyrone and Fermanagh had been burnt or entirely devastated. The only settlements that survived the ravages of the Rebellion in Ulster, along with two castles at Limavady, were the only two walled cities of the Plantation: the port towns of Coleraine and Londonderry (Forrest 2008, 33) (The British Academy 2002, 105). Thomas Moore (b. *c.* 1609), Edward's brother (b. *c.* 1612), would have died before 1644 doubtless as a result of the Rebellion; either at his property on the

Archdale estate (Macauley n.d., 2) or from trying to flee for safety towards the garrison town of Enniskillen.

The entire 1641 Depositions are available online from Trinity College Library Dublin at their website: http://1641.tcd.ie/depositions. They are grouped by County and then alphabetized thereafter. The Depositions were used to prove two things; who of the Irish were guilty of atrocities against the Protestants both English and Scot and secondly, to try to get restitution from the government for their (the Protestants) losses. The Irish who were found guilty were dispossessed of their lands and forced to abandon them. This opened up more and more Irish lands for further settlement all over Ireland, but mostly in Ulster.

> *The more rebellions, the more forfeited territory, the more opportunities to implicate, ruin, and despoil the principal men of the Irish race.* (Godkin n.d., 2)

It was a time of confusing allegiances among friends and even within families because of intermarriages involving brothers, brothers-in-laws and cousins. The above information only gives a small portion of the horrendous ordeals the planter people of Ulster, and all over Ireland, suffered during the Rebellion. It is still deep in the memories of the people of Ireland, both North and South. It was truly devastating for the Gaelic Irish and the old Anglo-Irish Catholic landowners as well.

In 1695, Hugh Reily, an influential Irish Catholic writer, is credited with saying that the Protestants *"took more pains to make the land turn Protestant than the people"* (Ford n.d., 93).

Dublin | 26 April 1644 & 25 Sept 1646

It appears that Edward Moore (b. *c.* 1612) was mustered twenty days after his Deposition on 26 April 1644 in Dublin into Sir Thomas Meredith's regiment (Historical Manuscripts Commission 1895, 168, 149) under the command of Col. Lawrence Crawford, a Scot. In the list of foot regiments now quartered in the city of Dublin on 16 July 1644, Sir Thomas Meredith's company, now under the command of Sir Patrick Weame, was quartered on *"the east side of New Street, and part of the west side from the gate to the Maypoule, mixed with troopers"* (Historical Manuscripts Commission 1895, 181). On 25 Sep 1646, Sir Thomas Meredith and a Sergeant-major Moore were named among those companies that watch within the city and suburbs of Dublin (Historical Manuscripts Commission 1895, 190–191).

Many people fled the terrors in Ulster, either by boat or otherwise. Some returned to Scotland, others to England and still others to the British Plantation of Virginia in the New World. Not being able to follow Edward into the army, Margaret and her 5-year-old child must have gone on to London without her husband to stay with friends, per their deposition above.

London | 1646

Edward Moore (b. *c.* 1612), a British subject, made his way to London to be with his wife sometime after his last entry of September 1646 as being in a militia regiment in Dublin. He was no longer mentioned amongst those files. It may have been that Edward Moore became involved in the London militia regiments; more specifically, that of the Tower Hamlet Trained Bands. The Tower Hamlet consisted of the villages of *Whitechapel*, Shoreditch, Hackney, Ratcliff, Wapping and Limehouse [fig. 27]. The titular colonel of the Tower Hamlet Trained Band was the Lieutenant of the Tower but the effective commander of the Tower Hamlets was Lt-Col William Whilloughby. This militia force was also used to guard the Tower of London both day and night (Nagel 1982, 98, 100). Men from the six trained bands of London, including those of the Tower Hamlet, were used to augment the Earl of Essex's Field Army as needed (Marsh 2016, 1–2, 5).

It had now become evident to Edward Moore (b. *c.* 1612) that his life would be that of a soldier. By the time of King Charles I's execution in January 1649 and the full power of Oliver Cromwell had become a reality, Edward Moore had been already living in the epicenter of the Commonwealth; in the city of London. Huge numbers of soldiers were mustered in and out of London and Moore would have been caught up in the military action; either voluntarily or by "impressment."

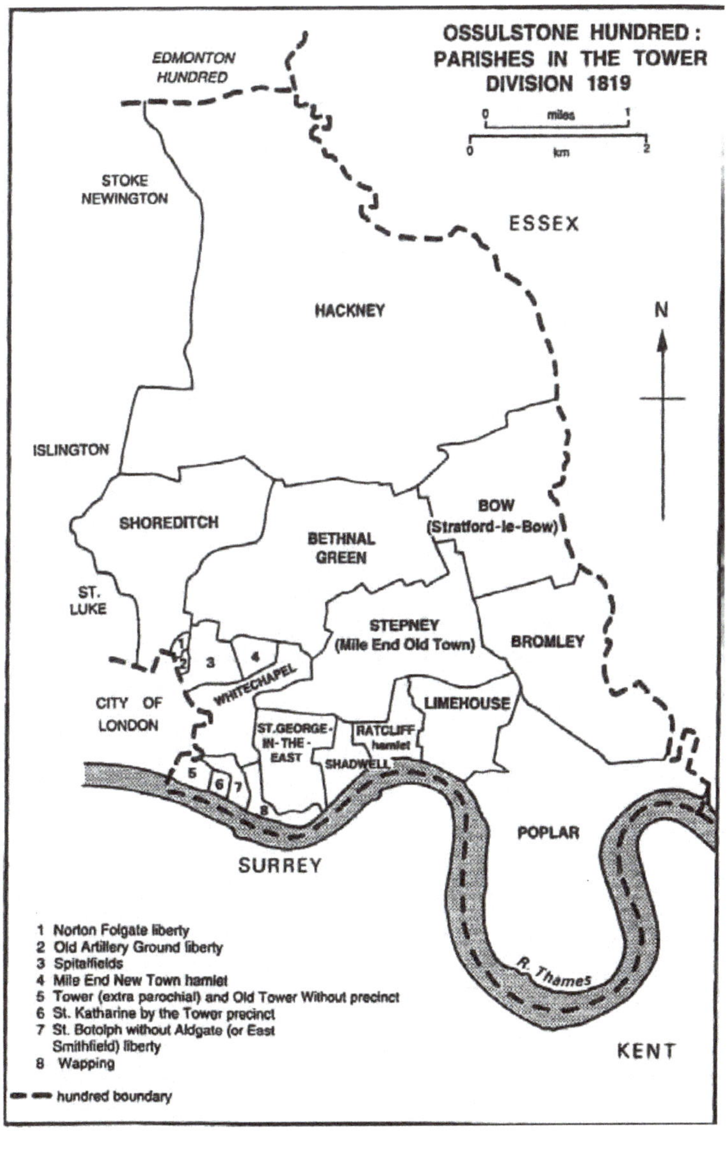

Figure 27. Ossulstone Hundred: Parishes in the Tower Division 1819

Source: (British History Online 1998) http://www.british-history.ac.uk/vch/middx/vol11/pp1-7

Whitechapel, a parish and populous suburb of the metropolis, in the Tower Division of Ossulstone hundred, and borough of the Tower Hamlets, County Middlesex, 1 ½ mile east of St. Paul's Catherdral. (The National Gazetteer 1868, v.12, 800)

"I am sorry that when I am in England,

I should be esteemed to be an Irishman,

and in Ireland an Englishman."

—CHRISTOPHER ST. LAWRENCE
10th Baron Howth

10

The Fight Between King, Parliament, Royalists and Covenantors

Scotland's National Covenant | 1638

IN SCOTLAND, ATTEMPTS BY CHARLES I to impose his authority upon the Church provoked a hostile response which eventually led to the National Covenant of 1638. This Covenant declared Presbyterianism the only true form of church government and bound the nation to the principles of the Reformation (Ulster-Scots Agency 2007). It swept the central and southern lowlands raising political consciousness like never before in Scotland; for the overthrow of popery (Lisle 2017, 95).

Many people in the north of Ireland also signed this Covenant. In response, the government insisted that all Scots in Ulster over the age of sixteen take an oath—the Black Oath as it became known—abjuring the Covenant (Ulster-Scots Agency 2007). This study's Moores may have been made to sign this oath if they had previously signed the Covenant; thus, remaining Anglican.

The 1641 Rebellion in Ulster, Northern Ireland, further divided the population along religious and political lines. The insurrection quickly escalated and resulted in significant loss of life and destruction of property. In 1642, an army of 10,000 soldiers under the command of Major General Robert Munro was sent from Scotland to Ireland to protect those Scots who remained in Ireland (Ulster-Scots Agency 2007).

Meanwhile in England, by August of 1642, King Charles I was embroiled in his own problems in a civil war against Parliament adherents.

In response to these widening political developments across the three kingdoms, the Solemn League and Covenant was drafted in 1643 by the Scottish Covenanters and the English Parliamentarians. In return for a promise to reform the Church in England and Ireland along presbyterian lines, the Scots agreed to provide military support to the Parliamentarians in their conflict with Charles I. The official signing in agreement of the Covenant was administered in the main squares of twenty-six Ulster cities by the Scottish Army from 4 April 1644 to 30 June

1644. People became further divided along national lines. Within three months, over 16,000 Ulster Scots had taken the Solemn League and Covenant Oath (Ulster-Scots Agency 2007).

The demands of the Scots, that episcopacy be abolished in all three kingdoms, became the shock that brought the Royalists party in England back to life. They did not want to introduce to England a Scottish-style Presbyterian system of church government (Lisle 2017, 120). However, among the Royalist forces in the British Civil Wars there were also numerous Scots, many of whom were Anglican and Episcopalians, who were quick to use "Britishness" as a way of affirming their anti-Covenanting position (Murdoch 2008, 258). Further splinters saw Royalists turn on Royalists and Parliamentarians turn on Parliamentarians (Lisle 2017, 162).

1st English Civil War | Aug 1642–1646

The 1st English Civil War was fought mainly between the King's Royalists and Parliament. The Parliamentarian war party was working on persuading the Scottish Covenanters into a military alliance; for the Scots to join the English civil war on the Parliament's side. The Royalists wanted King Charles I to match the size of the Scottish army with his own troops from Ireland (Lisle 2017, 182). There was huge pressure to resolve the Rebellion in Ulster in order to subjugate the soldiers to fight for the King in England.

Charles I quickly signed a peace with the Catholic Confederates and the English troops came back to England. The Royalist soldiers, as part of the Confederation, came to the aid of the King but Covenanters sided with Parliamentarians in January of 1644 (Lisle 2017, 183). It was ironic that the 10,000 men raised to defend the Protestant settlers in Ireland were to be used instead against the King (Lisle 2017, 160).

The New Model Army (NMA) was organized by the Parliamentarians in 1645 during this English Civil War, but there were many other Parliamentarian armies in the field at the same time. With Parliamentarian forces having been the decisive victor over the Royalists, the war was ended in 1646. At that point, the smaller Parliamentarian militia armies were either disbanded or absorbed into the New Model Army and in July 1647, Thomas Fairfax was made commander-in-chief of all Parliament's forces in England and Wales (Plant, David 2012).

> *Officers were appointed and promoted on merit rather than on their status in society; several high-ranking officers of the New Model Army were from humble origins.* (Plant, David 2007, 2)

The 1st English Civil War (1642–1646) complicated both the British and the Irish issues and several divisions of allegiances sprang up; both politically and militarily. By 1646, King

Charles I had lost the Civil War and on the nineteenth of May he surrendered to the Scots (Lenihan 2001, 90).

New Model Army

The New Model Army (NMA) Ordinance, passed on 17 February 1645, remodeled Parliament's army from simply regional militia regiments to a national army with no regional affiliations. Parliament's new army was ideally planned to consist of 22,000 men:

> *Twelve regiments of foot of 1,200 men each in the proportion two-thirds musketeers, one-third pikemen; eleven regiments of horse of 600 men each, one regiment of 1,000 dragoons (mounted infantrymen) and an artillery train of 50 guns* [cannons]. *The cavalry were mainly veterans drawn from the armies of Manchester, Essex and Waller. The infantry included some veterans, with a majority of pressed men drawn from London, the east and the south-east.* (Plant, David 2007, 1)

The majority of the officers lived in or near London. According to *The New Model Officer Corps in 1647* by Ian Gentles, the officers themselves stated this about their origins:

> *There are very few of us, but have most of this world's interest in the City of London, being chiefly and principally raised thence, and very many, especially of our officers, being citizens themselves, having their wives and children therein.* (Gentles 1997, 135)

Due to their lowly status in society, there exists hardly a trace of the ordinary men who served as regular rank and file soldiers in the New Model Army (NMA) (Gentles 1997, 130).

Thomas Fairfax led the occupation of London for Parliament in the summer of 1647 because the Presbyterian MPs were risking a new war by plotting to bring a Scottish army into England. In August 1647, Fairfax was appointed constable of the Tower of London and in January 1647/48 he was made commander over the trained bands (militia) and auxiliaries within the Tower Hamlets for two years (British History Online 1911) (Plant, David 2012).

2nd English Civil War | Feb 1648 – Jan 1649

The 2nd Civil war initially broke out in Canterbury with riots protesting against the strict Puritan rules of not celebrating Christmas. After the execution of the head of the riots in February of 1648, there were fresh riots, this time in London (Lisle 2017, 236–7). The unity of the NMA itself was crumbling and high taxes were angering ordinary people. Many former Parliamentarians declared for the king and joined Royalists against the NMA and the staunch

Independents of the Parliament. There became an out and out Royalist mutiny in many counties. Nine of Parliament's ships joined the small Royalist navy (Lisle 2017, 239).

Many men had also switched sides from King Charles I to the Parliament long before the king's execution due to the tendencies of Charles I to be lenient on the Papists. They were afraid that Charles I would revert England back to Catholicism. According to the Official Website for County Tyrone, by 1649:

> *The Confederation was occupied with endless debates and dissensions. Commanders changed positions so rapidly, the several causes for which men had been fighting became so confused in the unaccountable scene-shifting, giving glimpses now of the king, now of the commonwealth, and now of the Pope, that no one knew what to do, or what was to be the end.* (Godkin n.d., 4)

Ultimately, Fairfax and the NMA defeated the opposition with much bloodshed (Lisle 2017, 239). Having become the victor over the English and the Scots, the NMA no longer was interested in negotiations with the king (Lisle 2017, 250–1). However, Ireland was still in arms.

King Charles 1 Executed | 30 January 1649

Radical New Model Army officers forcibly purged Parliament of the king's supporters and brought about Charles I's trial and execution for inflicting a second civil war upon the nation. The king's death led to the establishment of a republican Commonwealth in England from 1649–1653; headquartered in London (Plant, David 2007, 2).

Charles II declared King of the Scots | 1649–1651

Charles II was in exile in Scotland when his father was executed. The primary condition for which Charles II could be crowned King of Scotland was that he was forced to sign the Covenant. He was coronated in Edinburgh and a Scots army was formed with which to fight for his English throne. Charles II and his sixteen thousand exhausted Presbyterian Scots army was defeated by the thirty thousand strong Commonwealth army (Fraser 1979, 134–5) at the Battle of Worcester on 3 September 1651 and Charles II fled back into exile (Lisle 2017, 285).

The Scots felt that Charles II would make Presbyterianism the official crown religion of Britain instead of Anglicanism. However, it was only a political move on Charles II's part. The reality was that, once the Restoration took place in 1660, the Covenanters were brutally persecuted for not falling in line with the King and the Church of England.

3rd English Civil War | 1649–1651

When Thomas Fairfax declined to lead the army against Charles II in an invasion of Scotland, Cromwell was appointed commander-in-chief in his place, leading the New Model Army to victory over the Scots and Royalists at the battles of Dunbar and Worcester (1650–51), which finally brought the civil wars to an end (Plant, David 2007).

The New Model Army activities officially changed from fighting an English Civil War to fighting a war in and against Ireland and Scotland (Wanklyn 2015, 15). Under Oliver Cromwell's leadership, the NMA army invaded Ireland in 1649 to defeat the Royalists and subjugate the Irish Catholics in retribution for the uprising against Protestant settlers in 1641 (Plant, David 2007, 2). Servitorships were sold for money to fund the war in exchange for escheated land as payment. The population and demographics of Ireland were to be changed forever.

Oliver Cromwell was declared the Protector of Great Britain 16 Dec 1653 until his death 3 Sept 1658. Ireland and Scotland were reduced to provinces of England under the new Commonwealth. The Scots lost their legal system and their national dignity. Twenty-five percent of the Irish population died from famine and disease and many were sent as slaves to the colonies in the Caribbean or as indentured labor to New England (Lisle 2017, 286). Irish Catholics were made to forfeit their estates "*meerly for being papists*" and entire families were completely transplanted to County Connaught or County Mayo. These lands were re-allocated to the Adventurers and soldiers who had fought for the Commonwealth by an act of Parliament called the Act of Settlement (O'Sullivan 2000, 75, 123).

There are two mentions of an [Edward] Moore in the ranks of the New Model Army:

Irish Confederate War: October 1641–April 1652

**An Edward Moore was a Captain in the NMA under Col. John Moore's Regiment of Foot serving in Ireland with the forces of Michael Jones. Edward Moore was in post in 6/49. Col. John Moore's Regiment had been shipped to Ireland in 1647 and were not disbanded by Cromwell in August 1649 (Wanklyn, Reconstructing the New Model Army, Vol 2: Regimental Lists 1649–1663 2016, 189). Edward Moore was part of the new recruits brought from England in July 1649 to continue fighting in the Irish Confederate War under Parliament's pay (Plant, David n.d.). He fought at the Battle of Rathmines in August 1649. Michael Jones' victory at Rathmines enabled Cromwell's army to land unopposed in Ireland and Jones became Cromwell's Lt. General (Plant, David 2011). Edward Moore was still Captain in 7/50 and 9/50 serving under Col. John Blagrave who had succeeded the late Col. John Moore by 7/50. The regiment was disbanded in the winter of 1650–1651. (Wanklyn, Reconstructing the New Model Army, Vol 2: Regimental Lists 1649–1663 2016, 212).

NOTE: This Edward Moore was the son of Col. John Moore. They are the Moore's of Bankhall and are not related to this study's Moores.

Regiments raised for the Scottish Campaign: Disbanded in 1651–2

**An XXX Moore was listed as a Captain in the NMA regiment serving under Col. Edmund Syler and Lt. Col. Henry Lillingston[44] (Wanklyn 2016, 256).

DISCUSSION

There is no paper trail to explain the specific whereabouts of this study's Edward Moore between late 1646 and 1652. One can only presume that he made his way to London to be with family who had fled from Northern Ireland due to the 1641 Rebellion. He may have been stationed and serving in one of the NMA regiments who fought during those years. He was feasibly in London by 1652, after having been disbanded at the end of the 3rd Civil War. Parliament was now in control of London, so he certainly fought for the Parliamentarians and was part of the Tower Hamlet Trained Band militia.

> *Between the years of 1640 and 1662, there was a period of great mobility. Impressment for the soldiers snatched men away from their crafts and husbandry; at the Army's insistence. Apprentice regulations were waived on behalf of disbanded soldiers. Military operations and the billeting* [housing] *of troops in private houses (which continued long after the war) helped to mix up the population. Scots and Irishmen fought in England; Englishmen in Scotland, Ireland, West Indies and Flanders. The marches of armies were succeeded by those of demobilized soldiers seeking work. The period was in general one of great mobility.* (C. Hill 1961, 151) ⚜

44 Col. Henry Lillingston was a Parliamentarian who also served as a Colonel in Flanders 1657–61. He was garrisoned at Dunkirk after the Battle of the Dunes from January 1659 to 1661. Coincidently, Edward Moore (b. c. 1612) may also have been garrisoned at Dunkirk at the same time as Col. Lillingston.

11

The Board of Ordnance & the Dutch Wars

Master Cannoneer

UNDER THE "ORDINANCE COMPANY" SECTION of an article regarding a *French* expedition in the *Journal of Medieval Military History*, a Master Cannoneer has the equivalent meaning as the English term Master Gunner (Spencer 2015, 186). The article goes on to say that the Master Cannoneer was an *"experienced professional with highly valuable skills"* (Spencer 2015, 187). In historical readings throughout many books, journal articles and academic papers, one does not often come upon the *French* term Master Cannoneer but, instead reads Master Gunner. It is necessary to keep in mind that the term of Master Cannoneer to describe his father Edward's occupation was used by Thomas Moore (b. 1654) in his 1690 Marriage Contract in the *French* Province of Quebec, Canada.

There are three different kinds of troops in an army: Foot Soldiers, aka Infantry; Horse, aka Cavalry; and Artillery, but not until recent history. The Artillery was not part of England's main army until 1714 when England developed the Royal Regiment of Artillery as a permanent force (Duncan 1879, 61).

A major text book titled *The Gunner's Glasse* was written in 1646 by William Eldred, Master Gunner of Dover Castle 1619–1629[45] (Atherton 2003, 9). It became the state-of-the-art reference for gunners for years to come. Edward Moore (b. *c.* 1612) would become very familiar with this book.

Board of Ordnance

There existed, since 1483, a Master Keeper of the Ordnance, as he was originally called, who had been initially in charge of that portion of the King's Wardrobe which was the king's suits of armor and his personal weapons (Barker 1993, 199). By 1604, the title became Master-General

45 William Eldred, b. 1580, had been at Dover Castle performing "Gunner's Watch" at least since 1613 (Atherton 2003). He may have served at Dover Castle for up to 30 years.

of the Ordnance and his duties had expanded to the *"arming of the ships and artillery regiments."* The Master-General answered to the Board of Ordnance who officed in the Tower of London. By the early seventeenth century, the Board of Ordnance dictated every decision made *"however temporary or trivial a nature."* The Board of Ordnance was an excellent national civilian institution (Ascoli 1983, 21). It provided efficiency for England in that there was one source for a national store of artillery, ammunition and men to drive the artillery train needed for various campaigns; both domestic and abroad (Ascoli 1983, 21) (Duncan 1879, 10–13).

The fee'd gunners at the tower, as they were called, worked either full-time or part-time, allowing them to continue to also work at their trades near the Tower of London. They were sometimes ordered to the harbor to mount guns onto vessels or to load or unload stores of equipment, for which they received working pay in addition to their regular salaries.

> *It was from their ranks that the vacancies among master-gunners and gunners of garrisons were almost invariably filled.* (Duncan 1879, 41)

The Board of Ordnance held power over the company of fee'd gunners at the Tower of London as well as garrisoned gunners in all castles; including Dover Castle. The Master-Gunner and gunners of the garrisons were *"the captain of the gun in war and its custodian in peace"* and they owed their allegiance to the Board of Ordnance (Duncan 1879, 39).

When a warlike expedition had been decided upon, the Master of the Ordnance was informed what size of a Train of Artillery was required. In addition, he appointed all the officers and attendants of the train. With the exception of any full-time gunners, it was understood that the services of any appointed gunners were only required while the expedition lasted. This type of organizing the Artillery forces of England continued until *"the commencement of the eighteenth century"* (Duncan 1879, 41–42) when the Royal Regiment of Fusiliers (7th Foot) was created in 1685 (Ascoli 1983, 21) .

The Board also supplied men, guns (cannons) and ammunition, sometimes referred to as fireworks, aboard England's fleet of ships. In the early days of the Board of Ordnance, its relationship with the navy was closer than in later years. The gunners of the ships were under the Board's control and had to answer to it for the expenditure of their stores [inventory] (Duncan 1879, 23). For transportation, the Master-General had to consult the Admiralty (Duncan 1879, 55).

First Anglo-Dutch War | 1652–1654

Men were mustered to fight specific wars and then disbanded when that war was ended. Edward Moore (b. *c.* 1612), presumably an infantry soldier in the NMA in the past, was living back in London in 1651/2 after the English Civil Wars and the Scottish Campaign ended. The NMA 5th infantry regiment's traditional role was that of garrisoning the Tower of London[46] (Wanklyn 2016, 15). Edward Moore was a resident of Whitechapel, Tower Hamlets and may still have been involved in the Tower Hamlet Trained Band militia which also was used to guard the Tower of London.

The 1st Anglo-Dutch War was fought over trading rights of the nation's merchants. It was a war that was fought entirely at sea between the Dutch Republic and the British Commonwealth. Although the NMA as a whole did not man the ships or operate the cannon, of exception were the soldiers of the 1st and the 5th Regiments of Foot who served onboard ships (Wanklyn 2016, 26, f.33).

In 1652, a proclamation was issued for the impressment of all seamen between the ages of 15 and 50 years of age in the South-eastern counties [of England] (Clowes 1898, 152). *"The 'press' had to be continually made use of ere [before] ships could be manned"* (Clowes 1898, 237). Due to lack of surviving resources, little is known about the rank-and-file soldiers [and seamen] in 17th century England. However, it is generally agreed that *"humble folk were more often recruited under compulsion"* and that *"bread and pay,"* were their primary motivations (McShane 2011, 106).

The Royal Navy had always had problems recruiting enough personnel to crew the ships of the fleet. The Navy would have needed many cannoneers [fig. 28] and soldiers; now seamen. Whether Edward Moore was impressed, volunteered or was part of the NMA's 5th regiment, it is most probable that Edward Moore (b. *c.* 1612), now age forty, was mustered into service out of London.

DISCUSSION

There are three scenarios which could have taken place for Edward Moore to serve:

First • That he volunteered or was impressed as a seaman working on a ship as part of the navy. It would be here that Edward would have experienced his first taste of artillery work by observing or assisting the gunners aboard ship.

Second • That he had been part of the fee'd gunners at the Tower of London and was assigned a position in the artillery aboard one of the many ships of the Commonwealth fleet in this war. He would have furthered his cannoneer skills at this time.

Third • That he was part of either the 1st or 5th NMA regiments who were placed aboard ships to augment the seamen's numbers.

46 Between the years of 1651 and 1660.

The new government of the Commonwealth had begun an unprecedented naval expansion and, between 1649 and 1651, twenty new ships of the Third, Fourth and Fifth Rates were built, and another thirty were approved in September of 1652 (Davies 2017, 41).

The following figure illustrates how many gunners, along with their wages, would have been needed to man the cannons per ship considering there would have been three or four men to each cannon:

	Third Rate	Fourth Rate	Fifth Rate
Gunner	3p(ounds)	2p 10s	2p 5s(hilling)
Gunner's Mate	1p 12s	1p 10s	1p 8s
# of Cannons	44–60	32–50	12–32

Figure 28. The pay of Officers per Lunar Month or 28 Days: 1649 –1660

Source: (Clowes 1898, 100)

In *The Military Dictionary* by William Duane, the definition of Gunner is, *"in the artillery,* [it] *is the title of the first and second artillerist at a gun in battery; all the rest are called aids"* (Duane 1810, 245). Edward Moore, eventually a Master Cannoneer/Gunner, would become familiar with all of the aspects of a cannon. Among these aspects, he would know about English brass guns vs English iron guns, how quickly the guns could cool, ascent and descent angles, and the various kinds of charges and shot regarding their weight vs their flight, altitude and range (Duane 1810, 247–251).

Upon the Commonwealth's win over the Dutch Republic on 5 April 1654 (Plant, David 2013), Edward Moore must have returned directly to London. Thomas Moore was born in 1654 in London, perhaps in December, as he claimed to the nuns at the L'Hotel Dieu in Quebec City while in hospital there in 1690 (L' Hotel Dieu de Quebec 1662–1757, A-33, #70). There doesn't seem to be any record of Thomas Moore's birth in London or its surrounding areas. Great amounts of ecclesiastical records were consumed in the 1666 Great Fire of London just twelve years later where 87 out of 109 churches were completely destroyed (Museum of London n.d.).

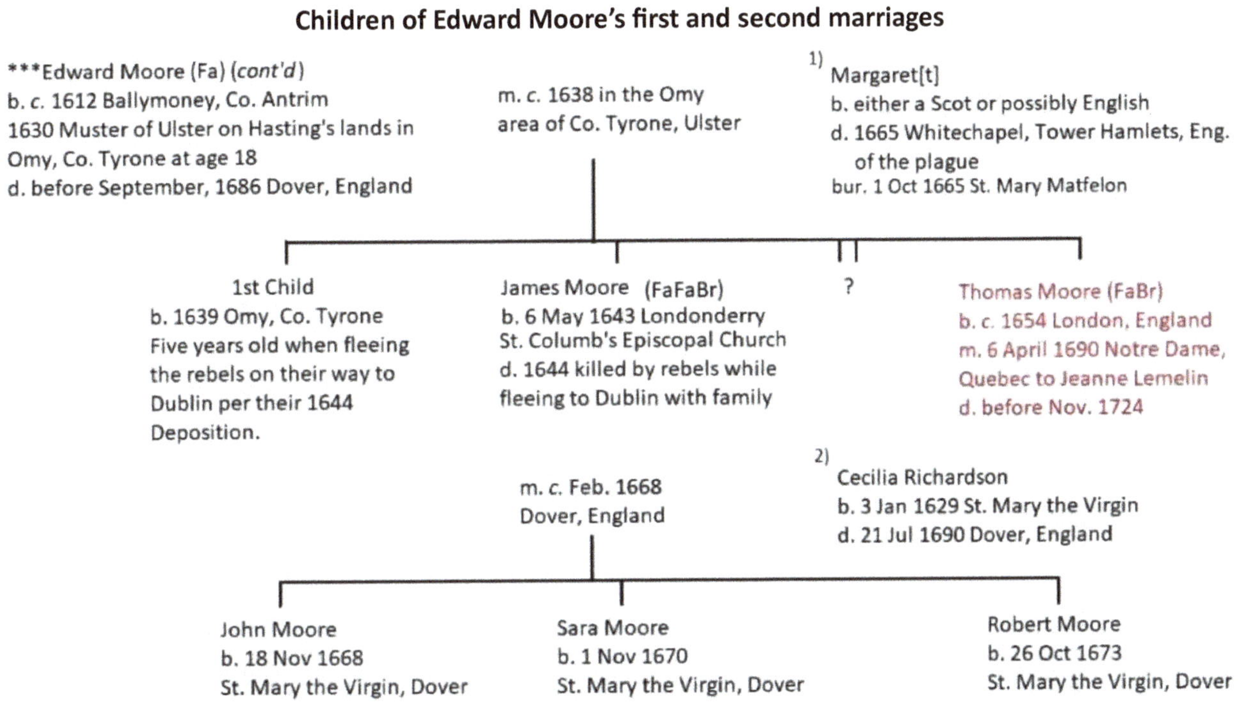

Figure 29: Children of Edward Moore

Chart by the author.

The genealogy chart above is a continuation from Figure 23 and illustrates how Thomas Moore could have been considered Irish given that his father was born in Ireland and, at the same time, thought to be English as he claimed to be a native of London. His prior Scottish roots proceeded to become totally unrecorded.

As of 27 May 1653, the Master Gunner for Dover Castle under the governor Lt.-Colonel Thomas Kelsey was a man by the name of Mr. Reader[47] who requested a *"supply of gunners and maltrosses for the castle and two forts"* in order to fight the Dutch (P. R. Great Britain 1878, #110, 356). From this record, it is conceded that Edward Moore was not Master-Gunner of Dover Castle as of yet.

Anglo-Spanish War | 1655–1660

The French were at war with Spain from 1635 to 1659. They were trying to weaken the Hapsburg Empire which was surrounding France. In order to gain a foothold on the continent, Britain's Commonwealth General, Oliver Cromwell, entered into an alliance with France against Spain in Flanders in March of 1657. According to the stipulations of the treaty, in exchange for

47 This was Godfry Reader who was a Gunner officer out of Kent nominated for a ship in Dec 1652 by the Admiralty Commission to fight the Dutch.

their help, Dunkirk and Mardyke were to be besieged by the Anglo-French army and handed over to the Commonwealth (C. H. Firth 1902, 76).

This left Charles II with making an alliance with Spain, his main goal being to invade England, along with Spanish forces once Spain defeated France, and to regain his throne (C. H. Firth 1902, 75). Charles II had been exiled with many of his Royalist followers since the assassination of his father in 1649. He was first at the French court then, when Cromwell allied with France, he was forced to look to Spain and became headquartered in Bruges, Flanders (S. F.-G. Hamilton 1874, 3).

In 1656, Charles II put a little army together which was raised in Bruges under Lord Wentworth. It consisted of his royal supporters who became his Regiment of Foot Guards. They had begun their career as a contingent serving in the Spanish Army under Don John of Austria[48] and the Prince of Conde[49] (C. H. Firth 1902, 75).

Eventually, Charles II brought together his subjects who had been fighting in the service of France and coerced them to join his English army in the service of Spain (C. H. Firth 1902, 68). In the spring through fall of 1657, Charles II was able to assemble six Royalist regiments. The first regiment put together was known as the King's Foot Guards under the command, after the death of the Earl of Rochester, of Colonel Thomas Blague. The second regiment was intended to be made up entirely of Scotsmen in exile in Flanders. It was initially commanded by Sir Thomas Middleton, later given to James Livingstone, Earl of Newburgh and later still became Sir William Urry's regiment of foot. The third regiment consisted of Irish soldiers who had deserted from the French service under the titular[50] command of the Marquis of Ormond, the real commander being Colonel Richard Grace. The fourth was the Duke of York's[51] which was an Irish regiment commanded by Lord Muskerry, Cromwell's nephew. The fifth regiment was also Irish and was that of the King's younger brother, Henry Duke of Goucester, commanded by, first, Lord Theobald Taaffe and in 1659, his son Col. William Taaffe. The last regiment formed was also Irish, previously in the service of France, and now under the command of, first, Lord George Digby, 2nd Earl of Bristol, and then under Col. Lisagh Farrell. Finally, there was one troop of Horse under the direct command of the Duke of York (C. H. Firth 1902, 69–72).

Oliver Cromwell sent a fleet to blockade the harbor of Dunkirk, as well as 6000 infantry and some guns (cannons) to be added to the army of Turenne (Longueville 1907, 258). The Commonwealth's forces were organized into six regiments under the commands of Sir John

---

[48] John of Austria (in Spanish: Don Juan Jose de Austria) was the only illegitimate son of King Phillip IV of Spain.

[49] Louis II de Bourbon was a French general and the son of Henri II Prince of Conde and Charlotte Marguerite de Montmorency.

[50] Titular means in name only.

[51] Charles II's brother, James. Stuart

Reynolds and, after his death, Sir William Lockhart, Thomas Morgan, Roger Alsop, Samuel Clarke, Sir Bryce Cochrane and Henry Lillingston (Colonel C. Field 1935, 102, f.*). Cromwell's initial 6000 men had joined with Commander of the Allied forces French Marshal-General Viscount de Turenne's army in June of 1657. By the time they had been three months in the field, they had lost a third of their troops owing to the hardships of the campaign (C. H. Firth 1902, 82). Col. John Reynolds, Commander of the English Parliamentary forces, went over to London to negotiate more troops to fill in his regiments and Cromwell complained of the lost time fighting inland sieges when what he really wanted was to get on with attacking the Flemish seaports of Dunkirk and Mardyke. It was agreed that Mardyke was a fort that must be captured before the siege of Dunkirk could begin. Cromwell then agreed to furnish the artillery, some of the supplies demanded, and to send a second dispatch of 2000 men to fill the gaps in the English contingent (Charles Harding Firth 1909, 283–4). The fort of Mardyke was besieged and taken over at the end of September 1657 and immediately handed over to the Commonwealth (C. H. Firth 1902, 83).

The winter of 1657/58 was extremely difficult for both the English Parliamentarian's Commonwealth garrisoned at Mardyke, now commanded by Sir William Lockhart, as well as Charles II's English Royalist regiments, in service with Spain, garrisoned at Dunkirk. There was much loss of life in the extreme, overcrowded conditions at both forts. At the end of January, the Commonwealth contingent, due to sickness and death, was reduced from 6,000 to 3,000 men, making a total loss of about 5,000 men since its landing in Flanders (C. H. Firth 1902, 83, f. 1).

By the end of May 1658, the Commonwealth forces were again reinforced with an additional 3,300 men dispatched to Lockhart's army (C. H. Firth 1902, 84). This was now the third influx of soldiers who were sent to Flanders to fight along-side the French army which was under the allied command of Marshall Turenne.

DISCUSSION

If this study's Edward Moore, now 46, had been sent to Flanders to fight, there would have been three separate times he could have been sent. There is no telling on which occasion this would have occurred. It appears that Moore, if he had been part of the Board of Ordnance's main artillery as a gunner, would have fallen under the command of Sir William Lockhart, a Scot, Cromwell's recent ambassador to France and now Commander of the Commonwealth Parliamentarian army in Flanders; ultimately to be used as Turenne saw fit.

Meanwhile, after the harsh winter of 1657/58, the weakened English Royalist army of five regiments[52] had to be formed into only three battalions. The first combined Charles II's footguards and the 2nd Earl of Bristol's Foot regiment and was commanded by Lt-Col Thomas Blague. The second consisted of the Duke of York's regiment under Lord Muskerry. The third battalion was formed by Ormond's regiments of Irish under Col. Richard Grace and Lord Newburgh's regiment of Scots under the command of Sir William Urry (C. H. Firth 1902, 84–5).

It is of note that a Royalist soldier named John Strode was Captain-Lieutenant in the 2nd Earl of Bristol's Foot regiment in Spanish service between 1656 and 1658. He then fought as head of a regiment for Charles II at the Battle of Dunkirk. Strode's father, Sir George Strode, who was a prosperous London merchant, had been financial adviser to the 1st Earl of Bristol (Henning 1983, 1–2). It was through this connection that John Strode received his commission with the 2nd Earl of Bristol. John Strode would go on to become Lt-Gov of Dover Castle at the same time that Edward Moore (b. *c.* 1612) was Master Cannoneer there. Strode's complete company, that had been garrisoned in Dunkirk after Charles II's Restoration in 1660, would form the permanent garrison of Dover Castle from August 1662 until his death in March of 1686 (Charles Dalton 1892, 6) (S. F.-G. Hamilton 1874, 85). Both Edward Moore (Commonwealth) and John Strode (Royalist) would have played their own roles in the Battle of Dunkirk, sometimes referred to as the Battle of the Dunes, albeit on opposite sides at first. ⚜

---

52 Gloucester's 6th Regiment had been previously captured by Turenne.

12

The Battle of Dunkirk and its Garrison

Battle of the Dunes | 14 June 1658

ABOUT FOUR IN THE MORNING on Friday 14 June 1658, having been alerted, the Duke of York hurried to the outpost. He could plainly see the whole French army forming in order of battle, the horse, with some guns (cannons) before them on each wing, the infantry in the center (Firth 1964, 192).

The Spaniards, under Don John of Austria, the Prince of Conde, the Marquis de Caracena, and the Duke of York, found themselves on the defensive instead of the offensive. Their heavy cannon and ammunition had been left behind, being slower with their advancement. Half of York's cavalry was scattered foraging; his infantry, composed of 2,500 Spaniards, 2,000 Irish and 2,000 Walloons, were inferior in number to the enemy (Grant 1897, 313).

From the French Allied point of view, Turenne, as his army marched leisurely on, could see:

> *. . . the enemy being pretty much puzzled to get themselves into order of battle, all the General Officers were busied therein, and we saw plainly that not one of them repaired to their advanced Guards, who retired to the main body of their army, without skirmishing.*
>
> In his memoirs, Turenne went on to explain,
>
> *We had . . . five pieces of cannon in each wing, which marched at the head of the foremost squadrons, and were at a reasonable distance from the enemy. We fired once or twice from each, and then put the horses to, and hasten'd them up again to the head of the squadrons. We made four or five discharges before we came up to the enemy.* (Tour 1735, 186)

The most common field gun (cannon) in the mid-1600's was the demi-culverin, which fired a cannonball of between nine and twelve pounds and could be fired about ten times an hour. The guns could be moved with the infantry as it advanced to bolster the firepower of the infantry. Transportation of artillery on campaign was the responsibility of the General of the Ordnance, who commanded the artillery train. The train also carried supplies of ammunition and gunpowder for the whole army, as well as all kinds of military tools and equipment. (Plant, David 2011).

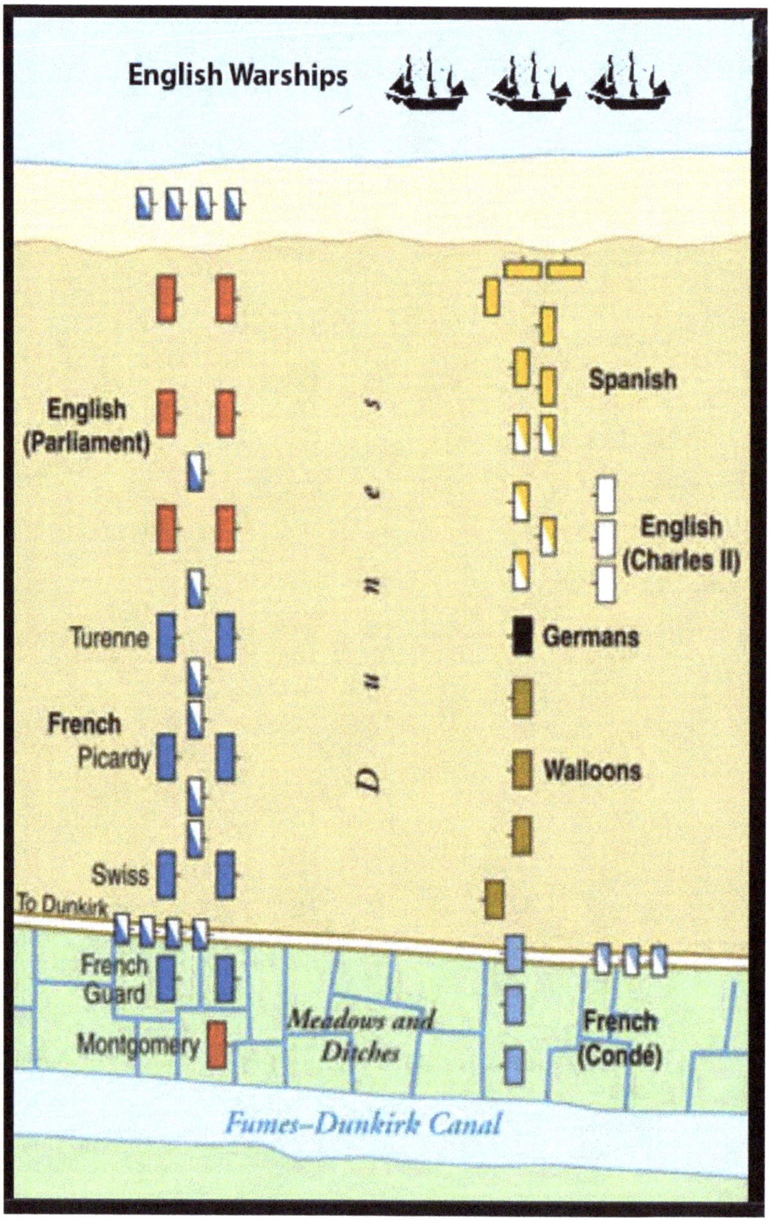

Figure 30: Battle of the Dunes

Source: Map taken from http://www.warfarehistorynetwork.com/2016/06/07/decision-in-the-dunes

The battle [fig. 30] is said to have begun soon after eight in the morning (Firth 1964, f. 193). Lockhart's own regiment of Cromwellian infantry attacked first. The Spanish had placed themselves at the top of a sandy dune so the English had to ascend a steep hill in the yielding sand to reach the summit where they lost several officers and men (Grant 1897, 313). As the fighting continued, Viscount de Turenne recalls in his Memoirs:

> *. . . the prince* [Duke of York] *had his horse wounded, and instantly took another: but his troops now beginning to be in confusion, he was hard put to it to make his escape . . . this happening just after the enemy's right wing was put into confusion, their whole army fell into disorder without rallying; and except some squadrons which dispers'd themselves, our whole army pursued the enemy a quarter of an hour in very good order. Part of the infantry got away on the left hand through the Morass; all the rest were taken. There were between three and four thousand of the enemy made prisoners, and a thousand killed or wounded. . . Being engaged in the siege* [of Dunkirk's fort] *we could not pursue the enemy very long: however, the cavalry push'd on as far as Furnes, behind which place the enemy retired.* Turenne further stated, *There fled to Furnes a good number of prisoners, whom our Troopers and Officers let go for their ransom.* (Tour 1735, 187)

By noon, the battle was over. About one thousand of the beaten army fell on the field and about four thousand were taken prisoners, including five hundred officers. The victorious army lost not more than four hundred men, of whom nearly half were English (Firth 1964, 199).

Suffice it to say that the Allied troops of the French/Commonwealth soldiers won handily over the Spanish/Royalists. The white flag regiments of Lord Lockhart's Foot and Horse as well as those soldiers of Lillingston's Foot under the blue flag bore the brunt of the fighting and became the decisive factors. Both of these regiments, as well as Alsop's, sustained heavy losses and several wounded, while the other regiments suffered only slight losses (C. H. Firth 1902, 85–6).

On the other side, two out of the three royalist battalions were almost annihilated. The King's Footguards stood their ground well, but were finally obliged to surrender and were taken prisoner. Bristol's and York's Irish regiments were routed and cut to pieces and the balance were made prisoners as well. Only Col. Grace's regiment was able to march off the field intact. The Duke of York's troop of guards suffered heavy losses but remained fit for further service. The king's forces after the battle numbered less than a thousand men, maybe not more than seven or eight hundred (C. H. Firth 1902, 86).

After the battle ended, the siege of Dunkirk began. In a letter from Colonel William Lockhart to Secretary of State John Thurloe dated 19 June 1658, Lockhart describes getting ready his cannon:

> *I am this day causing prepare a battery and platform for our mortar-pieces; and the fyer-master is making reddy all things fit upon his part; so that I hope they shall begin to play once more tomorrow. If the battery I am now desyning have that success I hope it will, I shall ere long be able to send your lordship good news concerning Dunkerke. Our greatest*

difficultie is how to get carriages to mount our cannon upon the doones; but we must wrestle over that, and I ame confident the Lord, who hath brought things to the birth, will give strength also to bring forth. (Birch 1742, June (1 of 6). vol. lix., 129)

Dunkirk surrendered ten days after the battle on 24 June 1658, and was immediately handed over to Cromwell's troops, as the treaty required. While part of the English Commonwealth contingent was left to garrison Dunkirk and Mardyke under the Command of Sir William Lockhart, the rest of the regiments continued to fight in the field with Turenne; that being the regiments of Morgan, Cochrane, Clarke and Lillingston. (C. H. Firth 1902, 86). The Train of Artillery would have also participated with these regiments in further pursuing the enemy in the next battle at Bergues, on June 27th. The Memoirs of Turenne mentions the use of *"some cannon to be brought openly and without the least cover close to the gates"* of Bergues (Tour 1735, 189). However, Bergues was in close proximity to Dunkirk (9.7 km) and there is further evidence in a letter sent about one week later from Lockhart to Secretary Thurloe that Turenne had no cannons, nor ammunition for them, as of the date of the letter which was 6 July 1658 (Birch 1742, June (5 of 6). vol. lix., 249). Therefore, the cannons at Bergues were most likely the Board's artillery and were presumably ordered to return and help garrison Dunkirk.

Commonwealth's Dunkirk Garrison

Colonel William Lockhart was made governor of Dunkirk (Grant 1897, 314). Three thousand of the English Commonwealth contingent were drawn off to garrison Dunkirk. The garrison consisted of Lockhart's regiment and the two English establishment regiments of Colonel Robert Gibbons' nine companies and the nine companies of Colonel Edward Salmon's. There was also a regiment of horse under Colonel Tobias Bridge (Firth 1964, 207, 209 f.2). Eventually, one half of Lillingston's regiment was also sent back to Dunkirk (C. H. Firth 1902, 88). In addition, in a 27 June 1658 letter from Colonel Lockhart to Secretary Thurloe, Lockhart states:

I have been forced to draw in ane other regiment, and made them cast lotts for it, which gave generall satesfactione: the lott fell upon colonel Alsopp's regiment, so that with colonel Gibbon's and colonel Salmond's regiments, and the two odd companies belonging to captaine Eaton and captaine Harrisone, we will have foure regiments in the towne, and foure in the field. (Birch 1742, June (2 of 6). vol. lix., 169)

In the same letter as mentioned above, Lockhart had taken an inventory of his cannon's stating that he had about 130 pieces, 63 brass and 67 iron, and that most of them were *"small guns."* He explained that he gathered all the ammunition that could be found and had paid the soldiers six pence for every ball of 29 lb. weight they brought in and a groat for 12 lb. balls. Tools such as shovels, spades and pickaxes were also gathered together from the towns people for the purpose of repairing Dunkirk.

Lockhart further stated that he had around 700 sick soldiers of which about 300 were also wounded and that he placed them in houses close to a nunnery to be cared for. In addition, he planned for both English and French money to be allowed for purchases *"at the rates they doe in England and France, which will free the soldiers of a greatt deale of troble they are putt to by changing their money"* (Birch 1742, June (2 of 6). vol. lix., 169).

Midday on June 25th, Louis XIV entered Dunkirk. That evening, the town was officially handed over to Lockhart; Louis XIV himself gave Lockhart the keys to Dunkirk with his own hand (Firth 1964, 201).

In Lockhart's 30 June 1658 letter to Thurloe, he continued to describe the work that had taken place in Dunkirk. He requested that food, ammunition and recruits be hastened to provide for the garrison. He included:

> *It will be necessary to send over good store of oats for the horsemen, as also some carpenters and gunners from the Tower. We shall serve ourselves with soldiers for mattroses* [gunner's aides]. Regarding the wounded and the sick, he wrote, *I have . . . at least 700 wounded and sick men, the greatest part whereof belong to the four regiments that are in the field. I erect eight hospitals for them, which is one for every regiment . . . finding the nuns not able to perform their promise.* (Birch 1742, June (3 of 6). vol. lix., 185)

Continuing to read what Lockhart himself had to say taken from Thurloe's State Papers, his letter from 6 July 1658 states that Dover Castle was full of infirm men being cared for from the recent war in Flanders:

> *I have this day mustered the forces here, and have done it with all the exactnesse possible. Their provisions shall be given out according to their rolles . . . I have also sent away by this tyde betwixt 2[00] and 300 sick and wounded. I have ordered them to go to Deale and Sandwitch, fearing that Dover may be already too full. And having occasione this day, upon the account of muster, to putt the whole garrisone under arms, I took that opportunity to disarme all the bourgoise, and other inhabitants of this towne, and have done it without clamour or noise.* (Birch 1742, June (5 of 6). vol. lix., 249)

Oliver Cromwell Died | 3 September 1658

Oliver Cromwell died at the Palace of Whitehall, London, only around two months after the Battle of the Dunes. His son, Richard Cromwell, was immediately confirmed by the Council of State as the new Protectorate (Fraser 1979, 207–8). Richard Cromwell proved to be a weak leader and as Parliament re-assembled on 7 May 1659, they voted to abolish the Protectorate. Richard Cromwell's renunciation of the Protectorship was read in Parliament on 25 May 1659, only eight months after his inauguration. Both the English army and its fleet accepted the change of regime and the Council of State was now in power (Plant, David 2007, 2). Nineteen months passed between the death of Oliver Cromwell and the restoration of Charles II in May of 1660 (Fraser 1979, 223).

The Royalist Prisoners

Turenne, along with the Cromwellian regiments of Morgan, Cochrane, Clarke and Lillingston, pursued the Royalists and the Spanish throughout the fall of 1658 as one place after another fell into the hands of the French which continually consolidated the opposing army's position. Bergues fell to Turenne on 27 June followed by Furnes on 3 July then Dixmunde by 9 July. Afterwards Gravelines fell on 27 August, Oudenarde by 9 September and Ypres on 26 September (Firth 1964, 207–09). With that, the campaign practically ended. Leaving garrisons in the important fortresses, Turenne went to Paris in December of 1658, about six months after the Battle of the Dunes and the main battle for France was almost over (Longueville 1907, 268). The war in Flanders and Cromwell's rule over Britain ended simultaneously on 8 May 1659 with the cessation of arms between France and Spain (C. H. Firth 1902, 89).

Despite the disaster of the King's little army at the Battle of the Dunes, although quartered in several towns in Flanders by the end of the year 1658, they continued to be recognized as distinct corps (S. F.-G. Hamilton 1874, 30). The exception was the King's own regiment which was picked up by the French as prisoners and remained so until June of 1659. "*Their condition was most miserable, for they had no clothes but those they were taken prisoners in, and were threatened with imprisonment by their landlords for former debts.*" The condition of the garrisoned men was little better, especially after the truce made between France and Spain in May 1659 had rendered their service to Spain of no value. They received their pay rarely and were often in danger of starvation (C. H. Firth 1902, 98). One Captain Gwynne, garrisoned at Nivelles, wrote in his memoirs:

> *Some of my souldiers one morning came to me grievously sharpe set, and in that hungry humour sadly complained of the hard measure they had, as to be forst to beg, steale, or starve, which was not always to be don, nor would they do it any longer; vowing that it was*

for my sake they staid there so long languishing at that rate. I could not take any thing ill that eas'd them with talking, because, to be sure, whatsoever they beg'd, stoale, or made a shift for, I had my share of it, or I might have gon and do as they did, or not live; therefore I seem'd to comply with them to gaine their patience but to the next day; and, in the meantime, I would fix upon something commendable for us all to do in so great an exigence; and so prevail'd with them. (Gwynne 1822, 132)

About the spring of 1659, the King's army was reorganized and by July 1659 the king once more had six regiments, at least on paper; the King's own, the Duke of York's, the Duke of Gloucester's, Lord Newburgh's, Colonel Grace's (once called Ormond's) and Colonel Farrell's (once Lord Bristol's). In all, there were eighty-six companies from which could be inferred as being about 2000 men (C. H. Firth 1902, 99–100). As of the Restoration of Charles II in 1660, they were still scattered in different parts of Flanders.

The Artillery as Part of the Garrison

From the English Secretary of State John Thurloe's papers dated 16 May 1659, a muster of the **"Train of Artillery"** garrisoned at Dunkirk and Mardyke had taken place (Ricardi Rawlinson 1862, 101 #17). If Edward Moore had helped garrison Dunkirk as part of the Artillery, he would have been among this muster.

Other examples that prove the Train of Artillery had been garrisoned in Dunkirk is evident in the House of Commons Journal dated 27 July 1659. An *"Address of the Officers and Soldiers"* in the regiments of Lockhart's Horse, Lockhart's Foot, Alsopp's and Lillingston's Foot and "***the Commissaries, Gentlemen of the Ordnance and the rest of the Train of Artillery of the Garrison of Dunkirk***" gave assurances of their loyalty to the Council of State (British History Online 1802, 734–36).

In the first half of the year of 1660, the garrison at Dunkirk consisted exclusively of the following Cromwellian troops: Colonel Lockhart's (the Governor) Regiment of Foot, Colonel Henry Lillingtons's, Colonel Roger Alsopp's regiments of infantry, the Governor's Regiment of Horse, four companies of Colonel Gibbons and Colonel Evelyn's regiments ***and the Train of Artillery*** (S. F.-G. Hamilton 1874, 33 f.*).

Charles II Restoration & the King's Dunkirk Garrison

On 25 May 1660, Charles II landed at Dover and on 29 May, his thirtieth birthday, he made his triumphal entry into London (Fraser 1979, 232–3).

Soon after being restored, the King appointed Colonel Edward Harley as governor of Dunkirk in Lockhart's place and Harley became his regiment-of-foot's colonel. Lockhart's regiment of horse was given to Robert Harley, the governor's brother. Both Alsop and Lillingston retained their commands. All four regiments escaped the great disbanding of the English army in the autumn of 1660 because it was necessary to retain a garrison at Dunkirk (C. H. Firth 1902, 96–7).

Charles II did not bring his army back to England with him. By degrees, however, they were drawn to Dunkirk, and were either incorporated in the garrison or otherwise provided for (C. H. Firth 1902, 101). The government of King Charles II had on its hands in Flanders not only the Cromwellian soldiers who garrisoned Dunkirk, but the remnant of the King's own army. To consolidate and unify the two to form a garrison for Dunkirk that was loyal to the King was top priority (C. H. Firth 1902, 96).

On 29 June 1660, it was ordered:

> . . . *that the Officers and Soldiers of his Majesty's Garrison of Dunkirk be injoined to take the Oaths of Allegiance and Supremacy*. The same day it was also ordered, *that the Troop of Guards to his Royal Highness the Duke of Yorke, consisting of a hundred Horsemen, besides Officers, be added to the Establishment of the Army*. (British History Online 1802, 77–8)

The next to be brought onto the establishment was the King's Regiment of Guards and on 26 August 1660 Lord Thomas Wentworth, on business at court in London, was appointed its colonel. Those regiments who were still quartered at Nivelles were sent to Namur for its winter quarters and it was not until early in 1661 that they received their orders to march for Dunkirk (C. H. Firth 1902, 102).

It was about at this time, March of 1661, that Lord Wentworth was ordered to augment the King's Regiments of Guards to consist of twelve companies of 100 men apiece to garrison Dunkirk. Therefore, Wentworth was authorized to raise 1,100 recruits for that purpose. The *officers*, John Strode among them, were already at their full complement. This augmentation of the regular troops was complete by the end of May. Lord Wentworth was directed by Charles II to communicate with the Duke of York for the transport of his 1,100 recruits and they were conveyed at the end of May to Dunkirk (S. F.-G. Hamilton 1874, 78–80). If Wentworth had to raise 1,100 troops, what had been left of the King's Regiment of Guards may only have totaled to about 100 soldiers in all. John Strode, future Lt.-Gov. of Dover Castle, is listed as one of the twelve Captains of a Company of the King's Regiment of Guards at Dunkirk as of June 1661 (Dalton 1892, 6).

In May of 1661, Lord Rutherford succeeded Edward Harley as governor of Dunkirk. Throughout his governorship, the Royalist regiments continued to live on the best of terms with the officers and men of the Cromwellian regiments who had already been occupying Dunkirk's garrison (C. H. Firth 1902, 102).

The public records note that there were still gunner's garrisoned at Dunkirk with the following entry:

1662- Sept 23, Commission to Thomas Fleetwood to be Master Gunner in Dunkirk garrison. (P. R. Great Britain 1861, 496) [Entry Book 2, p. 36]

Sale of Dunkirk

The Cromwellian acquisition of Dunkirk proved to be a financial drain on Charles II because it cost a fortune to maintain. Seemingly always at a loss for funds, it became a financial necessity to sell Dunkirk to his cousin, Louis XIV (Fraser 1979, 297). In November 1662, a series of warrants were ordered according to Charles II's Calendar of State Papers-Domestic:

Nov. 4. *Warrant [to Lord Chancellor Clarendon], to affix the Great Seal to Lord Rutherford's commission, empowering him to deliver up Dunkirk to the French King. [Entry Book 9, p. 32.]*

Nov. 4. Whitehall. *Instructions to Lord Rutherford for disbanding the forces at Dunkirk, and surrendering it to the King of France. The remaining companies of the King's Guard are to be sent over to England. The Duke of York's regiment is to enter the French service. The three troops of horse, his own and Lord Falkland's regiments, and the train and staff officers are to be disbanded before 17th Nov., if the money arrive in time. The arrears are to be computed from 24th Sept., 1660, when the garrison come into the King's pay, and the arrears of Sir Edw. Harley, the former governor, and of the officers are to be included. The arms of the disbanded troops are to be given up; the magazines of bread and cheese distributed among the soldiers, unless otherwise required; and the town delivered according to instructions, keeping only a sufficient number of soldiers for security, till the money has been received and embarked. Vessels are to be hired for the men to return; they are to have passes to their respective towns, and to be ordered to sell their swords and horses within 14 days of their arrival.*

Nov. 5. Whitehall. *Commission to Sir George Carteret* [treasurer of the navy] *to receive five million livres, to be paid by the French King for the surrender of Dunkirk . . . Having obtained satisfaction, he is to signify the same to Lord Rutherford, and on his intimation of the surrender of the place, embark the money on the yachts sent by the Duke of York, giving acquittances in due form, and convey it to the Tower, where he will receive orders for its disembarkation.* (British History Online 1861, 538–59)

13

The Troops Come Home

Figure 31: Dover Cinque Port and Castle c. 1720

Illustrator unknown. Print purchased in Dover, England by the author.

Dover Castle, England

DOVER HAD BEEN ONE OF THE FIRST PLACES in Kent to declare against Charles I (1625–1649) and the castle was captured by several townsmen and handed over to the Parliamentary authorities as early as 1642 during the English Civil War (Statham 1899, 116). Thus, it remained until the Restoration.

On 1 May 1660 at the Restoration of Charles II to the throne, Thomas Daniel was Lieutenant of Dover Castle in the Cromwellian Army. He had served in the past as a Lieutenant-Colonel of Horse in the Royalist Army (Dalton 1892, 7 f.8). Dover Castle came into the pay of the King on 1 October 1660 and Increased Collins was restored to the Keepership of Moat's Bulwark (P. R. Great Britain 1860, #58, 89). On 25 Jan 1661, Lt. Thomas Daniel marched the regular

Commonwealth garrison of Dover Castle to London and they were disbanded on 16 March 1661. In Feb 1661, only one gunner, two gunner's mates and two matrosses were left at Dover Castle besides two or three other individuals and the Lord Warden, who was proposing two companies be implemented (Atherton 2003, 13) (Lieut.-Gen. Sir F. W. Hamilton 1874, 70).

> *At the date of the restoration there were twenty-eight key points, or fortresses, in England, and these were manned by independent companies consisting of former Parliamentary soldiers . . . [soon placed] under Royalist officers, excluded from the provisions of the Disbandment Act [of Cromwell's Army], in the King's service and charged to the King's account. In June 1661, they were added to the establishment of what were strictly termed "Our Guards and Garrisons."* (Ascoli 1983, 15)

Parliament was in charge of the civilian militias (trained bands) and the King controlled his standing army of regular (professional) soldiers. Not until 1689 would Parliament recognize the King's soldiers as an army.

The garrison of Dover had been abnormally large during the Commonwealth but was reduced by Charles II to the *"Ancient Establishment"* similar to the times of his Royal ancestors for the *"Lessening of the Greate Charge and Burthen that is upon our Revenue."* By June of 1661, Dover Castle was guarded by one Gentleman of the Ordnance[53] and seventeen gunners who presumably had come from the Ordnance Board in London and consisted of disbanded Parliamentary soldiers. They were concentrated at Moat's Bulwark below the main castle. These gunners and infantry were often invalids and veterans of war who were relegated to be stationed in garrisoned castles. Residing in the Constable's Gate was Sir Francis Vincent the Lord Warden, one Lieutenant, one clerk, and one yeoman Porter, thus reducing its garrison to virtually the same size as that in the time of King Henry VIII. (Atherton 2003, 13, 15) (Salter 2000, 32).

It was 19 August 1662 that the Duke of York received directions from the King to give orders to the commander of the *Merlin* frigate to transport Captain John Strode's 9th Company of the Royal Regiment of Foot Guards from Dunkirk to Dover Castle[54] (P. R. Great Britain 1861, 464) [Entry Book 7, p. 189]. Captain Strode had served with the 2nd Earl of Bristol, Lord George Digby's Regiment of Foot in the Spanish service from 1656 to 1658. Strode had then served in the King's Regiment of Foot Guards ever since 1658, when he had joined it as a volunteer at the Battle of the Dunes (Dalton 1892, 6 f. 9). Now, Strode's 9th Company formed the permanent

---

53 *"Something more than an ordinary soldier, hath a little more pay, and doth not stand Centinel";* not an officer, but believed to be senior to a Master Gunner (Atherton 2003, 13).

54 For more in-depth detail of what happened to the rest of the Royalist and Commonwealth regiments who were stationed in Dunkirk, read *Royalist and Cromwellian Armies in Flanders, 1657–1662* by C. H. Firth, LL.D.

garrison of Dover Castle. The *Calendar of State Papers in the reign of Charles II* contains the following entry:

> *22 September 1662-Warrant to continue to Captain Strode's Company, removed to Dover, to Captains Jefferies and Sydenham, sent to Jersey, and to Captain Walter's, to Guernsey, the same pay as they had at Dunkirk. [entry Book 7, p. 258]* (P. R. Great Britain 1861, 494)

Therefore, John Strode's entire company had begun garrisoning Dover Castle late August to early September of 1662. His company formed the permanent garrison of Dover Castle until about 1685–6 (Atherton 2003, 15).

DISCUSSION

Was Edward Moore assigned Master Gunner as part of John Strode's Regiment, which had been augmented by Wentworth, coming from Dunkirk to now be stationed at Dover Castle between August and September of 1662? Could Thomas Fleetwood, who was commissioned as Master Gunner of Dunkirk in 23 Sept 1662, have taken the place of Edward Moore for that position? Or, could Moore have been assigned the Master Gunner position at Dover Castle coming from London with the Gentleman of the Ordnance as one of the seventeen gunners in June 1661? Being a veteran, he would have acquired highly valuable skills as a Master Gunner. If he had been in London sometime in 1661, he may have had the chance to visit his family there for a brief time. His son, Thomas, would have been seven years of age. It would be the last time Thomas would ever see his father.

Edward Moore was stationed as a Master Gunner at Dover Castle from either 1661 or 1662. This was a lifetime position (Ascoli 1983, 10). He possessed excellent mathematical skills taught by the Royal Navy. He knew the curves given the velocity for the distance of his ammunition and relied on the extensive information provide in *The Gunner's Glasse* which had been written by William Eldred, a former Master Gunner of Dover Castle. He would have been familiar with Queen Elizabeth I's 60 pounder "Pocket Pistol" cannon which was built in 1544 and which is still on display at the castle today. By now, he feasibly would have been very hard of hearing.

The Plague of London | 1665

In the spring and summer of 1665, the city of London experienced a devastating plague that killed 68,596 of its citizens (Champion 1993) [fig. 32]. Out of the capital city's population of up to 460,000 people, around twenty percent died. Many historians now accept a figure closer to 100,000 people dying (Jordan 2018, 194–5). The plague fell heaviest on the poor as the rich could easily escape to their country homes (Fraser 1979, 309–10).

Margaret (Margrett) Moore, died of the plague and was buried 1 October 1665 in the parish of St. Mary, Whitechapel, Middlesex, in the Borough of the Tower Hamlets (Find My Past n.d.) [fig. 27]. In fact, a total of forty-six of her fellow parishioners of St. Mary Matfelon's Episcopal Church[55], a.k.a. St. Mary's Whitechapel, died of the plague on that same day (London Metropolitan Archives 2010).

Whitechapel, Tower Hamlets, Middlesex is in the greater section of London called *London East End & Docklands* which is north of the river Thames and bordered by the river Lea; a canalized river attached to the river Thames to the east. It was an area which was very poor. Edward Moore's son, Thomas, would now be eleven years of age and possibly living and performing some form of labor down by the docks.

Second Anglo-Dutch War | 4 March 1665 to 31 July 1667

Thomas Moore's father, Edward Moore, was stationed at Dover Castle during October 1665 at the time of Margaret Moore's death and involved in a war with Dutch ships thronging the British coasts (Davies 2017, 201). He would have been unable to travel and aid Thomas in London. Furthermore, in 1665, the town of Dover ruled that *"no householder was to receive any person from London into his house"* due to the plague there (Statham 1899, 119).

---

[55] The church building, as well as all its records, was destroyed by fire on 26 August 1880.

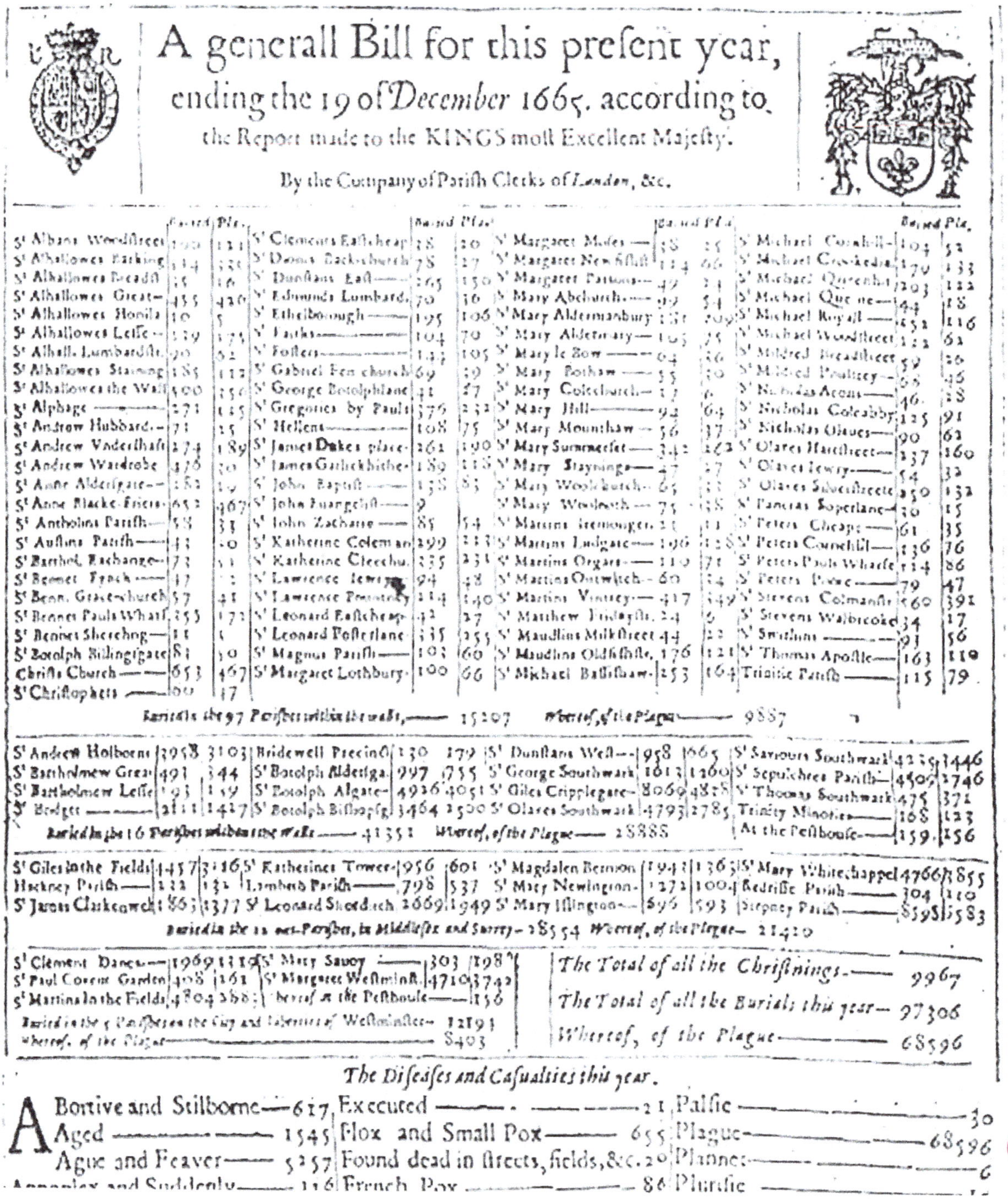

A generall Bill for this present year, ending the 19 of *December* 1665. according to the Report made to the KINGS most Excellent Majesty.

By the Company of Parish Clerks of *London*, &c.

	Buried	Plag.		Buried	Plag.		Buried	Plag.		Buried	Plag.
St Albans Woodstreet	[illegible]	121	St Clements Eastcheap	38	20	St Margaret Moses	38	25	St Michael Cornhill	104	52
St Alhallowes Barking	514	330	St Dionis Backchurch	78	27	St Margaret Newfishstr.	114	66	St Michael Crookedlane	179	133
St Alhallowes Breadst.	35	16	St Dunstans East	265	150	St Margaret Pattons	49	24	St Michael Queenhithe	203	122
St Alhallowes Great	455	426	St Edmunds Lumbard.	70	36	St Mary Abchurch	99	54	St Michael Quern	44	18
St Alhallowes Honila	10	5	St Ethelborough	195	106	St Mary Aldermanbury	181	109	St Michael Royall	152	116
St Alhallowes Lesse	239	175	St Faiths	104	70	St Mary Aldermary	105	75	St Michael Woodstreet	122	62
St Alhall. Lumbardstr.	90	62	St Fosters	144	105	St Mary le Bow	64	36	St Mildred Breadstreet	59	26
St Alhallowes Staining	185	112	St Gabriel Fen church	69	39	St Mary Bothaw	55	30	St Mildred Poultrey	68	46
St Alhallowes the Wall	500	356	St George Botolphlane	41	27	St Mary Colechurch	17	6	St Nicholas Acons	46	28
St Alphage	271	115	St Gregories by Pauls	376	232	St Mary Hill	94	64	St Nicholas Coleabby	125	91
St Andrew Hubbard	71	25	St Hellens	108	75	St Mary Mounthaw	56	37	St Nicholas Olaves	90	62
St Andrew Vndershaft	274	189	St James Dukes place	262	190	St Mary Summerset	342	262	St Olaves Hartstreet	237	160
St Andrew Wardrobe	476	308	St James Garlickhithe	189	118	St Mary Stayning	47	27	St Olaves Jewry	54	32
St Anne Aldersgate	282	197	St John Baptist	138	83	St Mary Woolchurch	65	33	St Olaves Silverstreete	250	132
St Anne Blacke-Friers	652	467	St John Evangelist	9		St Mary Woolnoth	75	38	St Pancras Soperlane	30	15
St Antholins Parish	58	33	St John Zacharie	85	54	St Martins Iremonger	21	11	St Peters Cheape	61	35
St Austins Parish	43	20	St Katherine Coleman	299	213	St Martins Ludgate	196	128	St Peters Cornhill	136	76
St Barthol. Exchange	73	51	St Katherine Creechu.	335	231	St Martins Orgars	110	71	St Peters Pauls Wharfe	114	86
St Bennet Fynch	47	22	St Lawrence Jewry	94	48	St Martins Outwitch	60	34	St Peters Poore	79	47
St Benn. Gracechurch	57	41	St Lawrence Pountney	214	140	St Martins Vintrey	417	349	St Stevens Colmanstr.	560	391
St Bennet Pauls Wharf	355	172	St Leonard Eastcheape	42	27	St Matthew Fridaystr.	24	6	St Stevens Walbrooke	34	17
St Bennet Sherehog	11	1	St Leonard Fosterlane	335	255	St Maudlins Milkstreet	44	22	St Swithins	93	56
St Botolph Billingsgate	83	50	St Magnus Parish	103	60	St Maudlins Oldfishstr.	176	121	St Thomas Apostle	163	110
Christs Church	653	467	St Margaret Lothbury	100	66	St Michael Bassishaw	253	164	Trinitie Parish	115	79
St Christophers	60	47									

Buried in the 97 Parishes within the walls, — 15207 *Whereof, of the Plague* — 9887

St Andrew Holborne	3958	3103	Bridewell Precinct	230	179	St Dunstans West	958	665	St Saviours Southwark	4235	3446
St Bartholmew Great	493	344	St Botolph Aldersga.	997	755	St George Southwark	1613	1260	St Sepulchres Parish	4509	3746
St Bartholmew Lesse	193	139	St Botolph Algate	4926	4051	St Giles Cripplegate	8069	4838	St Thomas Southwark	475	371
St Bridget	2111	1427	St Botolph Bishopsg.	3464	2500	St Olaves Southwark	4793	2785	Trinity Minories	168	123
									At the Pesthouse	159	156

Buried in the 16 Parishes without the Walls — 41351 *Whereof, of the Plague* — 28888

St Giles in the Fields	4457	3216	St Katherines Tower	956	601	St Magdalen Bermondsey	1943	1363	St Mary Whitechappel	4766	3855
Hackney Parish	232	132	Lambeth Parish	798	537	St Mary Newington	1272	1004	Redriffe Parish	304	210
St James Clarkenwel	1863	1377	St Leonard Shoreditch	2669	1949	St Mary Islington	696	593	Stepney Parish	8598	6583

Buried in the 12 out-Parishes, in Middlesex and Surrey — 28554 *Whereof, of the Plague* — 21420

St Clement Danes	1969	1319	St Mary Savoy	303	198
St Paul Covent Garden	408	261	St Margaret Westminst.	4710	3742
St Martins in the Fields	4804	2883	Whereof at the Pesthouse		156

Buried in the 5 Parishes in the City and Liberties of Westminster — 12194
Whereof, of the Plague — 8403

The Total of all the Christnings — 9967
The Total of all the Burials this year — 97306
Whereof, of the Plague — 68596

The Diseases and Casualties this year.

Abortive and Stilborne	617	Executed	21	Palsie	30
Aged	1545	Flox and Small Pox	655	Plague	68596
Ague and Feaver	5257	Found dead in streets, fields, &c.	20	Plannet	6
Apoplexy and Suddenly	116	French Pox	86	Plurisie	[illegible]

Figure 32: The Annual Bill of Mortality of London and its Environs, 1665

Source: (Champion, Epidemics and the Built Environment in 1665 1993, No. 1, 35–52)
http://www.archives.history.ac.uk/history-in-focus/medical/epichamp.html

Figure 33: St. Mary's Anglican Church in Dover, England

Source: Artist; C.V. Culver 1989. Sketch purchased in Dover by the author.

Of note is its prominent Norman style tower which was originally built in the early 12th century.

Having been a widower since 1665, Edward Moore married Cecilia Richardson at St. Mary's Anglican Church, Dover. They wed after 31 July 1667 when the 2nd Anglo-Dutch War ended; around late 1667 or early 1668. Their first child, John, was born 18 Nov 1668 followed by Sara, born 1 Nov 1670 and then by Robert, born 26 Oct 1673.

In June of 1670, gunner Edward Moore was part of *"a royal salute from the guns at Dover Castle"* welcoming back King Charles II's sister, Henrietta Anne, from a royal tour of the shores around Dover while she was there working out the terms for the secret treaty of Dover between England and France (Watkins 2019, pgs 129–132). Edward Moore would have used his skills as gunner in the 2nd Anglo-Dutch War March 1665 to July 1667 and the 3rd Dutch War 1672–74.

By 1678, the castle was *"so ruined there was no place habitable without repair."* From 1678–1702, there were many references that troops were quartered in the town doing duty in the castle over prisoners and deserters. By 1679, there were eighteen gunners. The army in Dover town was considered a *"grievance and vexation to the people"* (Atherton 2003, 17). The soldiers had been poorly paid and likely needed to beg for food and their other needs in town. It didn't help the situation that, in order to save money, Charles II made the mistake of using the same red uniforms for his army that the Commonwealth soldiers had worn (Ascoli 1983, 18 #11). By 1681:

> *Charles II's treasury again empty, the army unpaid and almost mutinous; however, the King formed an alliance with Louis of France . . . which guaranteed him an income independent of Parliament.* (Atherton 2003, 17)

In 1682, there were eight gunners in Dover Castle but in 1684 there were only five along with two companies of the 1st Foot Royal Scots Regiment. Colonel John Strode's company of 1st Regiment of Foot Guards were on parade at the coronation of James II, 23 April 1685, who was *"dressed in a coat of Cloth of Gold richly Imbroidered with Silver"* (Atherton 2003, 17).

Edward Moore would not have lived long enough to see the 1688 Glorious Revolution whereby the Catholic King James II was eventually defeated at the Battle of the Boyne by his Protestant son-in-law, William of Orange. Mary, William's wife, was James II's daughter. They became co-rulers following the deposition of James VII and II.

Both Edward Moore and John Strode died in 1686; September and March respectively. Their deaths were perhaps caused from wounds incurred from conflicts between the Catholic Royalists and those fighting for a Protestant England.

The Marriage Document for Thomas Moore and Jeanne Lemelin in 1690 states that Edward Moore's occupation was Master Cannoneer in Dover Castle. However, Edward Moore had died before the 19th of September 1686 as Nicholas Hunt had been commissioned to take his place by then. The Calendar of State Papers of Charles II, domestic series reads:

> *[1686] September 19. Windsor. Warrant in the usual form for Nicholas Hunt to be gunner in Dover Castle in the place of Edward Moore, deceased.* (P. R. Great Britain 1964, 267)

The other interesting note of information from the above entry is that a mention of "Master" gunner is not stated. It seems Edward Moore may only have occupied the station as one of many gunners at Dover Castle at the time of his death. When Nicholas Hunt was subsequently replaced, the new position for the person replacing Hunt is described as taking over the room of Nicholas Hunt.

[1688] September 17. Windsor. Warrant to Sir Edward Hales, Lieutenant of Dover Castle, to swear and admit John Tooth to be a gunner in Dover Castle in the room of Nicholas Hunt, deceased. Minute # 1511 (S.P. 29/359, p. 228) (British History Online 1972, 228) ⚜

14

Meanwhile, Thomas

Christ's Hospital

THE TERM "HOSPITAL" refers to a charitable institution providing housing or education for the children of needy families. With the dissolution of the monasteries in the 16th century, charity hospitals were founded to provide homes and schooling for poor, fatherless, or orphaned boys and girls in the larger cities such as London (Simmons 2007, 51). Part of Christ's Hospital was The Royal Mathematics School (RMS) which chose boys out of Christ's Hospital (after 1673) to specifically train in mathematics and navigation to be apprenticed, first on Merchant Navy ships and then aboard Royal Navy ships for the term of seven years. Boys upon leaving the Royal Mathematical School had their badges to prove that they were already apprenticed to sea service thus avoiding the press gangs (Jones 2015, 208). During these times, young boys were definitely taken from the streets to work on the ships at the age of fourteen and even younger. The RMS contributed several trained boys for apprenticeships for the East India Company and for the Hudson's Bay Company (Jones 2015, 36, 72).

In fact, there was a Thomas Moore registered at Christ's Hospital in London. He had been admitted at the age of two on 7 September 1657, father not given, and written off the register in 1665. This Thomas would have been only ten or maybe eleven when he was no longer on the register. It did not state an actual death date.

1665 was the year of the plague and in 1666, the Great Fire of London seriously damaged many of the buildings of the school on Newgate Street where all children had been safely evacuated (Jones 2015, 151). Sometimes, boys even ran away and were thus expelled (Jones 2015, 186).

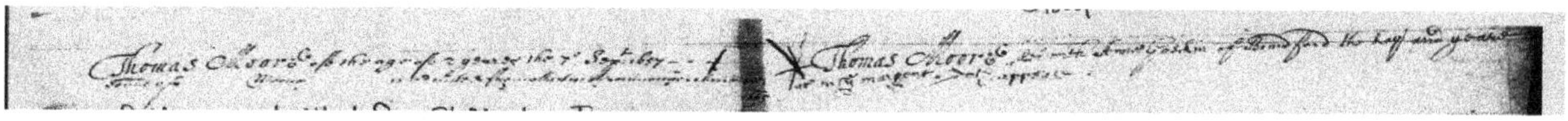

Figure 34. Register entry of a Thomas Moore admitted to Christ Hospital

Source: This entry was provided by Clifford Jones, volunteer at Christ Hospital, via internet.

DISCUSSION

I corresponded with volunteer archivist and author of *The Sea and the Sky; The History of the Royal_Mathematical School of Christ's Hospital,* Clifford Jones. He first cited that the *"register entry for Thomas Moore is very difficult to read and, in any case, incomplete*[56]*."* In a subsequent letter[57], Jones seemed to think that some of the illegible register's words were *"admitted from St. Martin* [Pomary] *Ironmonger Lane,"* which was an Anglican parish within the City of London. Further, he felt that:

> *. . . the right-hand page of the entry records the death in 1665 of Thomas at age ten while under the care of Anne Gardin."* Jones surmised that Thomas's discharge entry is *"most probable that Thomas is dead as pupils did not leave Christ's Hospital until aged fifteen, not even returning to parents on holidays. Thomas was admitted aged two, which implies that he was an orphan, then sent out to nurse until old enough for formal education.*

Given Clifford Jones's experienced knowledge, it appears that this Thomas Moore was not the same person as this study's Thomas Moore. However, it is not difficult to imagine that young Thomas, at age 11, was hanging out down by the docks and helping to do chores for the dockhands for money on which to live after the death of his mother in 1665.

Radisson and Groseilliers

Pierre-Esprit Radisson, born 1636 in St. Malo, France, and Medard Chouart des Groseilliers, baptized 31 July 1618 in the parish church at Charly-sur-Marne, St. Cyr, France, both but separately immigrated to the Quebec area; Radisson on 24 May, 1651 and Groseilliers in 1641 at the age of 16 (Radisson 1885, 1–2). While hunting near his home in Three Rivers (Trois-Riviere), Radisson was captured by the Iroquois and lived among them from 1652 where he learned of their ways, language, the surrounding areas and of the other indigenous peoples of the area.

By June of 1658, Radisson and his now brother-in-law, Medard Chouart des Groseilliers, joined in a two-year expedition exploring the Mississippi River. They returned to their homes in Three Rivers around 1 Jun 1660 and stayed there for the rest of the year. It was on this expedition that they found out from the Christinos (Cree Indians) about the great lake to the north, Hudson[58] Bay (Radisson 1885, 7–8).

---

[56] Correspondence dated 30 Nov 2015

[57] Correspondence dated 2 Dec 2015

[58] Hudson's Bay was its historric name. It is now correctly called Hudson Bay, which will be used throughout this book.

In the spring of 1661, an application was made to the Governor of Quebec, Monsieur Frontenac, for a journey[59] to explore for the fur trade around Hudson Bay, but the Governor's demands of them were too high. In addition, Frontenac did not grant permission for Radisson and Groseillier's voyage because he declared *"it would break the union between the two kings"*[60] who were then at peace against the Dutch (Radisson 1885, 19).

The two adventurers decided to set off anyway without Governor Frontenac's consent and in August, at midnight, they left to join a company of the nation of the Sault who were returning to their country. The Governor was *"greatly displeased"* at their disobedience and upon their return, Frontenac imprisoned Groseilliers and heavily fined them both. Receiving no justice in France, Radisson and Groseilliers resolved to *"go over to the English."* In early 1665, they were in New England engaging a New England ship, captained by Zachariah Gillam (Radisson 1885, 17), for a trading adventure into the Hudson Straits in 61 degrees north (Radisson 1885, 10–12).

While back in Boston, a Commissioner of the King of Great Britain, Colonel George Cartwright, convinced the two Frenchmen to go to England and offer their services to King Charles II, which they did aboard the ship *Charles*. They arrived in London around 25 October 1665 at a very bad time due to the plague. They were first in Oxford where the King's Court was residing to avoid the plague in the city of London. The King offered promise of a ship in the spring and in the meantime provided forty shillings for their maintenance and chambers in town, where they stayed three months. After Charles II returned to London, Radisson and Groseilliers were sent to Windsor where they stayed for the rest of the winter into 1666 (Radisson 1885, 12–14).

Plans for the expedition were further delayed due two other major events. First, the Great Fire of London, 2–6 September 1666, where one-third of London was destroyed and 100,000 people were left homeless. The fire consumed 13,200 houses, 87 out of 109 churches were destroyed as well as many other civic buildings (Museum of London n.d.). The second event was the 2nd Anglo-Dutch War which was from 4 Mar 1665 to 31 July 1667. The war was finally brought to an end by the Treaty of Breda (Fraser 1979, 325).

Finally, in 1668/69, three years after their arrival in London, Radisson and des Groseilliers set sail on their English expedition to the north of Canada headed for Hudson Bay. Among the trip's financial backers were Prince Rupert[61], the Duke of Albemarle and Sir George Carteret, Treasurer of the Navy. Charles II provided them with two of his own warships, initially the *Eaglet Ketch* with Captain Stannard and Radisson aboard and, after she was badly damaged in a

---

59 This was Radisson's 4th voyage.

60 Henry IV of France was "the two king's" mutual grand-father and so the King of England and the King of France were cousins.

61 First cousin to the King Charles II.

storm, the *Wivenhoe*. The expedition also acquired the *Nonsuch Ketch* after it was sold out of the navy at the end of 1667. The *Nonsuch* was captained by Zachariah Gillam and carried des Groseilliers aboard (Radisson 1885, 15–16). Both left Deptford, England on 5 June 1668. Radisson was forced to turn back off the coast of Ireland due to bad weather but des Groseilliers sailed on and established the first fort on Hudson Bay named Charles Fort (later Rupert House) which is at the mouth of Rupert River (Radisson 1885, 16). He successfully returned to London on 9 Oct 1669 laden with furs and the knowledge that trading directly into the bay was possible (Simmons 2007, 20).

The expedition's main achievement was that it led directly to the establishment of the Hudson's Bay Company, which received its royal charter on 2 May 1670, with Prince Rupert as its governor (Davies 2017, 187).

Gideon D. Scull states within his Introduction to the *Voyages of Peter Esprit Radisson*:

> *To des Groseilliers and Radisson must be given the credit of originating the idea of forming a settlement at Hudson's Bay, out of which grew the profitable organization of the Hudson's Bay Company. They obtained through the English Ambassador to France an interview with Prince Rupert, and laid before him their plans . . . Prince Rupert at once foresaw the value of such an enterprise and aided them in procuring the required assistance from several noblemen and gentlemen.* (Radisson 1885, 16)

Young Thomas Moore may have sailed on this early expedition of 1668/69 prior to the official establishment of the Hudson's Bay Company in 1670. Thomas would have been fourteen/fifteen years of age at the time. Boys were used on ships as volunteers (Ronald 2007, 164). He would have been exposed to the Cree language as well as the French language.

History has shown the precedence for young boys to be used onboard major expeditions. In the 1570's, Martin Frobisher was only fourteen years old when he went on his first Guinea voyage. Francis Drake's young cousin, John Drake, joined Drake's frigate *Falcon* as its "boy" at the age of thirteen (Ronald 2007, 185, 193). Lord Nelson was only twelve years of age when he began his naval career.

The Hudson's Bay Company hired able-bodied, but not necessarily well-educated, youths from the streets of London and the Orkney Islands (Simmons 2007, 52).

Whether Thomas Moore was part of an early 1668/69 expedition for English merchants with Radisson and des Groseilliers or not, it is a documented fact that Thomas Moore was officially hired by the Hudson's Bay Company from 1671 to 1678 at the age of 17. ⚜

15

Hudson's Bay Company

AT WHITEHALL PALACE on 2 May 1670, King Charles II authorized the Royal Charter that created "The Governor and Company of Adventurers of England Trading into Hudson's Bay," i.e.–The Hudson Bay Company (HBC). The investors were granted a monopoly of the trading and commerce of all the *"Seas Streightes Bayes Rivers Lakes Creekes and Soundes"* together with all the *"Landes and Territoryes upon the Countryes Coastes"* (Simmons 2007, 20). In his charter, the King declared that the lands adjacent to Hudson Bay or rivers flowing into Hudson Bay be *"from henceforth reckoned and reputed as one of our Plantacions of Colonyes in America called Ruperts Land"* (Simmons 2007, 305, f. 18).

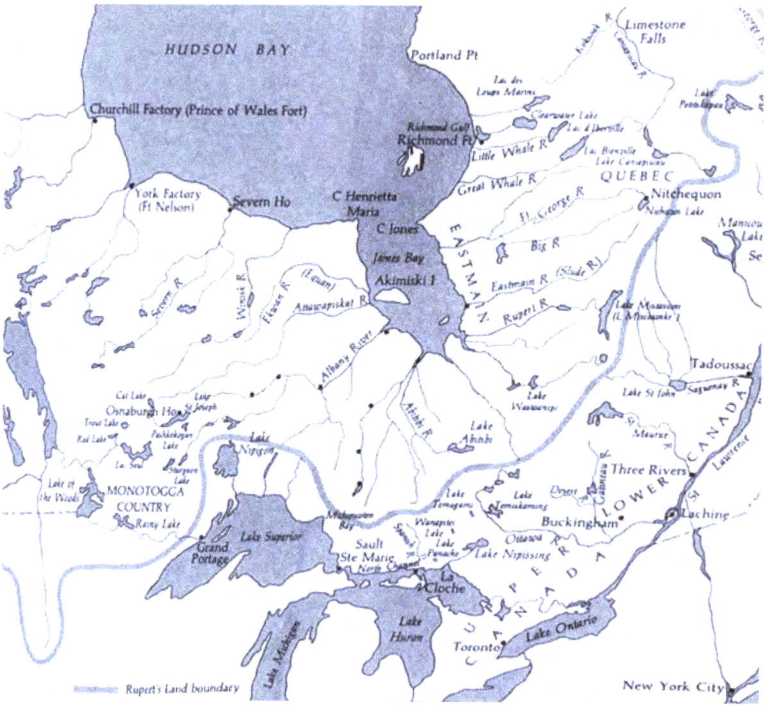

Figure 35. Rivers of Hudson and James Bays

Source: Map taken from location maps in *A Country So Interesting* by R. I. Ruggles, p. xvi.

Figure 36. Rivers with outlets into Hudson Bay or James Bay

Source: Map taken from www.researchgate.net/fig1_253141706.

The inset shows the overall contributing drainage basin for Hudson Bay shaded in grey.

Figure 37. Some HBC outposts on Hudson and James Bays

Source: Map adapted from www.redriverancestry.ca (Still last updated 2018)

York Factory (Port Nelson) is on the Hayes River, Rupert's House (Charles Fort) is on the Rupert River and Moose Factory is on the Moose River.

By early June 1670, the HBC sent out two ships from the Thames bound for Hudson Bay. *Wivenhoe,* captained by Robert Newland, had Pierre-Esprit Radisson aboard along with the newly appointed first Governor of the region, Charles Bayly[62]. The other ship was the *Prince Rupert,* which was captained by Zachariah Gillam, and carried Medard Chouart des Groseilliers. Upon the *Wivenhoe* reaching Port Nelson (later York Factory) in September, Charles Bayly went ashore and "*nailing His Majesty's arms 'in Brasse' on a tree, formally laid claim to the territory.*"

Finding that the Indians had already moved inland, the *Wivenhoe* sailed on and joined with the *Prince Rupert* at Charles Fort (later Rupert House) by the middle of October with her captain, Newland, and its chief-mate dead from scurvy. Here, they *"repeated and confirmed"* the trading agreements with the Indians and wintered at Rupert's River.

In the spring of 1671, Bayly and Radisson went to Moose River where they traded for all the beaver skins taken to London that year in the *Wivenhoe.* The two ships returned to London in October 1671, laden with 11,000 pounds of beaver pelts (Johnson, Charles Bayly 1966) (Simmons 2007, 21).

---

[62] Thomas Gorst, his secretary who kept a journal, was also aboard as well as *"ten or twenty men."* (Radisson 1885, 19)

It was in the year of 1671[63] in London that our Thomas Moore was hired by the Hudson's Bay Company (HBC) at the age of 17; undoubtedly after October with the return of the last expedition. He helped to unload the successful haul of furs brought into London's docks and to prepare for the large auction of beaver that took place on 24 January 1672 (Nute 2004 reprint of 1978 edition, 141) at Garraway's Coffee House near the Royal Exchange in London (Andra-Warner 2009, 35).

Thomas Moore would have been aboard one of three ships which left London for Charles Fort 22 June 1672. The ships names were the *Prince Rupert,* the *Messenger* and the *Employ* (Simmons 2007, 21). He worked with the adventurers, Radisson and des Groseilliers, who were essential to the early HBC expeditions. Governor Charles Bayly was his direct superior with John Abraham as Bayly's second, serving as governor of Port Nelson in James Bay from 1672–75 and 1676–78 (Johnson, John Abraham 1966, revised 1979).

Also in 1672, Father Charles Albanel was sent out of Quebec City in Canada to investigate the English of the HBC. He successfully demonstrated that James Bay could be reached overland and he laid claim to the territory in the name of French King Louis XIV (Johnson, Charles Bayly 1966). Albanel returned to Quebec in August of 1672 with knowledge of the new English location in the Bay (Giguere 1966, revised 2014).

While in post at Charles Fort, Governor Bayly had orders to settle a new post at Moose River, which he did on Hayes Island in 1673. That spring, Bayly sent des Groseilliers to trade at Port Nelson, but the trip was unsuccessful as the Indians were inland (Johnson, Charles Bayly 1966). Thomas Moore may have been assigned to accompany des Groseilliers on this trip. Des Groseilliers and Thomas Moore remained with Bayly at Charles Fort while Radisson returned to London in the fall of 1673 where he married an English woman, Mary Kirke, daughter of Sir John Kirke[64]. Radisson remained in London until 1674 (Simmons 2007, 21–22).

The winter of 1673/1674 was severe and the shortage of fresh food resulted in some scurvy (Johnson, Charles Bayly 1966). Difficulties also existed concerning trade with the Indians due to the competition from the French who had made a settlement *"not above eight days' journey"* up the Moose River from the place where the HBC traded. The French offered lower rates of exchange for furs to the Indians than those of the English (Radisson 1885, 19). By the summer of 1674, Bayly felt the effects on his business from the French trading on the rivers which flowed into the James Bay (Johnson, Charles Bayly 1966). Bayly sent des Groseilliers and others inland up the Moose River where they made a successful trade of two hundred and fifty skins (Radisson 1885, 19) by lowering the rigid prices of the Company (Johnson, Charles Bayly 1966).

---

63 Thomas Moore was hired by the Hudson's Bay Company from 1671 to 1678 (Thorman, Thomas Moore 1969, revised 1982).

64 Sir John Kirke was one of the London investors in the Hudson's Bay Company.

On 16 July 1674, Thomas Moore accompanied Charles Bayly, sailing most likely in the sloop *Employ*, *"to discover Shechittawam* [Albany] *River"* where *"no Englishman had been before."* There, Bayly entered into a treaty with the Indians and established Albany as a place of trade for HBC. They continued on 21 July sailing northwards towards Cape Henrietta Maria. They saw many signs of starvation among the Indians at Ekwan River and at New Severn. Hearing that there was no beaver and that the sea beyond the Cape was full of ice, they decided to return, arriving back at Rupert River's Charles Fort on 30 August (Johnson, Charles Bayly 1966).

Thomas Moore plausibly prepared a rough draft of the west coast of James Bay while on his voyage with Bayly (Thorman, Thomas Moore 1969, revised 1982). After that exploratory trip, Moore stayed for some time on the Albany River as evidenced by the extensive details in his 1678 map [fig. 38].

Radisson and des Groseilliers were at James Bay with the same group for several years. These men knew the country in the region of Lakes Superior and Nipigon, as well as the west shore of James Bay and the Albany route would have been familiar to them (Ruggles 1991, 276). Moore gathered extensive details from Radisson and des Groseilliers with whom he worked. He obtained further information of the river network from the Indians. Initially hired as a sailor, he was later promoted to a trader which would indicate he had gained a knowledge of the Cree language to some degree (Ruggles 1991, 26). Moore would have presumably also learned French while working with the French-Canadian adventures. Further detailed information about Thomas Moore's employment with the HBC are lost, unfortunately, as the minute book recording events from 1674 to 1679 is missing (Simmons 2007, 29). However, much can be garnered from the details of those surrounding him.

Meanwhile, Father Albanel was sent by Quebec's Governor Frontenac on a second overland trip bearing a letter for Governor Bayly dated 8 October 1673. Due to circumstances, Albanel did not arrive at Charles Fort until August of 1674 and Bayly did not receive the letter until after his return to Charles Fort on 30 August of that year. Bayly's letter was a request that he, as the HBC governor, would treat the Jesuit priest well and would let him winter with the English. A second letter, one for des Groseilliers, revealed the real reason for Albanel's journey; the French wanted Radisson and des Groseilliers back (Giguere 1966, revised 2014).

Two ships from England, the *Prince Rupert* and the *Shaftsbury,* arrived 17 September 1674 bringing a new Governor, William Lyddal, and provisions along with new crew. Captain Zachariah Gillam and Governor Bayly were supposed to return to England with the *Prince Rupert* in 1674, but the weather forced Gillam and his crew to winter in the Bay. The provisions being used up for so many additional men wintering in the difficult conditions of 1674/75 at Fort Charles forced the English to leave all but four men to guard the property and to hold the possession for England (Nute 2004 reprint of 1978 edition, 152). Lydall, *"disgruntled and disgusted,"* returned to England in 1675 and Bayly was left to resume the command which he held until his second recall in 1679 (Johnson, Charles Bayly 1966).

One can only assume that Thomas Moore was among the four men who stayed in the Bay along with Bayly, his direct boss. In fact, it appears that Moore stayed on in Hudson Bay until his return to London in 1678.

Father Albanel was ultimately arrested and forced to go to England, along with des Groseilliers aboard (Giguere 1966, revised 2014). Both ships arrived at Deal the 24th and the 25th of September, 1675 (Nute 2004 reprint of 1978 edition, 152).

While Albanel was being held in England, he was successful in seducing Radisson and des Groseilliers back into a French alliance (Nute, Medard Chouart Des Groseilliers 1966, revised 2016). Radisson said the cause for leaving was *"the bad intention of the Hudson's Bay Company to satisfy us"* (Radisson 1885, 21). The two Frenchmen spent the rest of 1675 in France and by 1676, des Groseilliers was back in Canada while Radisson stayed in France. It would not be until 1682 that the two adventurers would make it back to the Hudson Bay region.

1678 Map by Thomas Moore

The earliest map held by the Hudson's Bay Company Archives in Winnipeg is a map by Samuel Thornton and is dated 1709 (Ruggles 1991, 193). Thomas Moore's *1678 Map of the Western Shore of James Bay* predates Thornton's map by thirty-one years! Moore's map is held by the National British Library in London within their Maps and Manuscripts department. It is the oldest map held outside of the HBC Archives (Ruggles 1991, 237). There is only one other map which is older named *Map of Hudson's Bay according to Capt. James's Description* from a cartographer named Norwood dating to 1669. It is referred to in the '*HBC journals, letters or other documents*' but it is "*not located*" (Ruggles 1991, 241).

There is archival evidence that at least sixteen maps and charts were drafted for the company during the first fifty years of trading activity. Only three of these maps are found in the HBC Archives today; two others are in the National British Library's manuscripts department, one being that of Thomas Moore's [fig. 38]. The company ordered fourteen of these sixteen maps from leading chart makers in London. Only two were made by company servants; James Knight (1719) and Thomas Moore (1678). According to author Richard Ruggles in *A Country so Interesting:*

> *. . . Thomas Moore, a company seaman and trader,* [made] *the earliest map attributable to a company servant and the earliest detailed chart of the west coast of James Bay. It is also the first English map to conjecture the course of any of the great bay rivers, in this instance, the Albany, and its presumed connection through a large, island-strewn lake, probably Lake Nipigon, to Lake Superior. Moore's map includes inland elements such as river and lakes, although, not unexpectedly, the style is typical of sea charts at that time.* (Ruggles 1991, 25)

Figure 38. 1678 Map of the Western Shore of James Bay by Thomas Moore

Source: Map with permission c. The British Library Board, National British Library, Add Ms 5027A fol. 64
Original map dimensions: 18 x 13.5 inches, on paper.

Notice that Cape Henrietta Maria is on the bottom of the map at Latitude 55. The entrance into Lake Superior is depicted on the right-hand side of the map.

Private Trading

Although no official HBC records exist between the years of 1674 to 1679, it is known that Thomas Moore was in employment with the company until 1678 and that he completed his map while back in London that year (Thorman 1969, revised 1982), perhaps in an attempt to be rehired.

Initially, the company seems to have allowed some private trade by ship's captains and the first governor on the Bay, Charles Bayly. But, by 1673 the London based HBC committee was authorizing searches of the ships to look for smuggled furs (Mancke 1988, 25).

At the end of 1673, Radisson had informed the Company that some of its servants were engaged in private trading (Nute 2004 reprint of 1978 edition, 144). This was more strongly censured at the HBC's 8 May 1674 meeting which resolved that no private trade in furs would be permitted under any circumstances and that all private trade in other commodities was to:

> *bee by publicke License & brought into the Companyes warehouse to the ende that they may have cognizance thereof.*

At the same time, commanders of Company ships were strictly enjoined to suppress all manner of

> *privacy that may bee in the sayd shippes for Stoueing private trade, in order to prevente the same.* (MacKay 1936, 44–5)

Private trade undermined the Hudson's Bay Company's business and it constantly tried to curtail it (Bown 2020, 112–13).

Governor Charles Bayly was recalled back to London in December of 1679 to face charges made by John Abraham of mismanagement of company property due to lack of attention to detail and to slipshod, but not dishonest, methods. There is no doubt there were also accusations of the forbidden practice of private trade. These charges were being prepared when Bayly died one month later on 6 January 1680 (Johnson 1966) (Nute 2004 reprint of 1978 edition, 133).

There is good reason to believe that Thomas Moore's recall in 1678[65] and subsequent denial of further employment in 1680 (Thorman 1969, revised 1982) had much to do with the practice of private trading so prevalent at the time, especially since the lenient Charles Bayly was his direct boss.

---

65 It wasn't until 1680 that the iconic Hudson Bay point blanket began to be a staple of trade for HBC so Thomas Moore may or may not have owned one as a matter of principle.

Landwaiter at the London Port

It appears that Thomas Moore may have taken a Port of London Customs Landwaiter position in 1679. As stated in the Calendar of Treasury Books for 9 July 1679:

> *July 9 1679. Treasury reference to the Customs Commissioners of the petition of Thomas Moore for a landwaiter's place, London Port.* (British History Online 1913)

The Customs Commission was established in 1670. The Custom House was situated in the middle of the 600-yard Legal Quay that ran from London Bridge to the Tower of London on the north bank of the Thames. A Landwaiter was a clerical officer who worked on the Legal Quays at the Port of London as outdoors staff; they did not perform manual duties like weighing or portering. Landwaiters worked in pairs waterside and were part of an intricate operation of officers who monitored landed goods for taxation purposes. They were in daily contact with merchants as a result of their role in detailing all landed goods both imports and exports (Sweeting 2014, 22, 123–25).

Landwaiters usually had not attended University nor were they referred to as "gentleman" or "esquire." Most officers usually entered the Customs in their late twenties or thirties by which time they would have had jobs and acquired contacts elsewhere. An officer who had been a merchant and had attended his business at the waterside—being qualified by the Land Surveyor—was admitted without the usual instruction. The Custom Commissioners put a premium on expertise (Sweeting 2014, 140).

Thomas Moore was twenty-five in 1679. He had experience with fur imports and exports of trading-goods working with the Hudson's Bay Company for seven years. In addition, he would have had contacts at the docks, having feasibly lived and worked around the docks as a young boy. After trying to seek employment with the Hudson's Bay Company in 1680 and not being reinstated (Thorman, Thomas Moore 1969, revised 1982), Thomas Moore continued in the landwaiter's position at the port of London. With the large fur trade emerging on the London scene, Moore was a prized asset and would have surely been retained. ⚜

"There is not much difference
between correlation and coincidence
with historical events."

—GRACE LEE NUTE
Historian and Author

16

Compagnie du Nord vs. Hudson's Bay Company

RADISSON AND DES GROSEILLIERS had been living in France since late 1675 having been lured by Jesuit Father Albanel to abandon the Hudson's Bay Company and returned to the service of France. By 6 April 1676, they received a grant of a fishing license off the coast of Anticosti and from Anticosti to Montreal for twenty years from the King of France (Nute 2004 reprint of 1978 edition, 156).

While in still Paris in the year 1681, Pierre-Esprit Radisson was approached by the wealthy Canadian merchant Charles Aubert de La Chesnaye who was interested in establishing a Canadian fur-trading company to compete against the English Hudson's Bay Company. The following year in 1682, La Chesnaye was granted a secret charter by Jean-Baptiste Colbert, the French Finance Minister for Louis XIV, under the name of La Compagnie de la Baie d'Hudson or the Compagnie du Nord[66] (Nute 1969, revised 1982). The two Frenchmen were to use their fishing permit as their justification for exploration into Hudson's Bay.

1682/1683

Radisson, interested in the proposal, set sail from La Rochelle, France, and arrived in Quebec on 25 September 1682. He met directly with Monsieur La Chesnaye in Quebec City. They worked out the details of their new expedition and went over all things that were to be settled relative to each of their concerns and interests. Des Groseilliers made a contract with La Chesnaye for the same voyage almost on the same terms as Radisson (Radisson 1885, 231–32).

The ultimate objective was to establish a French colony for fur trade at the mouth of the Nelson and Hayes Rivers. Unfortunately for the Canadians, both the Hudson's Bay Company and a New England interloper out of Boston, Benjamin Gillam, had the same intent that summer (Nute 1966, revised 2016).

---

[66] The Compagnie du Nord was granted an official Royal Charter on 20 May 1685.

New England: The New England ship *Bachelor's Delight* with a crew of fourteen, captained by Benjamin Gillam[67] with John Outlaw as mate, arrived on 18 August 1682[68] (Moriarty 1966, revised 1979). They founded "Bachelor's Fort", a post twenty-six miles up the Nelson River (Thorman 1966, revised 1979) (E. H. Borins 1968, 60).

HBC: Sailing for the HBC was Zachariah Gillam[69] commanding the frigate *Prince Rupert* with John Bridgar, the new governor of Port Nelson, aboard. They arrived at the mouth of the Nelson River on 7 September 1682 (Moriarty 1966, revised 1979).

Compagnie du Nord: Radisson and des Groseilliers departed Quebec 11 July 1682 with a crew of thirty on board two poorly equipped vessels named the *Sainte-Anne* and the *Sainte-Pierre* (E. H. Borins 1968, 60). Radisson arrived before des Groseilliers on the west coast of Hudson Bay on 26 August and met up with des Groseilliers on 2 September at the entrance of the river called Kakivvakiona (Hayes River) (Radisson 1885, 234). One of the pilots for the Canadians was nineteen-year-old Pierre Allemand (Grenier 1966, revised 2014).

Therefore, in September 1682, three separate groups descended on the west coast of Hudson Bay albeit in different locations. Neither English expedition knew that each other were there, however, the Canadians were aware of both of them and of their locations.[70]

Radisson used his formidable knowledge of the area, his close relationships with the local Indians and deception to help him get the upper hand. Radisson captured the two rival posts in 1683 (Thorman 1966, revised 1979) along with a substantial quantity of furs each had accumulated (Nute 1969, revised 1982). Radisson, in preparation for returning to Quebec, left his nephew Jean-Baptiste Chouart des Groseilliers[71] instructions to carry on the trade in his absence until his return. The young des Groseilliers was left at the French fort with seven men and *"the absolute comand & disposall of all things"* (Radisson 1885, 276).

John Outlaw from the New England ship, along with some of the English prisoners, was made to captain the provisioned Canadian's unseaworthy ship, the *Sainte-Anne,* back into James Bay where he later returned to England on the HBC ship *Diligence* (Thorman 1966, revised 1979). Radisson sailed to Quebec on the captured New England ship, *Bachelor's Delight,* along with the rest of the English prisoners, including John Bridgar and Benjamin Gillam, and arrived 20 October 1683. In Quebec, Bridgar and Gillam were released by Governor Le Febvre de La Barre and given back their ship to return home to New England (Wilson 1966, revised 1979).

---

[67] Benjamin Gillam was the son of Zachariah Gillam.

[68] By the French calendar, that would have been 28 August. (Nute 2004 reprint of 1978 edition, 189)

[69] The same Zachariah Gillam who had captained the *Nonsuch* with des Groseilliers on board in 1668–69.

[70] Henceforth, the territory of Hudson Bay would be constantly contested by both England and France.

[71] Medard Chouart des Groseilliers' son.

Meanwhile, John Abraham had been promoted captain of the HBC *George* in 1683 and upon arrival at Port Nelson, finding that the post was abandoned and Bridgar was taken prisoner, he assumed command. The winter of 1683/84 was spent harassing and competing with Jean-Baptiste Chouart for the bulk of the fur trade (Johnson, John Abraham 1966, revised 1979).

Unfortunately, the 2000 furs Radisson and des Groseilliers had brought back with them were involved in a dispute over the "droit du quart" tax which the rival "Company of the Farm" felt was due them. The Company of the Farm held a right to impose a tax on all beaver pelts moved through the colonies. In opposition, the Compagnie du Nord's view was that Hudson Bay was not under the jurisdiction of the Company of the Farm tax (E. H. Borins 1968, 64–73). At the same time, the court in Paris was desirous for an account of what had happened in New France with the Compagnie du Nord's venture. As stated in Radisson's papers:

> *[Monsr. Cobert] desired that those which parted last yeare to make discoverys in the Northern parts of America being either returned or would soon return, hee desired one of them to give the court an account of what they had don, & of what setlements might bee made in those parts; & the Governour* [La Barre] *told me that I must forthwith prepare myself to goe satisfy Monsr. Colbert in the business. I willingly accepted the motion, & left my business in the hands of Monsr. De La Che[s]nay, although I had not any very good opinion of him, having dealt very ill by me: but thinking I could not bee a looser by satisfying the Prime Minister of State, although I neglected my owne privat affaires, I took leave of Monsr. La Barre, & imbark'd for France with my Brother-in-law, the 11 9ber[72], 1683, . . . and arrived at Rochell the 18 of Xber[73] . . .* (Radisson 1885, 280)

For these two reasons, Radisson and des Groseilliers arrived in Paris by 15 January 1684. By 10 April 1684, Louis XIV ruled that the 2000 furs imported through Quebec by the Compagnie du Nord were lawfully to be taxed by the Company of the Farm. It was after the "droit du quart" tax ruling that Radisson became disillusioned with serving the French and made his initial plans to return to the Hudson's Bay Company operations (E. H. Borins 1968).

Lord Viscount Preston, British minister to the Court of France, protested vehemently Radisson's recent actions against the English Hudson's Bay Company for which Radisson had to answer. Preston had an audience with Louis XIV himself. On 30 April, it was the King's decision *"that the French should restore the possession of Port Nelson, and of all which they had violently taken, to the English"* (Nute 2004 reprint of 1978 edition, 211).

---

[72] November

[73] December

At the same time, Radisson received letters from Monsr. Young, one of those interested in the Hudson's Bay Company, soliciting him in the name of the Company to return into England.

> *These letters, joined to those in which my Lord Preston continued his urgencies against me . . . decided me to determine, by the counsel of one of my friends, to yield myself at last to all their solicitations of passing over to England for good, & of engaging myself so strongly to the service of His Majesty, & to the interests of the Nation, that any other consideration was never able to detach me from it.* (Radisson 1885, 284)

Only some of Lord Preston's household and the friend who had counselled him, Gedeon Godet, knew of his plan to rejoin the HBC. It was not Preston, but Godet who succeeded in seducing Radisson back to the English interests. Godet was bribed by the HBC's Committee with the promise that his daughter, Margaret Charlotte Godet, should marry Radisson, which ultimately happened in 1685 (Nute 2004 reprint of 1978 edition, 207–8).

1684/1685

The ship for Radisson's second voyage with the Compagnie du Nord continued to be provisioned at Brest in France. He continued in conferences with the ministers of the Court of France discussing details of his obligations even up to the evening before his departure (Nute 2004 reprint of 1978 edition, 215). The ministers of France never doubted in the least his firm engagement with them. Radisson told the ministers that he needed to make a *"little journey"* to London for some family business first. He secretly left Paris on 24 April 1684. (Radisson 1885, 284). He travelled with Gedeon Godet on Godet's passport and, after ten days at Dieppe, they arrived in London on the 10th of May. Godet took Radisson to HBC and then to King Charles II who took Radisson to serve HBC *"as he desired"* (Nute 2004 reprint of 1978 edition, 216–17, 219).

HBC: Radisson knew he had to get back to his nephew, Chouart des Groseilliers, and the Port Nelson fort before the Compagnie du Nord's ships did. There were only a few days between Radisson's arrival in England and his departure to Hudson Bay. He left London from Gravesend pier[74] just seven days later on 17 May 1684 and sailed directly to Hudson Bay on the frigate *Happy Return*. His ship was accompanied by two other ships (Radisson 1885, 287); one being the *Lucy*, captained by John Outlaw, who had been the New England interloper just the year before (Thorman 1966, revised 1979). Radisson was successful in turning his nephew to the service of the HBC and getting the Indians to believe that he had made peace with the English *"for the love of them"* (Radisson 1885, 291–93). He loaded the HBC ships with a great cargo of around twenty

[74] 1.5 miles down the river from the Port of London.

thousand furs gathered that winter (Radisson 1885, 299, 311) and headed back to London 4 September 1684, arriving 23 October "*at the Downs*" (Radisson 1885, 321). Radisson's nephew, Jean-Baptiste Chouart des Groseilliers, had also been onboard and the two wintered in London well subsidized by the corporation (Nute 2004 reprint of 1978 edition, 228).

Meanwhile, Radisson's brother-in-law, Medard Chouart des Groseilliers, whom Radisson had left in Paris (Nute 2004 reprint of 1978 edition, 220), had no intention of going back into the service of the English. He rejected an HBC offer to re-enter its service, and it is surmised that sometime between April and November 1684, he returned to New France (Nute 1966, revised 2016).

Compagnie du Nord: In the meantime, back in Quebec, the Compagnie du Nord knew they needed to supply and relieve Jean-Baptiste Chouart des Groseilliers and the other Frenchmen who had been left by Radisson at Fort Nelson (Fort Bourbon) the year before. Due to "*Iroquois menacing*", the Canadian merchants sent word to France requesting another ship to help convoy the relief needed. The expedition, which departed Quebec on 19 June, was commanded by Claude de Bermen de La Martiniere (E. H. Borins 1969, revised 1982). Pierre Allemand was pilot along with Jesuit Father Antoine Silvy who kept a log of the expedition. (Grenier 1966, revised 2014).

Martiniere was forced to wait in the Bay St. Paul, fifteen leagues from Quebec, for the French aide ship *St. Antoine* to rendezvous, finally setting sail for Hudson Bay on 12 July 1684 (E. H. Borins 1968, 81–3, f. 5). It is not known if the already provisioned French supply ship at Brest in May of 1684, in which Radisson was supposed to have sailed, was the same ship that was sent to join Martiniere's convoy or not, but it would make sense if it were.

As a government official in New France, Martinierre was a legal councilor in the Conseil Souverain (E. H. Borins 1969, revised 1982) and knew nothing of the sea. It is possible that des Groseilliers, still in France, may have sailed on the *St. Antoine* to meet Martinierre's ship and that his ability as a guide and knowledge of the region were utilized by the Compagnie to help Martiniere with the convoy in this 50-man expedition. Radisson, reporting in the 1690's, stated that des Groseilliers was to have died[75] in the Bay about this time (Nute 2004 reprint of 1978 edition, 225).

Radisson avoided detection of Martiniere's coming into the Bay as he left. Upon arrival in September at Fort Bourbon (Port Nelson) where the Compagnie du Nord had established their post in 1682, Martiniere discovered that Radisson had already been there, had reverted his nephew back into the service of England and had destroyed Fort Nelson. He was forced to retreat into the Hayes River for the winter (E. H. Borins 1969, revised 1982) (Nute 2004 reprint of 1978 edition, 225). Pilot Pierre Allemand busied himself fur trading and was also sent as an envoy to

[75] It is not known exactly for sure when or where des Groseilliers actually died.

treat with the English commander, John Bridgar, who was at the mouth of the Hayes River at that time (Grenier 1966, revised 2014).

It was during Martiniere's 1684/85 expedition that the Compagnie du Nord's Committee realized they needed the financial backing of the crown of France, similar to that of the HBC 's reliance on the crown of England. This led to the official Royal Charter of the Compagnie du Nord in May of 1685 (E. H. Borins 1968, 87–9).

1685/1686

Compagnie du Nord: On the way back to Canada in July of 1685, Martinierre's expedition captured the English HBC vessel *Perpetuana Merchant,* commanded by Captain Edward Hume, who was just coming into the Hudson Straits (Nute 2004 reprint of 1978 edition, 235). That had been the Compagnie's only achievement for the whole season (E. H. Borins 1969, revised 1982).

HBC: A second HBC ship, the *Success* captained by John Outlaw and taking John Bridgar to his new post as governor of *"the Bottome of the Bay"* (Wilson 1966, revised 1979), saw Martinierre returning from Port Nelson with its English prize. Radisson's ship, the *Happy Return,* had already passed unnoticed by the returning French (Nute 2004 reprint of 1978 edition, 235–36). Radisson had been successful in establishing York Factory on the Nelson River replacing Fort Nelson which had been destroyed by the French in 1684.

Unfortunately, homeward bound in 1686, the *Success* became wrecked by ice and John Outlaw and his crew had to winter at Moose Fort with Governor John Bridgar (Thorman 1966, revised 1979).

DISCUSSION

It has been stated by authors NV. D. de Levis in *Bulletin des Recherches Historiques*[76] and Pierre-Georges Roy in *Les Petites Choses de Notre Histoire*[77] that Thomas Moore was "*most likely hired in France*" for work with La Compagnie du Nord in 1686. The big question is how would this have come about?

As it is in today's world, in the 17th century one used their connections to their advantage when trying to procure a position of employment. Moore's familiar connection and background with des Groseilliers could not fail to prompt Moore to contact him regarding opportunities which might be available with the French Compagnie du Nord in which des Groseilliers had been involved.

One reasonable way Moore's thinking could have developed would have been that, while working at the Port of London, Thomas Moore would have heard all the port gossip and of

---

[76] Vol., XXX, de Levis, Dec 1924, No: 12, p. 385–6

[77] Second series, Levis, Quebec, 1919, p. 116–119

particular interest for him would have been information regarding his old fur-trading friends; Radisson and des Groseilliers. He had worked closely with des Groseilliers from 1671 to early 1675 in the service of the HBC. In 1682/83, he would have heard about the two Frenchmen back fur trading in the Hudson Bay except now in the service of the French. That Thomas Moore had reapplied to the Hudson's Bay Company in 1680 is proof that he still had aspirations of being part of the fur trading scene in the Bay. Moore may have been aware that the two Frenchmen had returned to Paris in late 1683 and even that English forts had been seized by the French. It is quite possible that this is when Thomas Moore decided to travel to Paris in order to find des Groseilliers and persuaded des Groseilliers to help him get back into the realm of adventure of the Hudson Bay fur trade.

From des Groseilliers' point of view, he did know Thomas Moore pretty well from his HBC days. He could understand Thomas' circumstance in not getting rehired due to private trading as he had done some himself during those early years with HBC. He knew of the English company's tightening of rules and strict oversight in recent years. Des Groseilliers knew Thomas Moore's abilities and knew that Moore could help the Campagnie du Nord with fur trading and navigation around the Bay. Moore's knowledge of the Cree language was also a benefit. He had the wherewithal to help Moore return to what he knew and loved best and he was pleased to make it happen.

Moore may then have traveled with des Groseilliers on the *St. Antoine*, the same ship from France which rendezvoused with Martinierre's 1684/85 expedition.[78] Pierre Allemand and Father Antoine Silvy were also part of this trip. At that point, the French would have known Radisson had gone over to the side of the English and HBC, but not necessarily that he had already been to the Bay and turned his nephew against the French. Martinierre left the bay in June 1684 and returned to Quebec in the fall of 1685. Thomas Moore was officially hired by the Compagnie du Nord in 1686 (Thorman, Thomas Moore 1969, revised 1982).

1686/1687

Thomas Moore was doubtlessly hired out of Quebec as part of the Compagnie du Nord's 1686 overland trip from Montreal (Ville-Marie) to James Bay. Among those who were also part of this new expedition to Hudson's Bay were Pierre Allemand and Father Antoine Silvy, both from Martinierre's 1684/85 expedition. They could have recommended Moore to the Compagnie du Nord given all the experience he had proven on their recent trip together.

The Compagnie du Nord's 1686 expedition to Hudson Bay was led by Pierre Chevalier de Troyes who had been in Quebec as early as August 1685 (Bown 2020, 71). There is further

---

[78] Crew were hired under the captain's name, not by the sailor's name (E. H. Borins 1968, 36).

evidence that the French from Canada planned to oust the English from Hudson Bay as early as June 1685 from a letter written by Zacharie Jolliet from his post "Nemisko," about halfway to the Bay, to his English friend, Hugh Verner:

> *I am here to execute the orders of Monsieur le general [De la Barre] requiring the English to leave the Bay . . . For a letter has just come saying the General is sending men by land to seize you. So, having had the honor to see Mr. Bayly, to drink and eat and be lodged two or three nights with him in your fort, and having lived so long a neighbor with you, now to be forced to fight to obtain that place, would be my extreme grief."* H.B.Co. Archives, A/6/I, f. 122. (Nute 2004 reprint of 1978 edition, 241, f. 2)

De Troyes put together thirty professional French soldiers along with seventy explorers from Canada (Bown 2020, 71). It makes more sense that Thomas Moore was hired in 1686 out of Quebec by the Compagnie du Nord as a valuable explorer to the Hudson Bay region rather than having been hired out of France as a soldier.

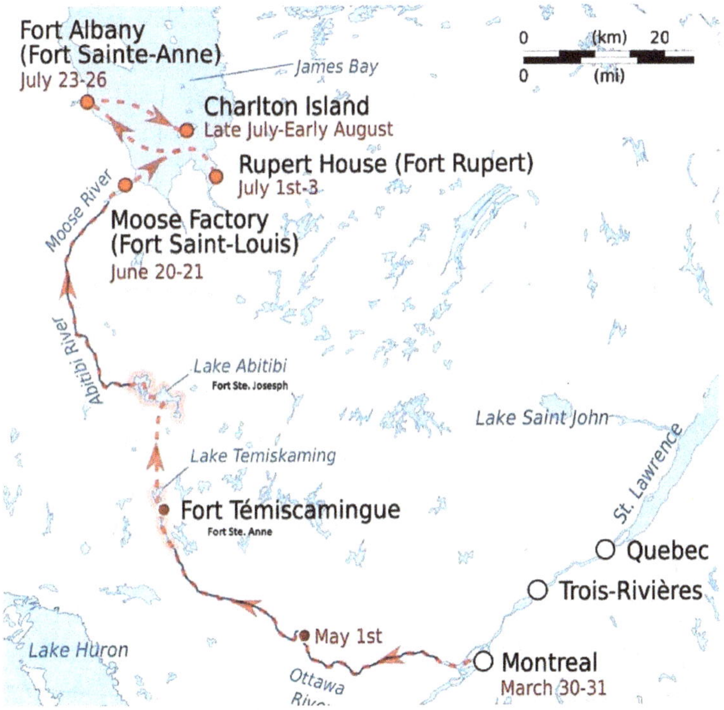

Figure 39. Troyes' 1686 Hudson Bay overland expedition[79]

Source: Map adapted from: Hudson Bay Expedition (1686) https://en.wikipedia.org/w/index.php?title=Hudson_Bay_expedition_(1686)&oldid=1038693492

79 Forts Ste. Anne and Ste. Joseph were set up prior to 1685 in order to support Troyes' expedition and his military force. The two forts were forced abandoned by the end of 1689 (E. H. Borins 1968, 99, 117).

Pierre Chevalier de Troyes' overland expedition of 1686

Compagnie du Nord: In 1685, news reached New France that the English were in possession of the forts at the Bottom of the Bay and had carried off a large shipment of beaver pelts intended for Quebec City. In response, around June of 1685, the French began planning an expedition to disrupt the English trading in Hudson Bay. Pierre de Troyes, Marine Captain in the Piedmont regiment, and his company of around 350 soldier reinforcements sailed up the St. Lawrence and arrived at Quebec on 1 August 1685. He brought the new governor of Quebec, Jacques-Rene de Brisay, Marquis de Denonville with him from France. La Chesnaye and the Compagnie du Nord soon persuaded the new governor to launch a military expedition overland north to capture English outposts at the Bottom of the Bay (Bown 2020, 71–2).

In February 1686, de Troyes was ordered by Denonville to put together a troop of thirty professional French soldiers and seventy young French Canadians who were accustomed to overland travel. The mission was to be financed principally by the Compaigne du Nord. Among them were Pierre Le Moyne, Sieur d'Iberville[80], as 2nd lieutenant, along with his two brothers Jacques, Sieur de Sainte-Helene, as 1st lieutenant and Paul, Sieur de Maricourt, as administrative assistant. They were joined by Jesuit Father Antoine Silvy as chaplain, experienced pilot Pierre Allemand as quartermaster, several skilled tradesmen such as blacksmiths and carpenters and a handful of Cree interpreters and guides (Lamontagne 1966, revised 1979, 1) (Bown 2020, 72). Thomas Moore was among them. (Thorman, Thomas Moore 1969, revised 1982).

The expedition left Montreal 20 March 1686 when ice was still on the Ottawa (Outaouais) River. They dragged their supplies and weapons on sleds through the snow along with thirty-five large canoes for use in the summer (Bown 2020, 72). They reached the junction at Mattawa on 10 May and continued north up the Ottawa and portaged into Lake Temiskaming. The company followed the portage route into the Abitibi River and reached James Bay on 20 June, three months after their departure date [fig. 39].

They captured three British forts without great difficulty—Monsipi (Moose Factory or Saint-Louis), Fort Rupert (Charles Fort), and Fort Quichicouanne (Fort Albany), as well as the British warehouse on Charlton Island, all without losing any of their men (Ottawa River Heritage Designation Committee 2005, 65).[81] After easily capturing Moose Factory, which was only guarded by sixteen men, de Troyes left forty men behind to guard the prisoners. The rest of the troops traveled 120 kilometers to the northeast along the coast of James Bay to take Fort Rupert

---

80 D'Iberville had begun his seafaring days at the age of twelve as a cabin boy on his uncle's ship trading from Montreal to Port Royal, Acadia.

81 The references for their paper were taken from the publication: *Ottawa Waterway, Gateway to the Continent* by Robert F. Legget, 1975: p.40.

which they again attacked at night. On 3 July, while de Troyes, Sainte-Helene and the bulk of the men were attacking Rupert House, d'Iberville and thirteen men canoed out to the HBC's supply ship *Craven* and captured it with a surprise attack. De Troyes burnt the fort and the captured men were taken aboard the *Craven* as prisoners back to Moose Factory. The *Craven* was fitted with cannons and Fort Albany was taken without the thirty men in residence even firing a shot on 25 July. Most of those prisoners were then taken to the outpost on Charleton Island. Leaving d'Iberville, who was made governor of the three posts with forty men total, de Troyes left for home in August 1686 and retraced his route overland back to Montreal arriving in October 1686 (Bown 2020, 73–5) (Pothier 1969, revised 1982). Pierre Allemand must have returned with de Troyes because he was back at Montreal at the end of October as well (Grenier 1966, revised 2014).

The previous English forts were renamed Saint-Louis (Moose), Saint-Jacques (Rupert) and Sainte-Anne (Albany). D'Iberville wintered at Saint-Louis fort during the winter of 1686/87. When no supplies had arrived by the late summer of 1687, d'Iberville returned south, first to Quebec, then to France, leaving his brother Maricourt in command with a dozen men at James Bay (Pothier 1969, revised 1982). He arrived in Quebec by sea aboard the *Craven* loaded with furs and English goods at the end of October 1687 (MacKay 1936, 51) before going to France for the winter of 1687/88 (Lionel Jean, reviewer updated 2019, 8.2). It is quite possible that Thomas Moore was aboard the *Craven* at that time, returning to Quebec. He would have been unaware that his father, Edward Moore, had passed away in September of 1686 while he was in Hudson Bay.

HBC: The day before the French attack at Moose Fort, Governor John Bridgar had left Moose in the *Craven*, piloted by John Outlaw, for Rupert House. Moose Fort was easily taken from the sixteen leaderless crew. Outlaw and Bridgar were at Fort Rupert when de Troyes next attacked that fort at night. When d'Iberville captured the *Craven*, John Outlaw was made to pilot the prisoners back to Moose Fort.

Outlaw and many of the English prisoners were picked up from the outpost on Charleton Island, where they had been prisoners for several months, by the HBC supply ship *Colleton* to winter at York Factory and Severn, now the only forts held by the English, subsequently returning to England in 1687. It was at that time that John Bridgar left the service of HBC. Outlaw and his crew were refused their wages for their loss of the ship *Success* in 1686 (Thorman 1966, revised 1979) (Bown 2020, 73–4).

1687/1688

Compagnie du Nord: While Pierre Le Moyne d'Iberville was in France for the winter, he succeeded in convincing King Louis XIV of the advantages of the sea approach to the fur trade of Hudson Bay. He also received support La Compagnie de la Baie d'Hudson needed in the form of a shipment of trade goods in order to consolidate the French positions in the Bay. The king supplied d'Iberville with a fast modern frigate as an escort vessel named *Le Soleil d'Afrique*. With the mandatory stop in Quebec first (Pothier 1969, revised 1982, 3), d'Iberville contracted with Thomas Moore in the spring of 1688 to be either master of a ship or his pilot (Thorman 1969, revised 1982).

At Fort Sainte-Anne (Fort Albany) in September 1688, while loading his ship with the previous year's fur stockpile, he noticed two large HBC ships—the eighteen-gun *Churchill* and the frigate *Yonge* crewed by eighty-five men—sailing up the river. D'Iberville had cunningly removed the channel markers that guided ships safely from the bay upriver to the fort and one of the ships ran aground. He had only sixteen men with him and one small ship; the larger *Soleil d'Afrique* being at Charleton Island (Bown 2020, 73–4). The onset of winter froze all three vessels in the river prolonging their confrontation with each other until the following summer (Pothier 1969, revised 1982, 3).

HBC: Company ships enjoyed peaceful trading the summer of 1688 with *John & Thomas* and *Dering* getting in and out of the Bay successfully (MacKay 1936, 51). The disgruntled John Outlaw joined John Abraham in an interloping expedition on the *Mary* but she was wrecked by ice in the Hudson Strait. They and their crew were happily rescued by the HBC ship *Churchill* with William Bond as captain, which, with the *Yonge*, was taking the new overseas governor, John Marsh, and men to Albany to establish a post near the former English fort captured by the French in 1686. The new English post was established but with difficulty from the French (Thorman 1966, revised 1979).

From 1685–1687, Pierre-Esprit Radisson was resident in Hudson Bay at Port Nelson (York Factory). He was given considerable authority in all trading matters by the company yet, before his return in 1687, many disputes had arisen between him and the other officials of the HBC (Nute 1969, revised 1982). On 24 October 1687, the Company entry states, *"Mr. Radisson now appeared and was welcomed home. . ."* That was his last trip to Canada (Nute 2004 reprint of 1978 edition, 251, 258).

1688/1689

Compagnie du Nord: The winter of 1688–89 was characterized by treachery and bad faith on both sides. In d'Iberville's favor, sickness raged on the *Churchill* and the *Yonge* and morale was poor. D'Iberville refused the English permission to hunt for fresh game, thus encouraging the spread of scurvy among them (Pothier 1969, revised 1982). In December 1688, when captain of the *Churchill,* William Bond, and his men were allowed to hunt for partridges, they themselves were *"caught like woodcocks"* and taken as prisoners (Johnson 1966, revised 1979).

With the lack of leadership in the English, d'Iberville moved cannons into place and began lobbing cannonballs into the camp until they surrendered (Bown 2020, 76). The French gained complete victory in the Albany River. After capturing another English vessel, the *Huband* (Thorman 1969, revised 1982), the previous July, d'Iberville and crew, including Thomas Moore, left James Bay in September arriving in Quebec on 28 October 1689. They brought with them English prisoners, considerable booty and prized furs (Pothier 1969, revised 1982).

HBC: The English were under the impression that they were at peace with the French per a December 1686 Peace Treaty of neutrality by both the English and French kings and were told not to fight unless provoked. Instead, they were defeated in their mission to re-establish a post on the Albany River and were made prisoners. Now, the only fort they still held for the English was York Factory and a recently established outpost at the Severn River (Bown 2020, 75).

Among the prisoners taken back to Quebec was John Outlaw who, having been taken prisoner by the French for the third time, deserted to the French either then or shortly afterwards. In 1690, the HBC warned its servants that Outlaw was a potential interloper (Thorman 1966, revised 1979). John Abraham, who was also taken prisoner to Quebec, changed his allegiance as well and apparently spent the rest of his life preying on English shipping among the St. Lawrence River islands (Johnson, John Abraham 1966, revised 1979). ⚜

17

Thomas Moore | 1689/1690

THOMAS MOORE RETURNED 28 OCTOBER 1689 TO QUEBEC from the 1688/89 Compagnie du Nord's Hudson's Bay expedition. About two months after his return, on 7 January 1690, a marriage contract between Thomas Moore and Jeanne Lemelin, daughter of Jean Lemelin dit Tourangeau and Marguerite Brassard, took place [fig. 40].

The event attendees gathered in the afternoon at the Quebec home of Charles d'Albert d'Ailly, 3rd Duke de Chaulne[82]. His first cousin's wife was the daughter of the French Finance Minister under Louis XIV, Jean-Baptiste Colbert. Colbert had sent Radisson and des Groseilliers from France to meet with Charles d'Aubert de la Chesnaye in Quebec. This meeting led to the latter three eventually starting the Compagnie du Nord (Nute, Pierre-Esprit Radisson 1969, revised 1982).

The de Chaulne family were close friends of de la Chesnayes. There were many connections between the two families. The 3rd Duke de Chaulne's father had been the Military Governor of Picardy stationed in the capital city of Amiens (Wikipedia contributers 2021). Charles Aubert de la Chesnaye's father became the Intendant of the fortifications of the town and citadel of Amiens. Charles Aubert's godfather was Charles Parmentier, the 1st Duc de Chaulne's "*maitre d'hotel.*" His sister Anne's godparents were "*a son and daughter of the 1st Duc de Chaulnes*" (Zoltvany 1969, revised 1982); most likely the oldest son, Henri-Louis. Being only seven years in age apart and both living at the citadel of Amiens, Charles d'Albert d'Ailly and Charles Aubert must have known each other since childhood.

---

[82] Per the Moore/Lemelin marriage contract

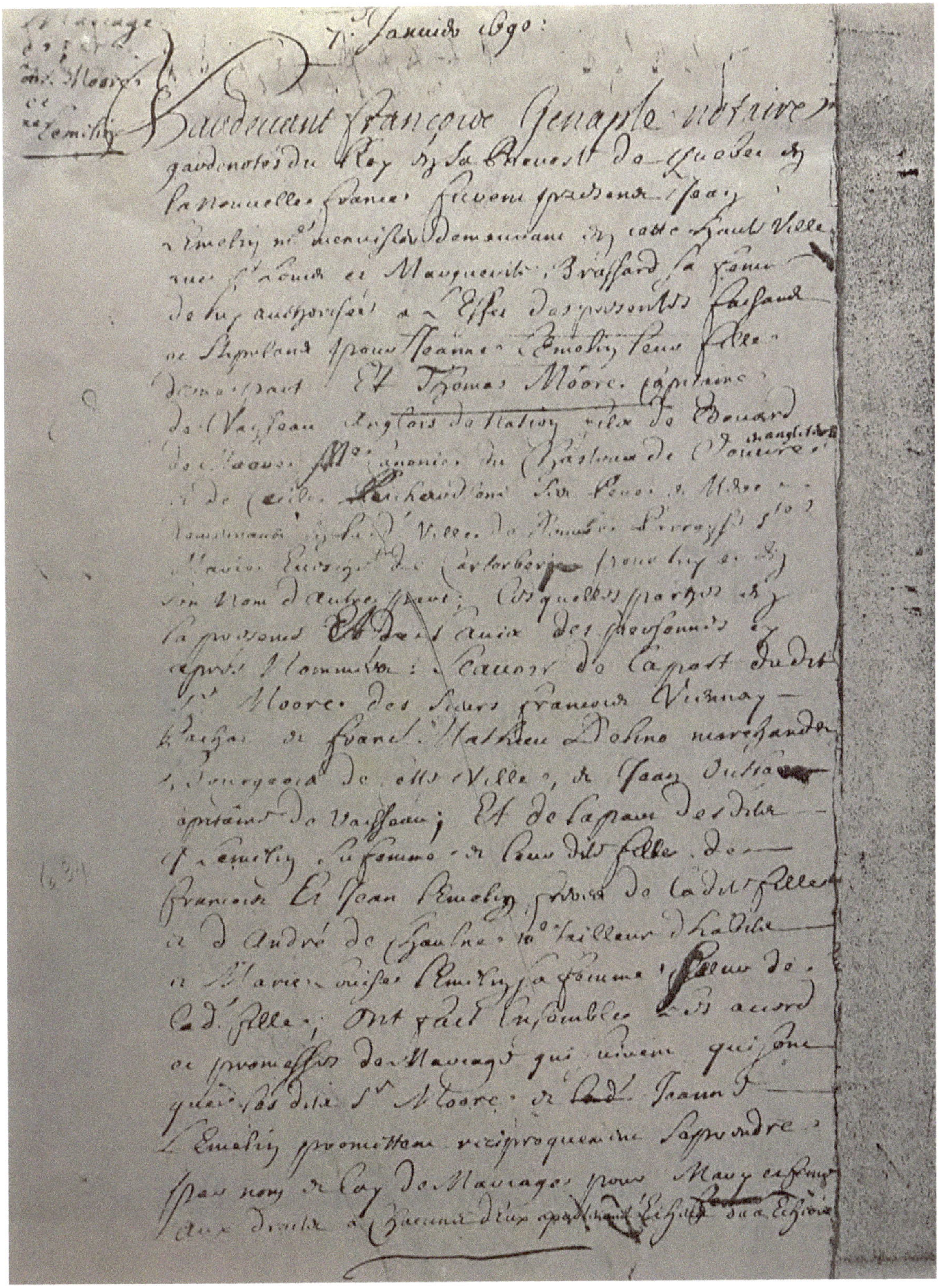
17 Janvier 1690:

Pardevant François Genaple notaire garde notes du Roy en la Prevosté de Quebec en la Nouvelle France furent presens Jean Emelin m[aîtr]e menuisier demeurant en cette haute ville rue St Louis et Marguerite Brassard sa femme de luy authorisée a l'effet des presentes faisant et stipulant pour Jeanne Emelin leur fille demeurant Et Thomas Moore capitaine de vaisseau anglois de nation fils de Edouard de Moore m[aîtr]e canonnier du chasteau de Douvres en angleterre et de [illegible] Richardson ses pere et mere [illegible]

Figure 40. Thomas Moore's marriage contract

Source: National Archives of Quebec.

Et led. Mariage sera celebré en face de
Notre Sainte Eglise Catholique apostolique et
Romaine, pour du Jour d'iceluy estre Uns
et Communs, suivant la Coutume de Paris, en tous
biens meubles et Conquests Immeubles; sans
estre neantmoins tenus des dettes l'un de l'autre
faites auparavant et quelles si aucunes y a, seront payées et acquittées
par le Sur d'iceluy dont elles procederont. Et a
led. futur Epoux Doué lad. future Epouse de la
somme de Cinq Cents livres de Douaire prefix, pour
une fois payer, a prendre quand Douaire aura
lieu sur les biens d'iceluy; Et pour l'amour et
affection qu'ils se portent Ils se font donation
mutuelle et reciproque de tous les biens meubles
acquests et Conquests Immeubles qui se trouveront
leur appartenir au Jour du decez du premier mourant
d'eux deux: pour en Jouir en pleine propriete a
toujours par le survivant, ses hoirs ou ayans
Cause; au cas qu'il n'y ait lors aucuns Enfans
vivants de ce Mariage: et au cas de predecez
par led. futur Epoux, sera libre a lad. future Epouse
de renoncer a lad. Communauté, et ce faisant
remporter tout ce qui paroistra luy estre echeu
pendant led. Mariage par succession ou autrement
avec ses d. douaire, hardes et habits a son usage
et linge; le tout sans estre tenue des dettes d'icelle
Communauté encor qu'elle y fut obligée ou
condamnée. Car ainsy a esté Convenu et accordé.
Et pour l'insinuation des presentes les parties
ont esleu leur procureur le porteur d'icelles
auquel elles donnent pouvoir de ce faire

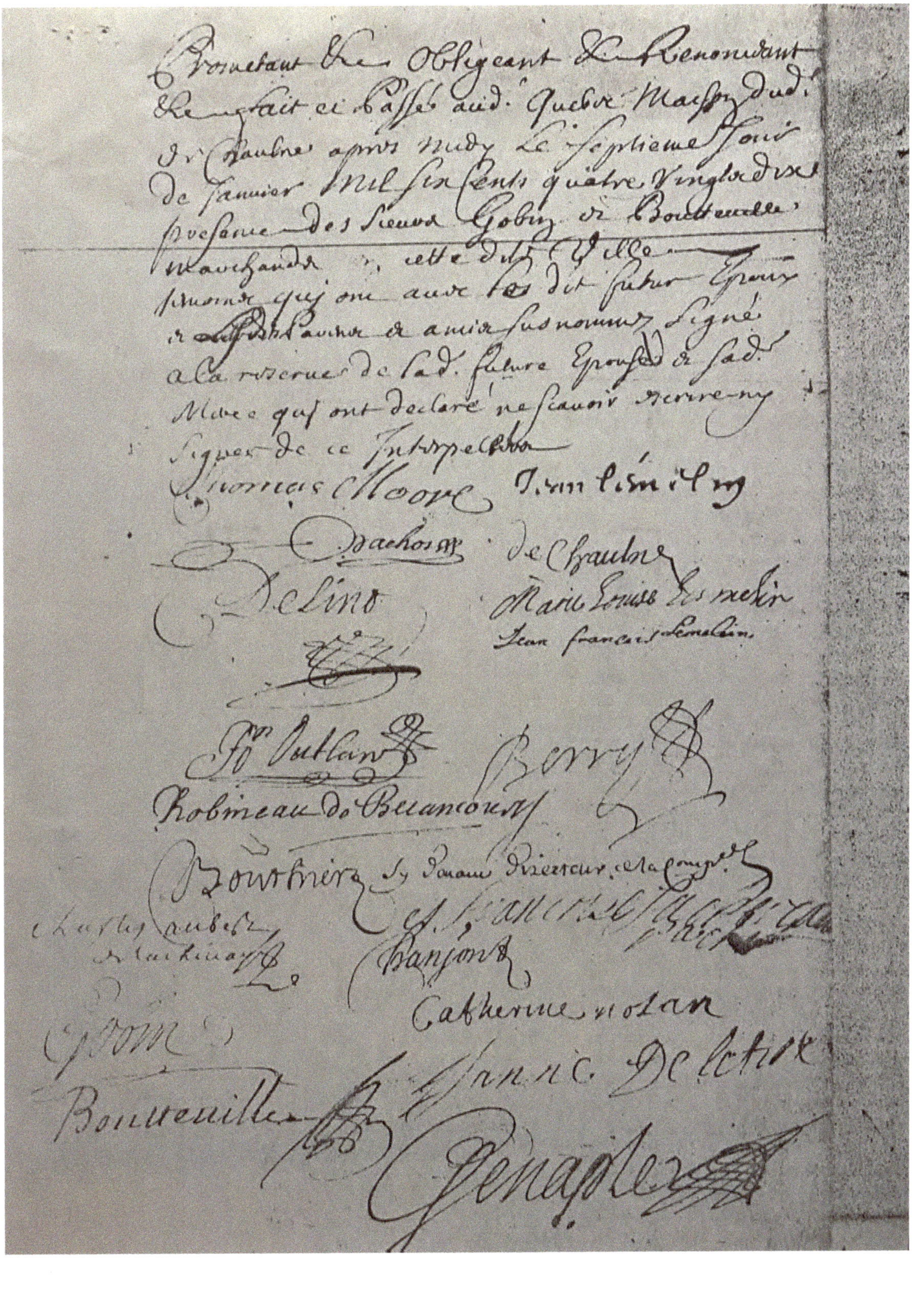
Promettant &c. Obligeant &c. Renonçant &c. fait et passé aud. Quebec Maison dud. sr Chaulne apres midy le septieme jour de janvier mil six cents quatre vingt dix presence des sieurs Gobin et Boutteville marchands en cette dite Ville temoins qui ont avec les dits futurs Epoux et susd. parens et amis sus nommez signé a la reserve de lad. future Epouse et sad. Mere qui ont declaré ne scavoir escrire ny signer de ce interpellées

Thomas Moore
Jean Lemelin
Bachoist
de Chaulne
Delino
Marie Louise Desmelin
Jean francois Lemelin
Fr. Outlaw
Berry
Robineau de Becancour
Bourbriere
Catherine Nolan
Gobin
Anne Deletre
Boutteville
Genaple

The marriage contract [fig. 40] between Thomas Moore and Jeanne Lemelin was witnessed by several Directors of the Compagnie du Nord and Quebec City merchants. Even the Englishman John Outlaw, a ship captain and three-time prisoner of the French, was in attendance.

Neither Jeanne nor her mother, Marguerite, knew how to *"write or sign"* the contract so the merchants Gobin and Boutteville represented them. The signatory's names and their descriptions (E. H. Borins 1968, table 2, 194–8) are as follows [fig. 40]:

Thomas Moore | Groom

Jean Lemelin | Father of the Bride

Charles d'Albert d'Ailly, 3rd Duke de Chaulne | French General and Diplomat

Jean Francois Lemelin | an older brother of the bride

Marie Louise Lemelin | oldest sister of the bride

Francois Viennay-Pachot | Quebec merchant and a director in the Compagnie du Nord (CdN)

Mathurin-Francois Martin de Lino | Quebec merchant and a director in the CdN

John Outlaw | ship captain, previous English prisoner and now part of the French adventurers

Monsieur Berry

Rene Robineau de Becancour | fur trader and chief road officer of New France

Guillaume Bouthier *"in front of the receiver of the company"* | a director in the CdN

Charles Auber de la Chesnaye | wealthy Quebec merchant, director and founder of the CdN

Francoise Juchereau | the wife of Pachot

Guillaume Chanjon | a militia captain and a director in the CdN out of France

Jean Gobin | Quebec merchant and a director in the CdN

Catherine Nolan | wife of De Lino

Jeanne Delettre (aka. Delestre) | wife of Charles Catignan, a director in the Compagnie du Nord

Boutteville | Quebec merchant

Francois Genaple | Royal Notary and clerk of the chief road officer of New France

A little more than a month later, Thomas Moore was hospitalized in l'Hotel-Dieu de Quebec on 12 February 1690 for seventeen days and re-admitted one day after his release on 1 March for twenty more days (Langlois 1998, H 452). Thomas Moore became a Roman Catholic one day before his release from L'Hotel-Dieu in order to marry Jeanne Lemelin, according to the Catholic religion.

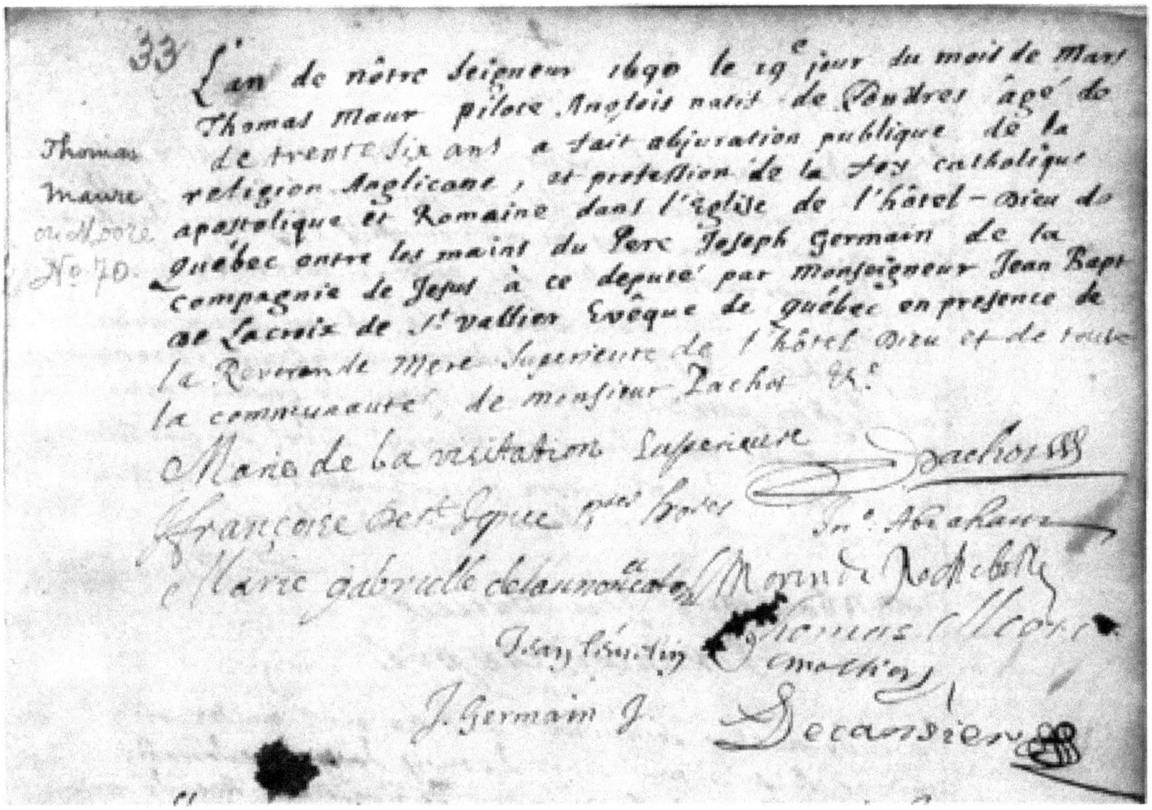
33 L'an de nôtre seigneur 1690 le 19e jour du mois de Mars
Thomas Maur pilote Anglois natif de Londres agé de
de trente six ans a fait abjuration publique de la
religion Anglicane, et profession de la foy catholique
apostolique et Romaine dans l'eglise de l'hôtel-Dieu de
quebec entre les mains du Pere Joseph Germain de la
compagnie de Jesus à ce deputé par Monseigneur Jean Bapt
de Lacroix de St Vallier Evêque de quebec en presence de
la Reverende Mere Superieure de l'hôtel Dieu et de toute
la communauté, de monsieur Zachar...

Thomas Maure
No 70.

Figure 41. Thomas Moore changes religions

Source: Archdiocese of Quebec Archives, Register of Abjurations 1662–1757: Abjuration of Thomas Moore, Hotel-Dieu de Quebec, 19 March 1690, p. 245. Reference: AAQ 66 CD, Abjurations, vol. A: 33. (#70).

Thomas Moore abjured his Anglican faith and became Catholic on 19 March 1690 while in Hospital at the L'Hotel Dieu in Quebec City.

TRANSLATION:

In the year of our Lord 1690 the 19th day of the month of March, Thomas Moore, pilot, English native of London, age 36 years, made a public abjuration of the Anglican religion and professed the Roman Catholic Apostolic faith in the Church of the Hotel-Dieu of Quebec before the hands of Father Joseph Germain of the Company of Jesus to this deputy by

Monseigneur Jean Baptiste Lacroix of St. Vallier, bishop of Quebec in the presence of the Reverend Mother Superior of the Hotel-Dieu and of all the community. . . [the undersigned —including Thomas Moore].

The actual Register Entry reads:

Moore, *Thomas*, pilote anglaise natif of Londres, 36 ans, abj RA [religion anglicane] Eglise Hotel-Dieu de Quebec 19 mars 1690 [ABJ. A–33 (N 70)].

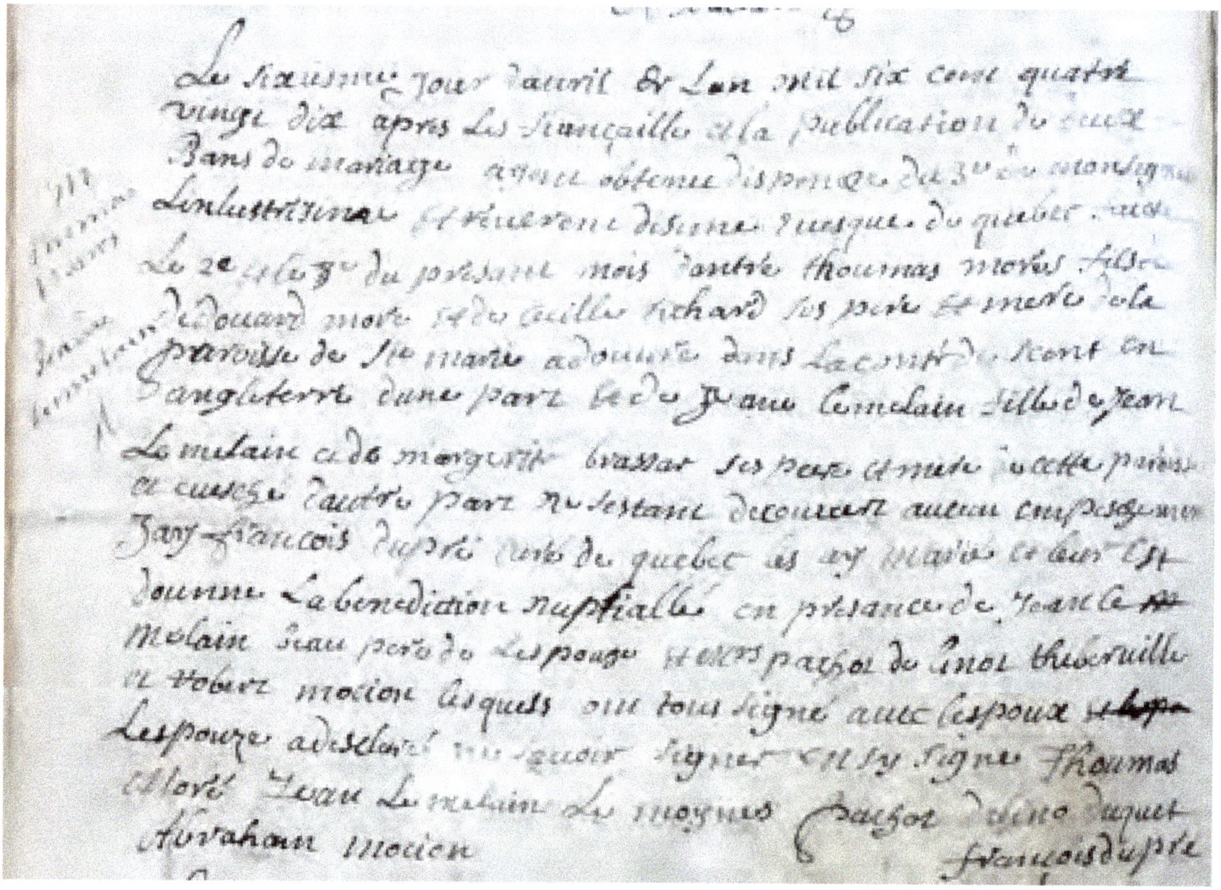

Le sixiesme jour d'avril de l'an mil six cent quatre vingt dix apres les fiançailles et la publication de deux bans de mariage [illegible] Lillustrissime et reverend evesque de quebec [illegible] le 2e [illegible] du present mois entre thoumas more fils d'edouard more [illegible] richard ses pere et mere de la paroisse de Ste marie [illegible] dans la comté de kent en angleterre d'une part et de Jeanne Lemelain fille de Jean Lemelain et de marguerite brassar ses pere et mere de cette paroisse [illegible] d'autre part ne s'estant decouvert aucun empeschement [illegible] Jean-françois dupré curé de quebec [illegible] leur a donné la benediction nuptialle en presence de Jean Lemelain [illegible] pere de l'espouse [illegible] pachot [illegible] thiberville et robert mouton lesquels ont tous signé avec l'espoux [illegible] l'espouse a declaré ne sçavoir signer [illegible] Thoumas More Jean Lemelain [illegible] Pachot [illegible] Abraham mouton françois dupré

Figure 42. The marriage entry for Thomas Moore and Jeanne Lemelin

Source: Registre Des Baptemes, Mariages, & Sepulcres from the E.N.D. de Quebec, 1687–1692 in the National Archives of Quebec.

Thomas Moore (36) and Jeanne Lemelin[83] (17) were married 6 April 1690 at Quebec, Notre-Dame Cathedral. Among the signatures on the marriage certificate as witnesses were:

---

83 Jeanne Lemelin had been married before to Pierre Brunet on 16 April 1689 but it had been annulled. One possible reason for the annulment in those times was for being married too young.

Thomas Moore

Jean Lemelin | Father-in-law

Pierre Le Moyne d'Iberville | Soldier, ship's captain, explorer, colonizer, adventurer, privateer and trader

Francois Viennay-Pachot | Quebec merchant and a director in the Compagnie du Nord (CdN)

Guillaume Chanjon | a militia captain and a director in the CdN out of France

Mathurin-Francois Martin de Lino | Quebec merchant and a director in the CdN

John Outlaw | Englishman and pilot who changed allegiance to France

John Abraham | Englishman and pilot who changed allegiance to France

Robert Mossion | a Quebec tailor

Francois Dupre | Notre Dame parish priest

The marriage for Jeanne and Thomas in Quebec's Notre Dame Church was special to Jeanne in particular as her father, Jean Lemelin dit Tourangeau, had constructed the left side altar which was dedicated to Saint-Anne. He had presented *"the best composition"* to the Brotherhood of Sainte-Anne.

DIMENSIONS | *19 feet high; width proportional.*
DECORATIONS | *two columns adorned and enriched with their complete decorations and two frames, one of which will be for the placement of the painting of Sainte-Anne.*

Jean Lemelin dit Tourangeau, Master Cabinet Maker, designed and created a frame within a frame for the painting of Saint-Anne as well as the two columns on each side of the altar which adorns the left side chapel in the church of Notre Dame, Quebec City [fig. 43]. He was paid 400 livres and the work was completed for Pentecost 1661 (Laforest 1999, vol. 28). The present frame and columns are replicas of the originals due to a fire of the church in 1922 caused by the KKK of Canada.

The Church's formal name is the Cathedral-Basilica of Notre-Dame de Quebec. It was founded in 1647 and was originally named Notre-Dame de la Paix.

Figure 43. The Chapel of Saint-Anne in the Notre Dame of Quebec Basilica

Source: Photo taken by the author.

Nine days after his marriage, Thomas Moore was again readmitted to l'Hotel-Dieu on 15 April 1690 for six more days. However, only two months later, Thomas Moore was ready to return to Hudson Bay.

Figure 44. D'Iberville contracts pilot Thomas Moore, 1690

Source: Bibliotheque et Archives Nationales du Quebec (BAnQ)

This historic piece of paper was discovered by Maurice Moore from the Bibliotheque et Archives Nationales du Quebec (BAnQ) which obtained them from the family of an ancestor of J.-Camille Pouliot, Judge of the Superior Court. It is a contract for Thomas Moore to be a pilot for Pierre Le Moyne d'Iberville for an expedition to the Hudson Bay in 1690. It is signed by Pachot for the Compagnie du Nord. This piece of paper is now lost. (M. Moore 2016, 333)

D'Iberville left Quebec for Hudson Bay in July 1690 but with and inadequate complement of three small vessels carrying only thirty guns and eighty men. Thomas Moore was one of the ship's pilots. Arriving before York Fort in late August, they found the English on the alert, and were forced to flee from an enemy ship of thirty-six guns. They escaped and decided to attack New Severn instead, an outpost of York Fort some 250 miles southeast. This station was so weak that its commander, Thomas Walsh, blew up the buildings and fled without resisting. D'Iberville, Moore and the rest of the crew likely wintered in James Bay before returning to Quebec in October 1691 and from there, d'Iberville went on to France (Pothier 1969, revised 1982).

Found in the files of the Pouliot family were two additional pieces of paper[84] regarding Thomas Moore's pay for the 1690 expedition: one an account by Thomas Moore and the other a receipt from the Compagnie du Nord.[85]

NOTE: *[page torn]*
. . . years currency of the country, starting from the first of April from this present year to continue three years. And for all the services he rendered to the Company until the first of April, he will be paid the sum of two hundred pounds, Canadian currency. And for all advances, he will be paid in the month of May and June before his departure.

Quebec, 13 April, 1690
So signed, Thomas Moore

The above two hundred pounds are paid to said Moore and [he] received in addition the sum of three hundred and thirty-three pounds fourteen sois and three deniers [as] witnessed with the entry in the Compagnie's journal, folio II to this day of June 27, 1690.
So signed, Pachot for the Compagnie du Nord.

[84] Information from *Thomas Moore: Collection of Family Archives* by Maurice Moore p.329

[85] Both accounts are translated by the author.

18
Settling on the Isle d'Orleans

ON 7 FEBRUARY 1693, Thomas Moore, ship pilot, bought from Jean Lestourneau (Letourneau) three acres of frontage along the St. Laurence River in St-Paul[86], with house, barn and stable, for 1,050 pounds; between Anthoine Gaudeboust (Godbout) and Joseph Regnard (Renaud). Letourneau had originally received the three acres of land as a concession from Charles Auber de la Chesnaye on 13 March 1664 (L. Roy 1978, 296–7).

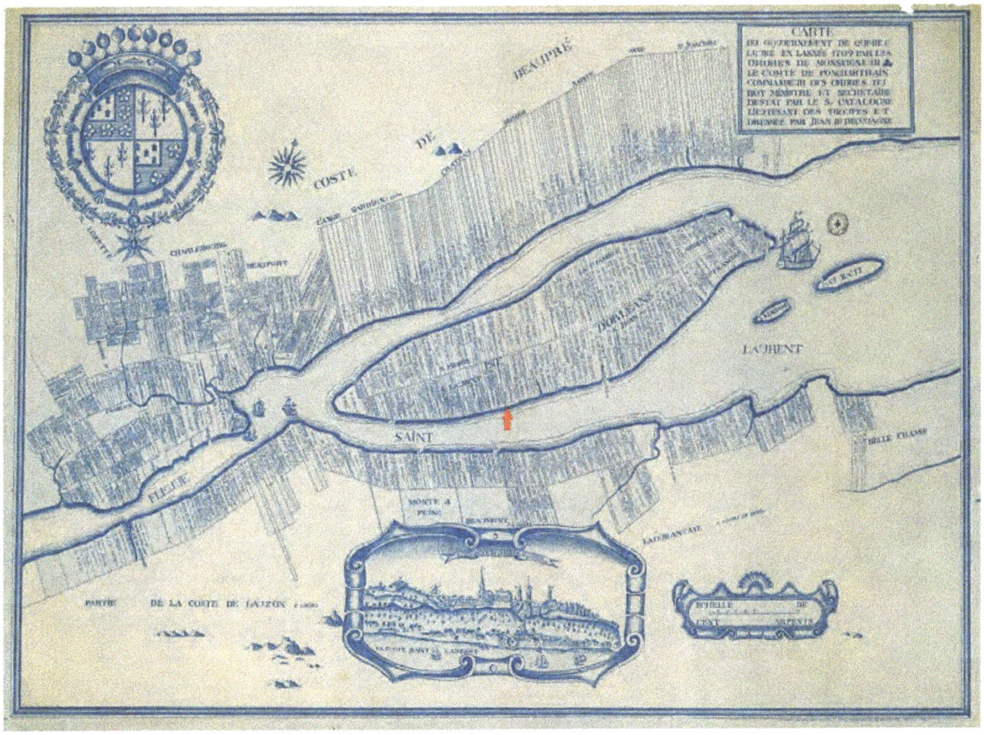

Figure 45. 1709 map of Isle d'Orleans and the Surrounding Area by Gedeon

Source: https://commons.wikimedia.org/wiki/File:Cadastral_map_of_Quebec_city_region,_1709.jpg

Thomas Moore's land was on the left bank of the River Maheu in St. Laurent, Ile d'Orleans.

[86] St-Paul was established in 1678, the town name then changed to St-Laurent in 1698.

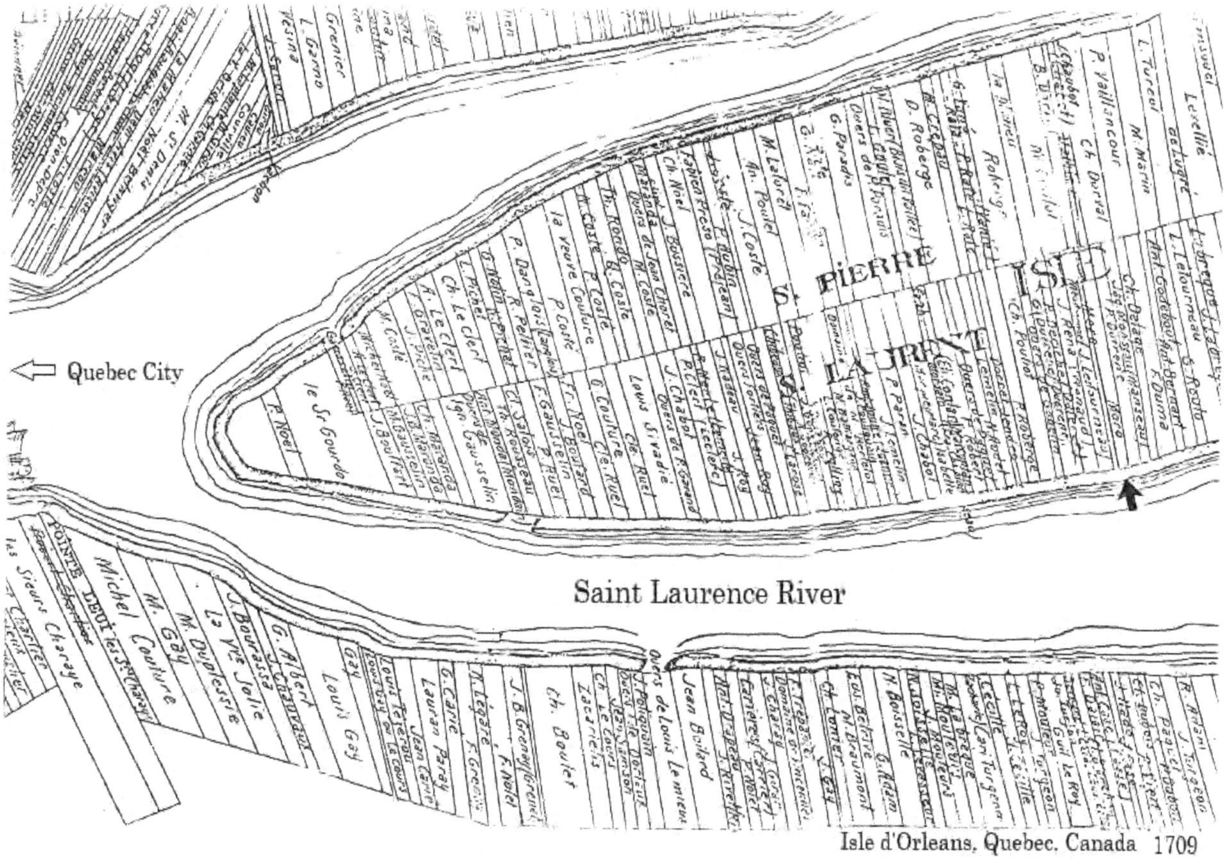

Figure 46. A closer look of Figure 45

On Gedeon's map from 1709, Moore's neighbors are shown as Joseph Renaud and Letourneau on the one side and P. Dufrene and Jaques Manseau on the other. The address which corresponds to Moore's land today is 730 Chemin Royal, Saint Laurent, lots 42–3. An old house dating from 1789 still stands on the property and its back yard is the old golf course. The land can be immediately identified as being above the present-day restaurant of *Le Moulin de Saint-Laurent* which is adjacent to the Maheu River.

At the western extremity of the village of St-Laurent, the Maheu River offered a natural inlet which was used by the first sailors (Helene Bourque 1999, 33). This area of the St. Laurence River was deep and a ship could get very close to shore. In the fall and when the tides went out and the river was frozen over, the ship was aground and could receive well needed repairs during the winter months so as to be prepared for the following spring (Pouliot 1927, 200).

On the 17th day of November in 1692, Thomas and Jeanne's first son, Antoine, was born in St-Pierre, I.O., presumably where they were living at the time. He was named after Jeanne's grandfather, Antoine Brassard. After the purchase of their St-Laurent land in 1693, Moore began to farm on his property while still continuing his work as a navigator, as he was always denoted as *"ship-master and pilot."* The couple had three more sons and, by 1706, three of the four born had died; only Pierre was living. Louis was born while Thomas was at sea in June 1706, however, he also died one year later.

> *Antoine Moore | b. 17 Nov 1692, St. Pierre, I.O.; d. 22 Apr 1705, St. Laurent*
> *Louis-Augustin Moore | b.7 Feb 1694, St. Laurent; d. 24 Mar 1703, St. Laurent*
> *Thomas Moore | b. 30 Jan 1697, St. Laurent; d. young*
> *Pierre Moore | b. 10 Sep 1704, St. Laurent; d. 22 Nov 1759, St. Laurent*
> *Louis Moore | b. 10 Jun 1706, St. Laurent; d. 10 Jun 1707, St. Laurent*

In 1706, Moore was in command of the vessel *La Marie.* On 2 June 1706, Governor Philippe de Rigaud de Vaudreuil wrote to Mr. Joseph Dudley, Governor of New England, regarding an exchange of prisoners:

> *Referring to what you have done with regard to sending 57 prisoners to Port Royal, and as you are my only informant on this subject, since there has been no agreement of exchange signed on either side, I am sending in the ship "la Marie", commanded by Thomas Moure* [Moore], *43 of your prisoners to Port Royal, the list of whom I am conveying to Monsieur Brouillan with instructions to forward them on to you at Boston.*
>
> *As "la Marie", which I am ordering off, will return direct here from Boston, I beg of you to send back to me the Canadian prisoners that you detain and who are from this part of the country, to wit: Monsieur Gourdeau and his family, the persons named Dion and Pierottiere and le Fenoc and his children.*
>
> *I beg you to treat the captain of this ship and the crew with the courtesy and humanity common to all nations towards vessels bearing the flag of truce . . .*[87] (P. G. Roy 1928, 345–6)

About one year later, in an act signed on 6 May 1707 before the notary Chambalon, Guillaume Gaillard went into partnership with Alexandre Leneuf de Beaubassin, a lieutenant in the colonial regular troops, and Joseph Riverin, another merchant, with the intention of fitting out the ship *Nostre-Dame de Victoire "to go privateering . . . on and in the neighborhood of Cape Breton, the island of Newfoundland, the Grand Banks, and surrounding areas."* Beaubassin provided

---

87 According to *Collections de Manuscrits,* Vol. II, p. 452.

the ship, of eighty to ninety tons draught, which was under construction at Quebec, and which would be armed with six iron cannon and manned by 100 officers and men. Gaillard was to obtain the provisions and *"all utensils that will be required both for the service of the cabin and for the crew."* Riverin was to rig out the vessel with sails, grappling-irons, and so on. The profits were to be divided between the three partners and the crew. Thomas Moore was taken on as ship's master and pilot (Biron 1969, revised 1982). Thomas was to have *"the chest, clothing, navigation instruments and personal belongings of the master pilot of each ship that was captured."*

Unfortunately, they had arrived too late for sailing that far north and they returned in the autumn having captured nothing. A letter from Raudot, dispatched in November of 1707 proves that nothing was accomplished (P. G. Roy 1928, 346). Coincidently, according to the book titled *The Hudson's Bay Company* written by George Woodcock, *"no ships went out from England in 1707 or 1709"* due in part *"from the risk of losing its ships to French men-of-war or privateers"* (Woodcock 1970, 59).

Thomas Moore appears to have stayed home a while after this venture as he and his wife, Jeanne, had two more children. Out of their seven children in total, only two lived to become adults and have children of their own; Pierre and Marie-Louise.

Marie-Louise Moore, b. 19 Nov 1708, St. Laurent; d. 2 Jul 1736, Lower town of Quebec[88]
Francois Moore, b. 31 Dec 1709, St. Laurent; d. 31 Mar 1710, St. Laurent

On 6 November 1713, Charles Couillard, Sieur de Beaumont, contracted with Thomas Moore for a voyage to Labrador. Moore was to be his ship's master and pilot from 15 April 1714 until his return from the country of Labrador at the rate of seventy pounds per month plus food. Moore promised to follow his orders and serve him loyally and honestly. He was required to stay in Labrador for as long as Couillard required him to and then to return back to Quebec. This contract was witnessed by two Quebec merchants; David Pauperet and Etienne Regnault. It was signed by Couillard and Thomas Moore and notarized by Louis Chambalon[89]. It is unknown for what reason Moore was to go to Labrador for Couillard, but it could have had something to do

[88] On 2 July 1736, Louis Mallet and his wife, Marie-Louise [Moore] were convicted and hanged in the public square of the lower town of Quebec the very same day for a crime of "lese-mafeste" against the king of France which was counterfeiting money. They had imitated monetary tokens from the Intendancy which were legal tender at the time known as "Card Money." Their child was eventually sent back to France.

[89] Information from BAnQ #4 M00 2107 Engagement of Thomas Moore a Charles Couillard, Sieur de Beaumont. (M. Moore 2016, 388–90)

with the Treaty of Utrecht of 1713 in regards to French property or French fishing rights in the Labrador/Newfoundland area.

Thomas Moore must have returned within the year due to the fact that by 8 May 1715 Charles Couillard died from an epidemic during the winter of 1714–15 that had wreaked havoc on the Beaumont seigneury (Cournoyer 2021 edition).

Moore would have missed the wedding of young Jeanne Lemelin, a niece[90] of Thomas' wife Jeanne Lemelin, to Charles Jolliet on 7 November 1714 at St. Laurent, I.O. Charles was the son of the famous adventurer Louis Jolliet[91] (1645–1699.) Thomas Moore and he would have known each other. Assumably, Thomas' wife Jeanne would have attended the wedding.

Thomas Moore died sometime before November 1724. The documents from the marriage of his son Pierre and his wife Genevieve-Louise Gendreau (Gendron) on 26 November 1724, declare that Pierre's father, Thomas Moore, is deceased. Many historians believe he may have been lost at sea, however there is no proof of that being the case.

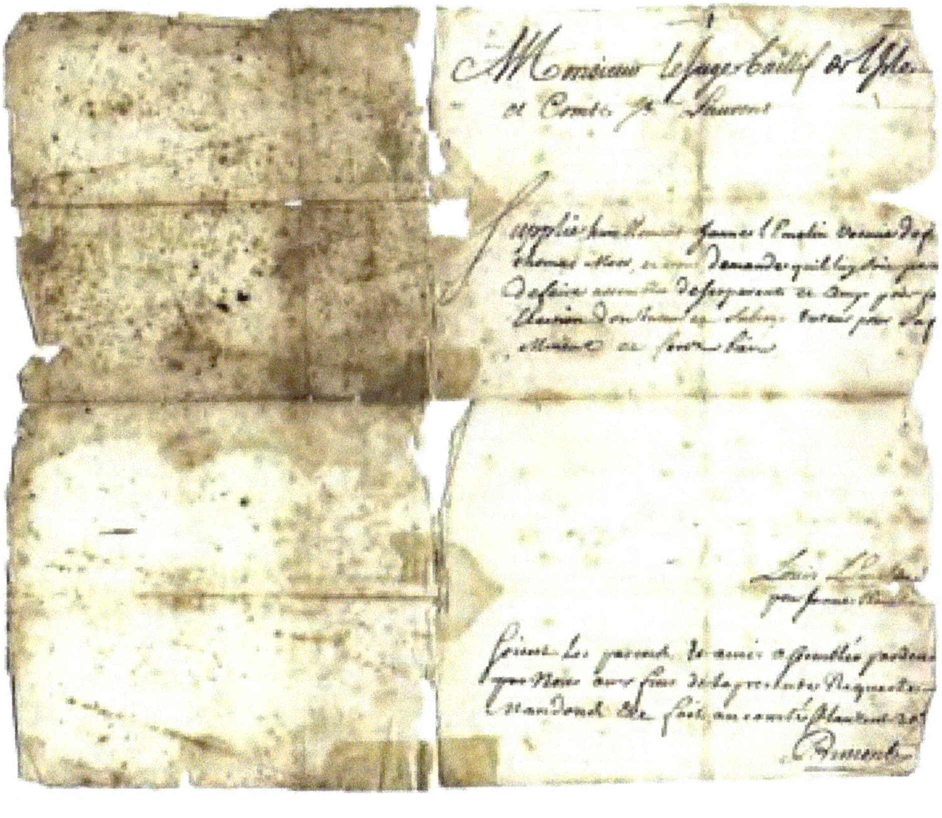

Figure 47. 1725 document from Jeanne Lemelin

Source: BAnQ, Pistard, file #P436, S999, P21 from documents found in the files of the Pouliot family (M. Moore 2016, 394–6).

[90] Jeanne Lemelin's oldest brother, Louis, named his daughter Jeanne Lemelin.

[91] Louis Jolliet's wife, Claire-Francoise Byssot (b. 1656), was the great granddaughter of Louis Hebert, the 1st citizen of Quebec.

The request of Jeanne Lemelin [fig. 47]:

Monsieur Judge bailiff of the island and county of Saint-Laurent.
Humbly pleads for Jeanne Lemelin, widow of the late Thomas Moore, and asks you that he be allowed to assemble his parents and friends to elect a guardian and substitute tutor for her minor child's [Marie-Louise] *best interest.*

[signed] Louis Lemelin for Jeanne Lemelin

Relatives and friends are assembled in front of us for the purpose of this request.
Writ made in Saint-Laurent County through us by the son of this request.
Writ made in Saint-Laurent County the 20th (not complete)

[signed] Primont

This request for help in raising Marie-Louise by her mother, Jeanne Lemelin, makes one think that Marie-Louise may have had a very troubled childhood. Here, Jeanne's older brother, Louis, tried to help Jeanne in the wake of her missing husband, Thomas Moore.

All those people related to Thomas Moore, the subject of this book, also share the common ancestry with Thomas Moore's only surviving son, Pierre Moore and his wife Genevieve-Louise Gendreau (Gendron). Pierre Moore was born 10 September 1704 in St. Laurent, Ile d'Orleans, Quebec and he died 22 November 1759 in St. Laurent. He married Genevieve-Louise 26 November 1724 in St. Laurent, I.O. She was the daughter of Jacques Gendreau (Gendron) and Marie-Anne Daleret and was born 15 January 1702 in St. Laurent. She died 9 March 1776 in St. Charles, Bellechasse. Genevieve-Louise had lived just down the street from Pierre Moore as a child. In 1741, she and her new husband, Pierre, bought the land from the estate of her father who had died in 1739. Its present-day location is 1032 Chemin Royal, St. Laurent, I.O. Pierre and his wife, Genevieve-Louis, had eight children.

Pierre, age 55, along with his son also named Pierre, age 26, both died in 1759. Their two deaths may have been, in some way, due to the invasion of the English General James Wolfe and his troops on the island in that same year. Being warned of the fleet of approaching troops up the St. Laurence River, preparation had begun as early as 22 May 1759 for all the people living on the island to abandon their homes and go into the woods around Charlesbourg near Quebec City. This escape was directed by Monsieur de Saint-Vincent, an official of the colony.

These orders, so sudden and, no doubt, ill-advised, were clumsily interpreted and badly carried out . . . Blunders and haste did far more harm to thousands of owners of property than the enemy would have done. Numbers of families were ruined by this panic; three-quarters of the animals perished, and for a long time the farmers of . . . the Island of

Orleans, who owned at least 5,000 head of cattle, did not recover from this loss, to say nothing of people, women and children who, unfortunately, perished, too, in the tumult, having been assembled at one extremity of these islands, without boats sufficient for their transport or any provision made for their nourishment. Still less, had there been any thought of putting up shelters to harbour them.

What must have been the grief of the Islanders when they found themselves so suddenly compelled to leave their houses and yield them to the looting of the soldiers! The parishioners bade a weeping farewell to their hearths and withdrew to Charlesbourg under the guidance of their venerable cure. The aged and sick were removed on beds, destined never again to sleep under the paternal roof. Several children were born and baptized in the woods.

It was on 27 June 1759 that the English first disembarked at Saint-Laurent, Isle of Orleans before continuing on to capture Quebec City.

The people of the Island spent three long months in this part of the country, suffering the greatest apprehension and complete privation . . . Ile d'Orleans was devastated [from] one end to the other . . . more than 1,400 houses were reduced to ashes in the campaigns. . . Six company troops circled the island and returned to the camp with a quantity of effects . . . From Ste. Famille to the beginning of St. Pierre, there remained only an old masure [tumbled down cottage]. (Turcotte 1867, 41–3, 45)

After this major event, the family of Pierre Moore (1704–1759), the only child of Thomas Moore and Jeanne Lemelin to live to adulthood, made its way to Saint-Charles, Bellechasse to settle with many other families from the Island.

One of Pierre's sons, Francois Moore (1733–1768), married Marie Louise Desmeules on 26 November 1753 in Saint-Jean, I.O. They had six sons. Other than the oldest son, Pierre, who was born pre-invasion in St. Laurent, I.O., all of their children were born in Saint-Charles, Bellechasse. The 1762 government census for Saint-Charles in the Archives of Quebec shows Francois Mort [Moore] with his wife, four infant males below the age of fifteen years old, on three arpents of land with one horse.

DISCUSSION

As is explained in the Introduction at the beginning of this book, we can follow three of the six sons of Thomas Moore's grandson, Francois Moore (m. 1753) and his wife Marie Louise Desmueules. The descendants of the oldest son, Pierre Moore (1754–1795), along Eric Moore's direct line moved first to Quebec City for a short while then to Sherbrooke, Quebec for three or so generations ending up with Eric now living in Trois-Rivieres, Quebec. Their second son was Francois Moore (1756–1802). His descendants along Maurice Moore's line made its way back to St. Jean, I.O. in the mid 1800's before leaving the Island all together, first settling in the Lauzon and Levis areas and then across the river in Quebec City. The descendants of the fourth son, Laurent (Laurence) Moore (1761–aft. 1818), along Norman Moore, Sr.'s side moved to the Detroit French settlers' region around Mount Clemens, Michigan and eventually became United States citizens when Michigan became a state in 1837. From there, Norman Moore's direct line eventually moved to homestead in Fraser township in 1910 around the Pinconning area. They then spread out into the Linwood and Bay City areas of Michigan.

Six generations later, the descendants of these three sons of Francois Moore (m. 1753) and Marie Louise Desmeules met each other in Quebec City on 20 June 2016. At the lunch were Maurice Moore of Quebec City, Eric Moore of Trois-Rivieres, two daughters of Norman Moore, Sr.; Vicky Moore Jacobs of Golden, Colorado, and Christine Moore Skrocki of Bay City, Michigan, and the daughter of Norman Moore Sr.'s sister, Dianne; Kathy Kelly and her daughter, Gabriella Kelly, both of Sammamish, Washington. It was a momentous occasion indeed! ⚜

19
Moore Ancient Journey

IT HAS ALREADY BEEN DEMONSTRATED AND PROVEN in the Introduction that this study's Moore ancestors were of Viking stock. In addition, the Y-DNA origins show that they are part of the R-Haplogroup which originated in the Russian Steppes (grasslands) and Central Asia in the Paleolithic era about 27,000 +/- 4,000 years ago. They then subdivided into the R1a subclade of R-M420, around 18,000 +/- 3,000 years ago. They headed north and the branch R-M417 was formed. As it is, 99% of modern R1a descends from the R-M417 branch which expanded from the Bronze Age onwards about 5,600 +/- 800 years ago (Hay 2021).

This branch, living along the Voronezh River in the modern area of Western Russia, split into two branches forming a Northeast Europe route and a Western Europe route. The Northeast Europe branch also split into two which are known as the Central & East Europe branch and the Northeast Europe to Asia branch. Our ancestors were part of the former, specifically the R-Z283 subclade otherwise known by Dr. Bowes as the Pomeranian branch. They spread along the coast of modern Poland and Germany into Denmark and crossed into the modern borderlands of Norway and Sweden as part of the subclade R-Z284, with its epicenter in central Norway during the Copper to Early Bronze Age. By the beginning of Europe's Viking age in 793AD, having spread north along the Norwegian coast, they were living on the banks of the Namsen River (Hay 2021) (Bowes 2017).

The study *Reconstructing the Moore Ancient Paternal Ancestral Journey* by Dr. Tyrone Bowes in Appendix 6 illustrates the progression discussed above. Bowes forms his study based on Y-DNA genetic markers of people who share paternal ancestry prior to the appearance of surnames. By opening up the Ysearch.org database criteria to less Y-DNA matches and mapping these matches with the earliest known ancestor of these matches, his study began to unfold. Just as the more Y-DNA genetic markers that two people share the more recent their common male ancestor once lived, so the less genetic markers shared show distant relatives further back in time.

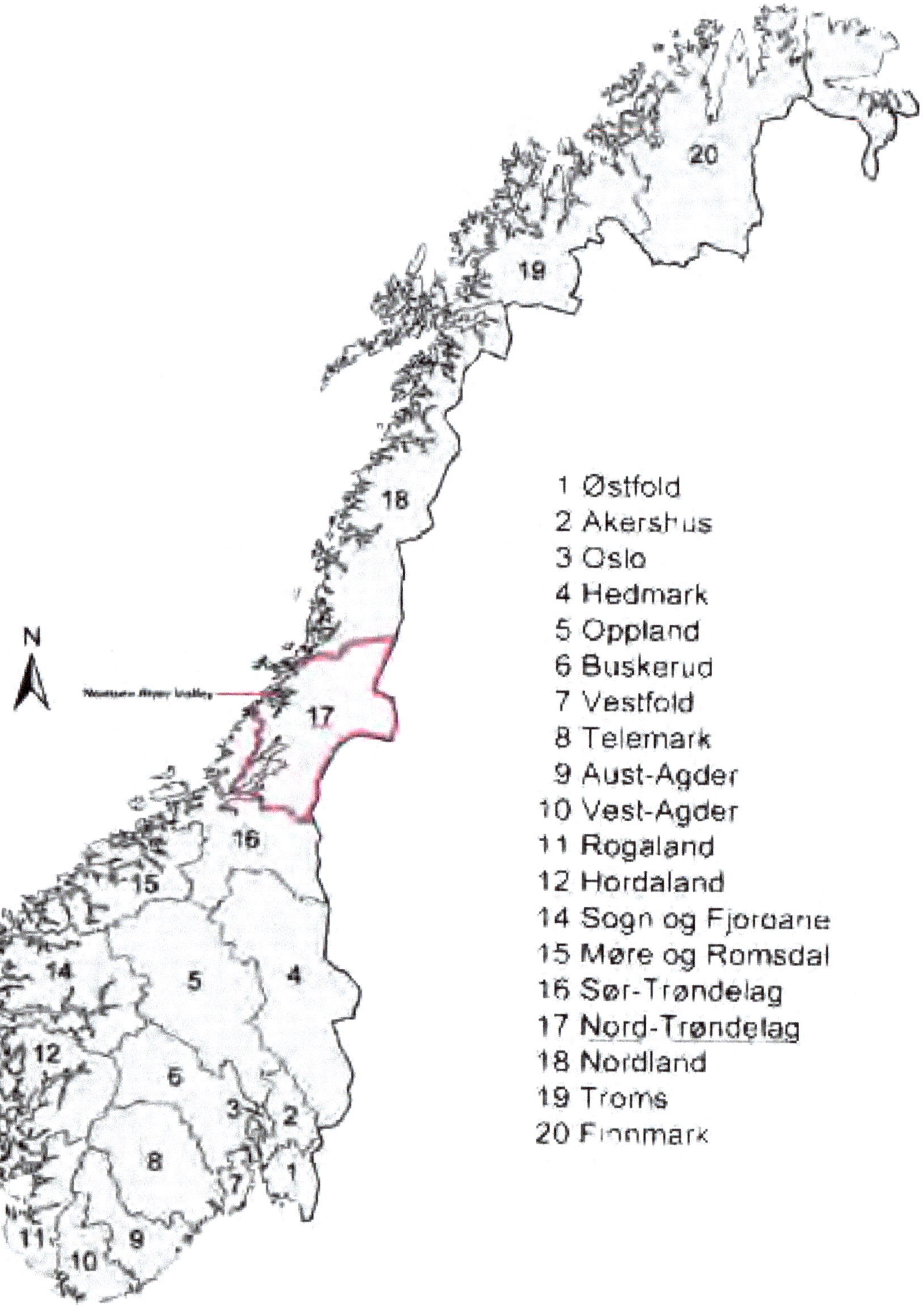

Figure 48. The County Map of Norway

Source: Map adapted from https://www.researchgate.net/figure/Counties-in-Norway-per-December-2107.

The Namsen River Valley in Nord-Trondelag is highlighted in red.

Some surnames found to match this study's Moore ancestors are names that we have no clue as to where they came from, but are, in fact, ancient remnants of past relations. Appendix 6 lists such surnames as Kielec and Konczak from Poland, Bonorden and Panzer from Germany, Gryskiewicz from Belarus, Kniznik from Ukraine, Crnkovic from Croatia as well as Johansen from Norway (Bowes, Reconstructing the Moore Ancient Paternal Ancestral Journey 2017) [App. 6]. Again, this makes sense now and it correlates with the migration documented for the R-Haplogroup as well [fig. 6].

History shows that the western counties of Norway from Rogaland in the south up along the coast to Nord-Trondelag in the north were the areas from where most Norse Vikings set sail (Edwards 1999, 173). It is from the Namsen River Valley in Nord-Trondelag that our past ancestors left as they sought adventure and their future in the distant Isles of Scotland. They made their way to the Isle of Bute towards the end of the first millennium (Bowes, Pinpointing the Moore Scottish Paternal Ancestral Genetic Homeland 2017). The Phylogenetic Tree for Norman E. Moore, Sr. subsequently shows him as being part of the subclade R-CTS4179 [fig. 4]. This subclade is the most common Scottish variety of R1a. It came from Norway with the Vikings (Hay 2021). ⚜

20

Conclusion

THE NORWEGIAN WESTERN COASTAL COUNTIES of Hordaland, Sogn og Fjordane and a few other parts of western Norway, including Nord-Trondelag, were the areas from where most Norse Vikings set sail (Edwards 1999, 173) (Yirka, Bob 2019). According to Dr. Tyrone Bowes, this study's Moore ancestors originated from along the Namsen River Valley, which is located in the present-day County of Nord Trondelag (Bowes 2017) [fig. 48, Appendex 6]. They sought new lands and opportunities and eventually settled on the Isle of Bute post 800AD to 1100AD (Reid 1864).

They first took the surname Moore or Muir around the turn of the millennium. They would have spoken Norwegian. As they assimilated into the Isles of Scotland, they would have started to speak Gaelic. Linguistic and cultural ties between western Scotland and Northern Ireland were strengthened in the 15th and 16th centuries through the influence of Clan Ian Mor (MacDonnells) and the Campbells, Earls of Argyll. Much of Antrim's Ulster lands had been secured by Sorley Boy MacDonnell by 1586. As a result, those areas not included in James VI & I's official Plantation in county Antrim, continued as Gaelic enclaves into the early 17th century (Lenihan 2008, 7). With the overlaying of the Lowland and Central Scots' English language and the Isles' and Borders-Southwest's Gaelic language across the northern half of Ulster, a bilingualism had resulted by 1600 that was a major factor in the plantation's acculturation process. The result was that people in Ulster started to speak a distinct "country" Ulster-English (J. M. Hill 1993, 27–29). A video posted on youtube.com called *Forged in Ulster* by comedian Tim McGarry states that people spoke: *"Scots to your King, French to your Lady and Gaelic to your God"* which formed a language he jokingly called *"EnglishFrenGaeluca"* (McGarry 2015, 16:28–16:43)!

When our Moore ancestors ended up in Ulster can only be surmised. They left Bute to settle on Antrim lands in Ulster, Northern Ireland, plausibly pre-plantation in the mid-16th century. They were possibly part of a private settlement into northern Antrim with either the MacDonnells of Antrim or the Stewarts of Ballintoy as these families incorporated their fellow

Scots onto their lands in a significant way. However, it is also possible that our ancestors arrived as part of the Plantation of Ulster onto the Earl of Antrim lands between 1603 and 1610.

There is a high probability that one or two of the younger sons of our initial Ulster settlers would have moved on from their family; leaving their first assigned location. It was a common occurrence for younger siblings to look for new lands and opportunities of their own. All men who were eighteen years and older would have participated in the *1630 Muster* of Ulster. Whole families, as well as the larger community, would have been displaced due to the 1641 Irish Rebellion and sought refuge in the closest fort for safety.

Subsequently fleeing Ulster, Edward Moore (b. c. 1612) served in the trained bands (militia) in Dublin for Parliament on the side of the King for a short time. Edward finally joined his wife and child in London. He was either "pressed" or volunteered for the 1st Dutch War which was held entirely at sea. He would have gained some knowledge of cannons during this time. After the war ended in 1654, he returned to London where his son, Thomas was born later that year, likely in December.

Edward and his family were presumably living in Whitechapel, which is part of the Tower Hamlets near the Tower of London. The Tower Hamlet Trained Bands helped guard the Tower of London. The Tower was also the location of the Board of Ordnance which used the fee'd gunners and guards of the Tower of London to be assigned to various wars in their Artillery Divisions.

In 1658, it is probable that Moore was sent to Dunkirk in the Train of Artillery to fight in the Battle of Dunkirk, also known as the Battle of the Dunes. He eventually became part of the Commonwealth's Dunkirk garrison. He was mustered with the Train of Artillery in 1659. He remained in the Dunkirk garrison until around the year 1661/2, of which England was then in command.

After King Charles II of England sold Dunkirk to the French King Louis XIV, Edward was possibly sent back to London and the Board of Ordnance then stationed him as a gunner at Dover Castle. Alternatively, he could have been sent directly from Dunkirk to Dover at the same time as Colonel John Strode's Regiment of Foot was commanded to its garrison between August and September of 1662. Strode's Regiment stayed intact at Dover Castle until 1685. Moore's position as gunner of Dover Castle was a lifetime position.

It appears that Edward Moore may have been married prior to his marriage with Cecilia Richardson, who was born and raised in Dover. It would make sense that, since Thomas Moore was born in London in 1654, London was where both of his parents lived at the time. Edward's first wife and children, including Thomas, were in London during the 1665 London Plague which killed thousands of people. Thomas Moore's mother died of the plague and was buried on

1 October 1665 at Whitechapel in the borough of the Tower Hamlets. The dates of 4 March 1665 to 31 July 1667 kept Edward Moore busy at Dover Castle with the 2nd Anglo-Dutch War.

Becoming a widower in 1665, Edward Moore and Cecilia Richardson probably married in Dover in January or February of 1668, six or seven months after the end of the 2nd Dutch War, and their first child named John was born 18 Nov 1668. They went on to have two more children. Edward remained a gunner at Dover Castle until his death in 1686. Coincidently, John Strode died that same year.

Meanwhile, young Thomas Moore, a dockhand at the London Docks, may have volunteered to be on Medard des Groseilliers' ship at the age of thirteen or fourteen for his June 1668 – Oct 1669 expedition into Hudson Bay. The Hudson's Bay Company's Royal Charter was formed on 2 May 1670. Thomas was officially hired after October of 1671 until 1678 by the Hudson's Bay Company at the age of seventeen. Thomas Moore charted one of the earliest maps for the HBC in 1678 which depicted the Western Shore of James Bay.

Pierre-Esprit Radisson and des Groseilliers left the HBC and went into the service of the French from 1675 to 1684. After July 1679, Thomas Moore was a Customs' Landwaiter at London Port working with imports and exports. Wanting to return to the Hudson Bay where he had found adventure for seven years, Thomas reapplied with the HBC in 1680 but he was not rehired.

Thomas may have travelled to Paris in 1684 to meet up with des Groseilliers for the purpose of regaining employment into the fur trade. He may also have travelled with des Groseilliers to meet up with Martinierre's expedition into Hudson Bay in 1684 which returned to Quebec in 1685. Thomas Moore was one of seventy men hired out of Quebec by the French Campagnie du Nord's[92] overland expedition in 1686[93]. The mission, led by Chevalier de Troyes and assisted by three senior officers, brothers Pierre, Paul and Jacques Le Moyne, was to expel the British from their Hudson Bay posts. Thomas Moore was hired as pilot for Pierre le Moyne d'Iberville's second expedition of 1688 to 1689 to Hudson Bay, this time by sea. Thomas Moore abjured Anglicanism and his Catholic marriage contract to Jeanne Lemelin was in January 1690. Their marriage was held on 6 April 1690 in Quebec City at Notre Dame Cathedral. He signed a piloting contract with d'Iberville for June 1690 to capture York Factory back from the English in Hudson Bay but it failed. Moore continued working on ships a few more years for various people in the Quebec area as he was always denoted as a pilot. He is thought to have died prior to 1724, possibly being lost at sea.

---

[92] Compagnie du Nord was founded by Charles Aubert de La Chesnaye and other Quebec merchants with the assistance of Radisson and des Groseilliers in 1682 but not given a Royal Charter until May 1685.

[93] Sept 1686 was also the year that Thomas's father, Edward Moore, died.

In conclusion, our Protestant Ulster-Scots ancestor, Edward Moore (b. *c.* 1612), had a son born in London named Thomas Moore (b. 1654) who, abjuring his Anglicanism, married in 1690 in Quebec City, a Catholic French-Canadian woman named Jeanne Lemelin. Over time any remaining trace of our Ulster Irish and Scottish roots were lost as our family assimilated into the St. Laurence River French Settlers of Canada.

To this day, 25% of all Moore's in Ireland are in Co. Antrim alone and the name is also common in County Derry and County Tyrone (Bell 2021, 199–200). ⚜

APPENDIX 1

An Irish Seaman in 1690

THE THING SEEMS STRANGE AT FIRST SIGHT, but it is none the less true, that in 1690, an Irish seaman settled at Saint-Laurent on the Island of Orleans.

The North Bay Company, founded in 1684 by some Quebec merchants, played an important part, for some years. It was this enterprising company which helped Lemoyne d'Iberville undertake his first voyages to Hudson Bay.

In 1686, the North Bay Company had engaged, probably in France, an Irish Catholic from Dover, England, one Thomas Moore, to command and pilot one of their ships.[94]

Moore sailed several times to Hudson Bay, for the North Bay Company. He must have met Le Moyne d'Iberville there.

On April 6th, 1690, Thomas Moore married, at Quebec, Jeanne Lemelin, daughter of Jean Lemelin, alias Tourangeau, joiner, and Marguerite Brassard.

Moore settled the same year at the Island of Orleans at Saint-Laurent, where he began to farm, though still continuing his work as a navigator, for he is always denoted as "ship-master and pilot."

In 1706, Moore was in command of the vessel la Marie. Governor de Vaudreuil instrusted him with an important mission. On June 2nd, 1706, M. de Vaudreuil wrote to Mr. Dudley, Governor of New England:

> *Referring to what you have done with regard to sending 57 prisoners to Port Royal, and as you are my only informant on this subject, since there has been no agreement of exchange signed on either side, I am sending in the ship 'la Marie', commanded by Thomas Moure (Moore), 43 of your prisoners to Port Royal, the list of whom I am conveying to Monsieur Brouillan with instructions to forward them on to you at Boston.*
>
> *As 'la Marie', which I am ordering off, will return direct here from Boston, I beg of you to send back to me the Canadian prisoners that you detain and who are from this part of the country, to wit: Monsieur Gourdeau and his family, the persons named Dion and Pierottiere and le Fenoc and his children.*
>
> *I beg you to treat the captain of this ship and the crew with the courtesy and humanity common to all nations towards vessels bearing the flag of truce . . .**

---

94 It was actually an overland expedition.

It is a curious coincidence that M. Gourdeau and his family, whom Moore was under orders to repatriate, were also from the Island of Orleans.

The next year, a certain number of Quebec merchants armed a frigate, Notre-Dame de la Victoire, in order "to go privateering against the enemies of the State," that is to say, the English. It was Alexandre Leneuf de Beaubassin et de la Valliere, a lieutenant in the troops of the naval detachment, who was given command of this outfit. Moore was chosen as master and pilot of Notre-Dame de la Victoire.

What was the result of M. Leneuf de Beaubassin's expedition? A letter from Raudot, dispatched in November, 1706, proves that nothing was accomplished.

We lose all traces of Thomas Moore after this date. We think that he died in the course of one of his expeditions. Thomas Moore's descendants became complete French Canadians.

—*The Isle of Orleans* by Pierre Georges Roy | 1928, pg. 345–6

* According to *Collection de Manuscrits*, Vol. II, p. 452.

APPENDIX 2

Various Genealogy Descriptions of Thomas Moore

1) *Genealogie des Familles Originaires des Comtes de Montmagny, L'Islet, Bellechasse* by Eloi-Gerard Talbot, B.A., B.P., p. 206

   Thomas Moore, pilote, fils d'Edward Moore et de Cecile Richardson, natif de Londres, se marie a Quebec, le 16 avril 1690 (contrat Genaple N.P. 7 janv.) aJeanne Lemelin, fille de Jean Lemelin et de Marguerite Brassard, (B.R.H. 1924 p. 385). Un Irlandais a Quebec, en 1687. P.-Georges Roy et chanoine D. Gosselin, B.R.H. 1925, page 755. Il avait adjure le protestantieme a Quebec, le 19 mars 1690.

2) *Dictionnaire Genealogique des Familles du Quebec* by Rene Jette, p. 826

   Moore ou Maure, Thomas (Edouard & Cecile Richard) de Ste-Marie, v. Douvres (Dover), comte de Kent, Angleterre, d. avant 26–11–1724, St-Laurent I.O.; cite 12–02–1690 Hotel-Dieu Quebec. 36 ans; abjure l'anglicanisme 19–03–1690 Quebec, pilote. [DBC II 509]

3) *Genealogy of the French Families of the Detroit River Region, Revision 1701–1936, Vol II* by The Rev. Fr. Christian Denissen, p. 862

   Thomas Moore a sailor son of Edmund Moore and Cecilia Richard who r. Dover, England Parish of St. Mary the Virgin where the old Anglo-Saxon Church with its Norman tower still stands came to Canada m. 6 Apr 1690 Quebec Jane Lemelin, b. there 24 Dec 1673 bur 27 Mar 1732 St. Laurent dau of John Lemelin dit Tourangeau and Margaret Brassard.

APPENDIX 3

Pinpointing the Moore Scottish Paternal Ancestral Genetic Homeland

by Dr. Tyrone Bowes

27 May 2017

Person tested | Norman Moore, Sr.

A Scottish Case Study | www.scottishorigenes.com

—Dr Tyrone Bowes

Introduction

A simple painless commercial ancestral Y chromosome DNA test will potentially provide one with the names of many hundreds of individuals with whom one shares a common male ancestor, but what often perplexes people is how one can match lots of individuals with many different surnames? The answer is quite simple. Roughly 1,000 years ago one's direct medieval male ancestor, the first for example to call himself 'Muir' was living in close proximity to others with whom he was related but who inherited other surnames like Lamont, Livingstone and MacEachern. Given that 1,000 years have passed since paternally inherited surnames became common, there will be many descendants of those individuals some of whom will today undergo commercial ancestral Y-DNA testing. Hence the surnames of one's medieval ancestor's neighbors will be revealed in today's Y-DNA test results. Early 19th century census data demonstrates that Scottish surnames could still be found concentrated in the areas from which they originated. One can therefore use census data to determine the origin of the surnames that appear in one's Y-DNA results, identifying an area common to all, and reveal ones '**Paternal Ancestral Genetic Homeland**.' The genetic homeland is the small area (usually within a 5-mile radius) where one's ancestors lived for hundreds if not thousands of years. It is the area where one's ancestor first inherited his surname surrounded by relatives who inherited others. It is the area where one's ancestors left their mark in its place names, its history, and in the DNA of its current inhabitants. Since modern science can pinpoint a paternal ancestral genetic homeland, it can also be used to confirm it by DNA testing individuals from the pinpointed area.

Notes of caution!

1. In Scotland each of the estimated 1,500 distinct surnames had a single founding ancestor, that's an estimated 1,500 Adam's from whom anyone with Scottish ancestry can trace direct descent. But science has demonstrated that only 50% of individuals with a particular Scottish surname will be related to the surnames founding ancestor, the other 50% of people will have an association that has arisen as a result of what are called 'nonpaternal events' usually a result of adoptions or maternal transfer of the surname. Since Scotland adopted a similar Clan based society these scientific findings can be applied to Scotland and people with Scottish ancestry.
2. Often people are looking for their DNA results to trace back to a specific area. One must remember that the results typically reflect one's ancestor's neighbors from around 1,000 years ago. As a result, if one's Scottish ancestor was descended from an Anglo-Saxon settler, Viking raider, or 12th Century Norman one's DNA results will reflect earlier English, Welsh, French, and possibly Scandinavian origin. One must approach this process with an open mind!

Interpreting the Y-DNA test results

To pinpoint a paternal ancestral genetic homeland, one must first identify the surnames that appear as one's Y-DNA genetic matches. Those surnames, particularly one's that *recur* throughout one's Y-DNA results will typically reflect the surnames of one's medieval ancestor's neighbors. With no genetic matches at the 37-marker level in the FTDNA database, the test subject's Y-DNA results were analyzed at Ysearch.org where one can drop the match criteria to reveal close genetic relatives, see **Figure 1**. Upon Y-DNA testing the test subject did not match other individuals named Moore. This indicates that the test subject may not be directly descended from a Moore-Adam;' literally the first male (Adam) to take that surname who lived approximately 1,000 years ago (when surnames first appeared). However, Moore is a very common surname which is associated with England, Scotland and Ireland, and it may simply be that other Moores with whom the test subject shares common founding ancestor, have simply yet to Y-DNA test. The dominance of Scottish associated surnames among the test subject's Ysearch.org matches reveals a most recent paternal ancestral link with Scotland, see **Figure 1**. It is the test subject's closest Scottish-associated genetic surname matches as a snapshot of his medieval ancestor's relatives/ neighbors which will reveal where his Scottish Moore ancestors lived. This is because those Scottish surnames arose among related males living in a specific location an estimated 1,000 years ago.

Ysearch.org Matches						
Last Name	**User ID**	**Origin**	**Haplogroup**	**Tested With**	**Markers Compared**	**Genetic Distance**
Moore (test subject)	K7HDW	Ireland	R1a1a (tested)	Family Tree DNA	67	0
LaMons	3ZGXW	**Scotland**	Unknown	Family Tree DNA	37	5
D'Audney	E8FFG	Unknown	R1a1a1b (tested)	Family Tree DNA	37	6
Lamons	W597B	**Scotland**	Unknown	Family Tree DNA	37	5
McCain	WK8S9	**Scotland**	R1a (tested)	Family Tree DNA	37	6
Jeffery	7D6BD	Unknown	R1a1a (tested)	Family Tree DNA	37	6
Lee	T3HD2	Unknown	Unknown	Family Tree DNA	34	4
Livingston	QRMJS	Crane Hill, America	Unknown	Ancestry.com	34	5
Hailstone	HHFN2	Unknown	Unknown	Ancestry.com	34	6
Newton	JKQ74	Bures St. Mary, Suffolk County, England	Unknown	Family Tree DNA	34	6
MacEachern	VWQPW	**Argyllshire, Scotland**	R1a1*	GeneTree	30	4
Sharypov	YVHP9	Russia	Unknown	Other - SMGF	30	6
Riebel	R35HG	Unknown	R1a*	Other - Genex	29	5
Livingston	Q7XH4	America	Unknown	Ancestry.com	28	5
Hawthorne	B943D	Greaugh,Drumsnatt, Monaghan, Ireland	R1a1a (tested)	Family Tree DNA	27	5
MacDonald/McDaniel	MRNBR	**Skye,35w20, Western Isles, Scotland**	Unknown	Family Tree DNA	27	4
McArthur	BQXRU	**Isle of Mull, Argyllshire, Scotland**	Unknown	Other - Genebase	27	5
king	8H8ZU	Unknown	Unknown	Ancestry.com	27	6

Figure 1: *Snapshot of the test subject Moore's closest genetic matches in the Ysearch.org database. The more genetic markers two people share the more recent their shared paternal ancestor once lived. Upon commercial ancestral Y-DNA testing the test subject matched many individuals with Scottish associated surnames. The surnames that appear among his closest genetic matches are* ***NOT RANDOM****; some like Livingstone and MacDonald recur among his genetic relatives. Lamons/LaMons is a spelling variant of Scottish 'Lamont,' while McCain is an Irish spelling of a number of Scottish surnames.*

The Scottish 'Muir' Surname

Early Scottish census data reveals that Moore in Scotland is spelled 'Muir.' Since surnames arose in an agriculturally based society, farmers with each surname can still be found concentrated in the area where their surname first appeared or in the areas where one's ancestors first settled. An examination of the distribution of farmers named 'Muir' reveals that they not distributed evenly but occur within 9 distinct geographical locations, see **Figure 2**. This indicates 9 distinct groups within Scotland associated with the Scottish Muir surname, see **Figure 2**. Each group was potentially descended from an unrelated Muir-Adam, and since the test subject may be descended from a Scottish Muir-Adam his paternal ancestry is linked to one of these 9 distinct locations. An examination of the Scottish Origenes databases reveals castles and place names associated with the Scottish Muir surname which are associated with areas where that surname is common, see **Figure 3**.

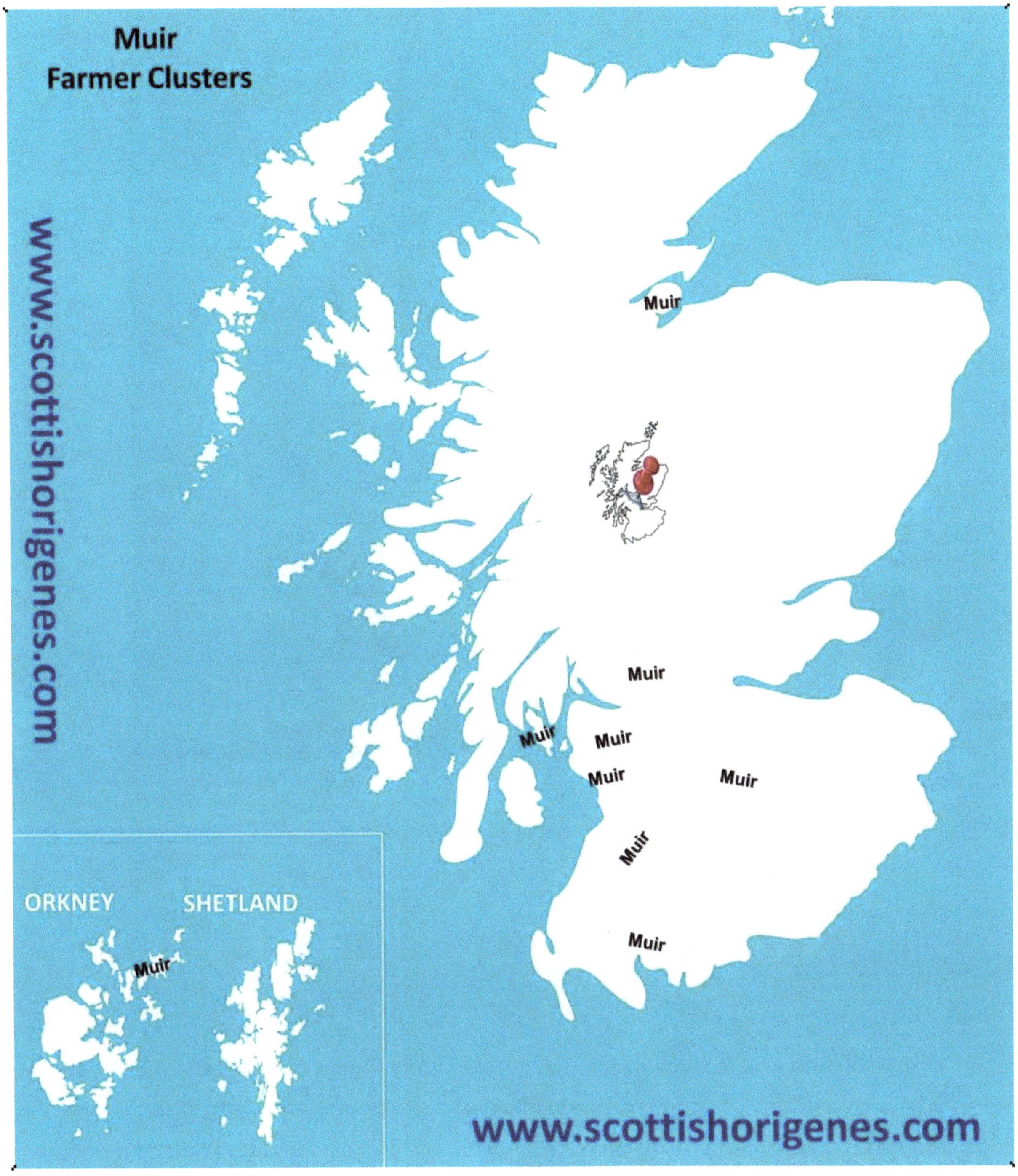

Figure 2: *The Scottish Muir farming community in 1841. Early census data reveals at least 9 distinct groups of Scottish Muir farmers; each group may be genetically distinct and hence founded by an unrelated Muir-Adam. Each surname is placed on the map in the area where farmers with that surname concentrate in early census data. The most common spelling is detailed in each location.*

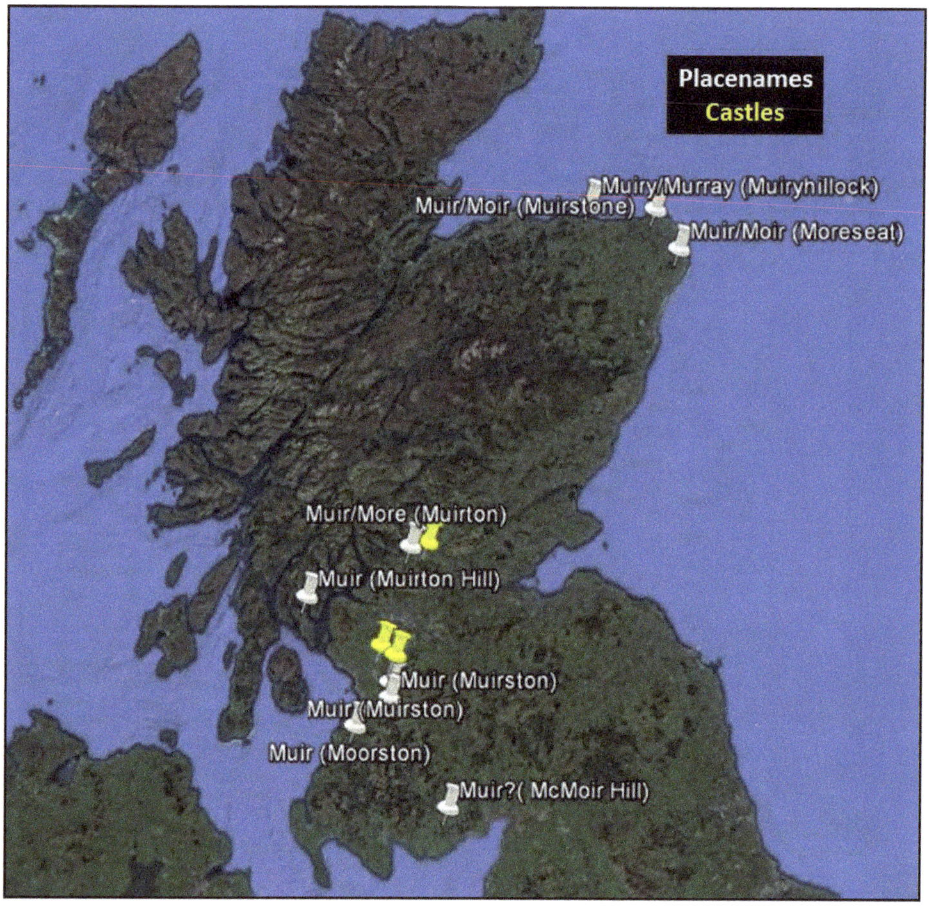

Figure 3: *Scottish Muir Castles and Placenames. An examination of the Scottish Origenes castles and placenames databases revealed a number of castles and placenames that are associated with the Muir surname and which are found in areas where the Muir surname is common.*

Y-DNA, Surnames, and Land

The method of using genetic surname matches as revealed by commercial ancestral Y-DNA testing to pinpoint a paternal ancestral genetic homeland works by exploiting the link between the Y chromosome, surname and land; which are typically passed from father to son through the generations. In the absence of a link to the land the process becomes more challenging. The link with the land is greatest among the farming community and since farmers in Scotland can still be found farming the lands where their ancestor lived when he first inherited his surname, or where one's ancestors first settled within Scotland, one can plot where farmers with the surnames that appear in one's Y-DNA results cluster and identify an area common to all. Hence, it is Mr. Moore's closest Scottish-associated genetic surname matches (*identified in Figure 1*) which will reveal where his paternal ancestors originated within Scotland.

Mr. Moore's closest Scottish-associated genetic matches are to people named Lamont, Livingstone, MacEachern and Jeffrey, see **Figure 1**. By overlaying maps of where farmers named Muir, Lamont, Livingstone, MacEachern and Jeffrey concentrated in early census data it reveals a paternal ancestral link with West Central Scotland, see **Figure 4**. The Scottish Origenes Surnames and DNA Map of Scotland details where farmers with each surname concentrated in early census data, and an examination of West Central Scotland as it appears on that map reveals Muir farmers on the Isle of Bute surrounded by farming communities with surnames that appear among the test subject's closest genetic relatives, see **Figure 5**.

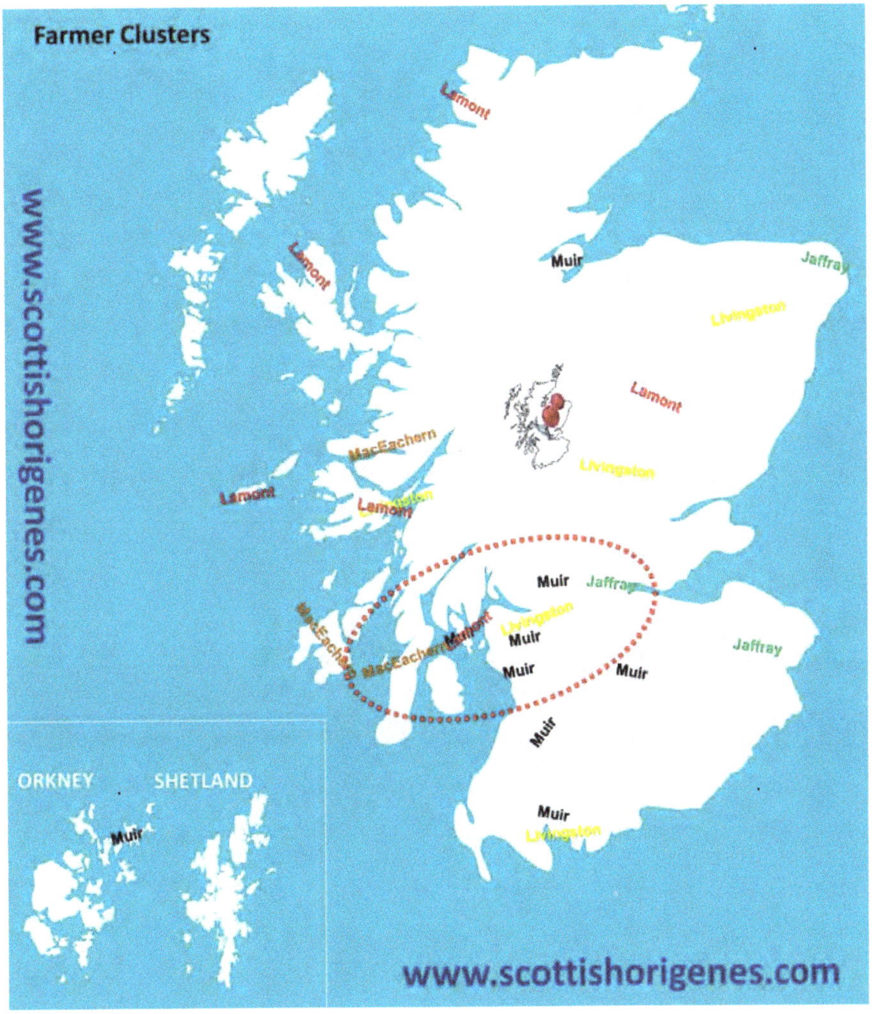

Figure 4: *Mr. Moore's genetic surname matches reveal a paternal ancestral link with West Central Scotland. By plotting the locations where Muir, Lamont, Livingstone, Alexander and Jeffrey (Jaffray) farmers concentrated in 1841 it reveals a paternal ancestral link with West Central Scotland (**red broken circle**).*

Figure 5: *The Surnames of the Clyde Estuary in West Central Scotland. The Muirs of the Isle of Bute (red arrow) lived surrounded by farming communities with surnames that appear among the test subject's closet genetic matches (orange arrows). The MacArthur surname (yellow arrow) appears as a more distant match in the ysearch database. The McCain surname may be an Irish variant of Scottish MacCunn (green arrow). Each surname is positioned in the location where farmers with each surname concentrate in early census data. Surnames in red font are associated exclusively with a single location within Scotland.*

The Clan Territories of West Central Scotland

By examining the locations of the castles and towerhouses that are historically associated with a particular surname, it reveals that Medieval Scotland was a patchwork of territories dominated by notable Clans and Families. Almost everyone with Scottish paternal ancestry will be genetically related to at least one of these prominent Clans or Families that once ruled over one's paternal ancestral genetic homeland. An examination of the castles and towerhouses of the Isle of Bute and its surrounding area reveals Clans and Families of predominantly Viking (Norse), NorseGael, Picto-Gael, Norman and Ancient Briton origin, see **Figure 6**. The test subject's Lamont and MacDonald genetic relative's ancestors dominated much of the land that surrounded the Clyde Estuary, see **Figure 6**.

Figure 6: *The principal Medieval Clans and Families of West Central Scotland. West Central Scotland was dominated by a diverse mix of Clans and Families of predominantly Viking(Norse), Norse-Gael, Ancient Briton, Picto-Gael and Norman origin. The test subject's 'Muir' ancestors lived in an area dominated by his Lamont (red arrows) and MacDonald (yellow arrows) genetic relatives. The Lamont surname appears as the test subject's closest genetic relative, while the MacDonald surname appears as a more distant, but frequently recurring genetic match in the FTDNA Y-DNA database.*

Mr Moore's Paternal Ancestral Genetic Homeland

Early census data reveals that Muir farmers concentrate in the parish of Rothesay on the Isle of Bute; and it is there that the test subject's paternal ancestral genetic homeland is to be found, see **Figure 7**. It was there that the test subject's direct male ancestor lived when he first inherited the 'Muir' surname, which over time and distance morphed into 'Moore.' His paternal ancestors lived surrounded by male relatives who took surnames like Lamont, MacEachern, MacDonald, MacArthur and Livingstone among many others. When one's ancestors have been associated with an area for long enough, they often leave evidence of their ancestral links in the placenames and historical monuments one finds there. An examination of the area surrounding Rothesay town revealed '*Muir*ton Hill' which is a clear reference to the test subject's paternal ancestors, see **Figure 7** and **8**. The Muirs of the Isle of Bute will undoubtedly have left evidence of their ancestral links with this area in both its history and in the DNA of any Muirs who may still live there.

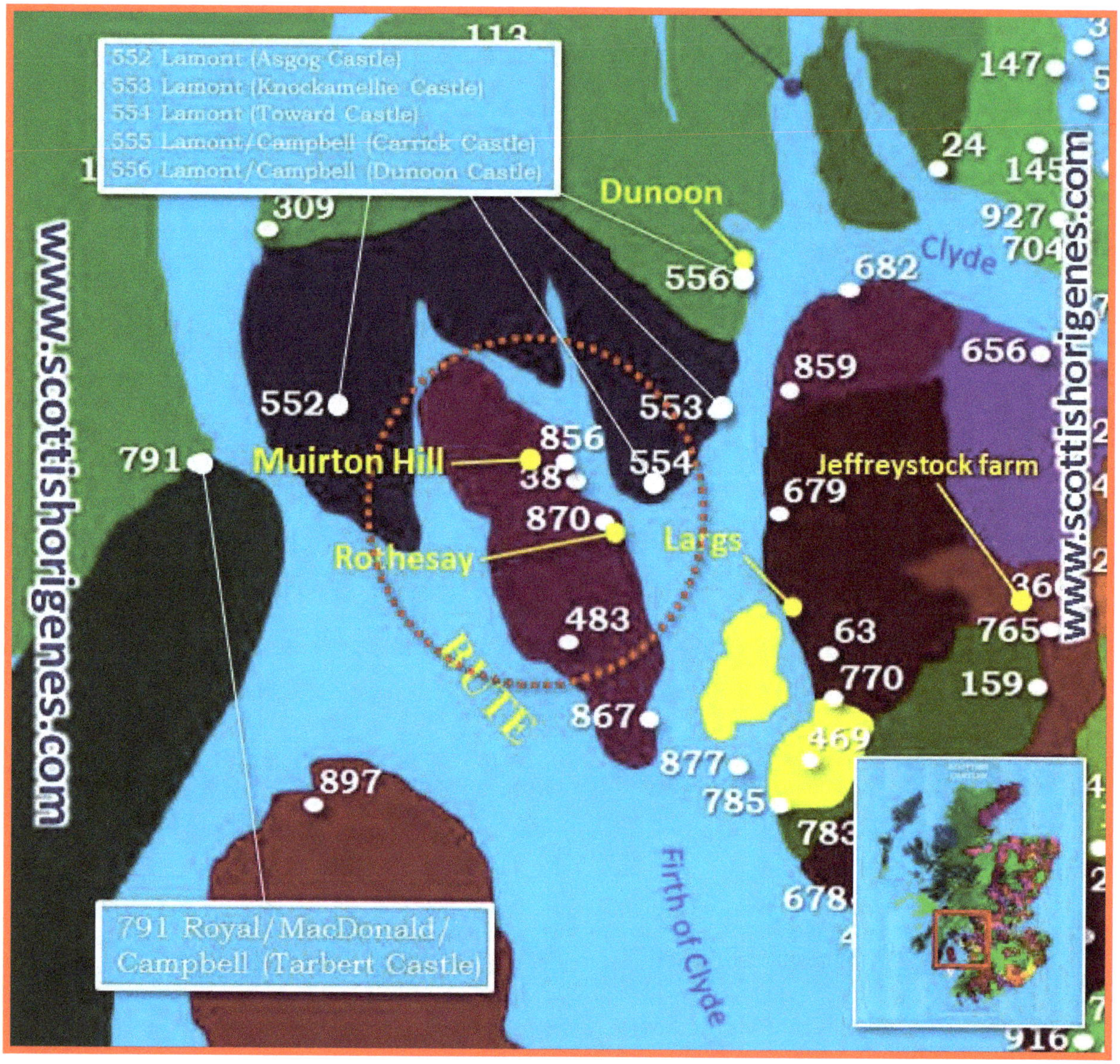

Figure 7: *Mr Moore's Paternal Ancestral Genetic Homeland. Early census data reveals that the Muirs concentrate in the parishes that surround Rothesay town (**orange broken circle**); and it is there that the test subject's paternal ancestral genetic homeland is to be found. It was there that the test subject's paternal ancestor lived when he first acquired the Muir surname approximately 1,000 years ago. His Muir-Adam ancestor lived surrounded by male relatives who inherited other surnames like Lamont, MacDonald and Livingstone among many others, some of whom (including the Muirs) have left evidence of their long ancestral links with this area in the surrounding placenames and castles. All of these Clans will also have left evidence of their ancestral links with this area in its history, but also in the DNA of the current inhabitants*

Figure 8: *Muirton Hill on the Isle of Bute.*

Mr. Moore's Viking origin

The test subject's R1a Y-DNA Haplogroup, his genetic matches to individuals with Viking-associated surnames (Lamont, MacDonald) and his more distant matches to Scandinavian surnames (at the 25 and 12 marker levels) indicate that his ancestors were descended from Vikings who settled on the Isle of Bute approximately 1,000 years ago.

How to confirm the Moore Genetic Homeland

One must keep in mind that this is a scientific 'DNA' approach. The DNA does not lie, and a simple painless commercial ancestral Y-DNA test of Muirs who live and farm the land that surrounds Rothesay town would confirm the paternal ancestral link with that area.

APPENDIX 4

Eric Moore
An Autosomal DNA Case Study

by Dr. Tyrone Bowes

25 July 2019

Person tested | Eric Moore

www.irishorigenes.com

—Dr Tyrone Bowes

Introduction

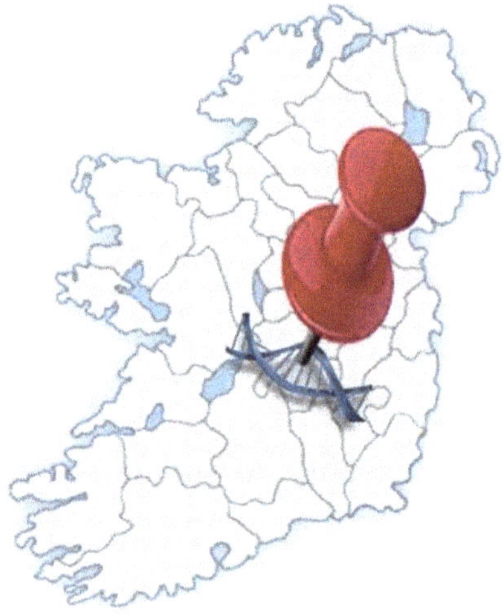

There are a number of commercial ancestral DNA tests that can be used to explore one's ancestry. By far the most popular is the 'autosomal test' which sheds light over all of one's recent ancestral lines. With autosomal DNA testing one will typically match many individuals (both male and female) and making sense of those relationships can be quite challenging. However, as with every DNA test the same golden rule applies; the more DNA that two people share the more recent their shared (paternal or maternal) ancestor once lived. In addition, many of one's autosomal matches will reveal surnames and placenames associated with their family tree, and those surnames and locations can hold clues as to where the various branches in one's own ancestral tree originated. The challenge of modern autosomal DNA test analysis is linking a common location revealed in the DNA test results with a particular ancestral surname.

Interpreting the Autosomal Results

An examination of the test subject's FTDNA Family Finder 'autosomal' DNA test results revealed 3,077 genetic relatives, 1,203 of whom record details of their ancestral surnames or locations, see Figure 1. What is quite striking is that the locations revealed by the test subject's 'autosomal' genetic relatives are NOT RANDOM; given its respective population size, Ireland dominates, see Figure 1.

A

FamilyFinder STATS	
Matches	3077
Ancestral details	1203
Percentage	39

B

Country	Frequency	Percentage
Ireland	201	16.7
Scotland	85	7.1
England	157	13.1
Wales	17	1.4
Germany	102	8.5
France	178	14.8
Spain	6	0.5
Italy	28	2.3
Norway	18	1.5
Poland	29	2.4
Finland	4	0.3
Russia	24	2.0

***Figure 1**: Family Finder Stats. Approximately 39% of the test subject's Family Finder matches record some sort of ancestral information (surname and/or location, panel A). The locations revealed by those genetic relatives are NOT RANDOM, compared to a selected number of European countries, and given its respective population size; Ireland dominates, panel B.*

Irish Autosomal Matches

Ireland is divided into 32 counties, and an examination of the Irish counties revealed among the test subject's autosomal genetic relatives who record ancestral links within Ireland, revealed ancestral links with Counties Antrim and Donegal within Ulster in Northern Ireland, see Figure 2. An examination of the ancestral surnames revealed by the test subject's genetic relatives with recorded links within County Antrim reveals that they are dominated by surnames of 16th and 17th Century Scottish Plantation origin. In contrast, a mix of pre-Plantation Gaelic Irish and Plantation Scottish surnames dominate within Donegal. The majority of the test subject's autosomal DNA links with Northeast Ireland are the result of relatively recent Scottish settlement.

A

IRELAND

	County	Frequency	Percentage
Ulster	Antrim	11	5.5
	Down	8	4.0
	Derry	4	2.0
	Donegal	11	5.5
	Tyrone	4	2.0
	Fermanagh	5	2.5
	Monaghan	3	1.5
	Armagh	6	3.0
	Cavan	2	1.0
Leinster	Longford	0	0.0
	Meath	0	0.0
	Louth	3	1.5
	Dublin	5	2.5
	Wicklow	3	1.5
	Kildare	0	0.0
	Westmeath	1	0.5
	Offaly	0	0.0
	Wexford	0	0.0
	Laois	3	1.5
	Carlow	2	1.0
	Kilkenny	0	0.0
Munster	Tipperary	2	1.0
	Limerick	6	3.0
	Cork	7	3.5
	Clare	3	1.5
	Waterford	2	1.0
	Kerry	2	1.0
Connaught	Leitrim	3	1.5
	Roscommon	4	2.0
	Sligo	5	2.5
	Mayo	3	1.5
	Galway	7	3.5

B

***Figure 2**: Autosomal matches reveal ancestral connections to two distinct areas within Ireland. The ancestral locations revealed by the test subject's genetic relatives with recorded ancestral links within Ireland are **not random**, and a search of the Irish counties revealed by the test subject's genetic relatives (**panel A**) reveals potential ancestral connections to Antrim and Donegal in Ulster, (red arrows **panel A** and red broken circles **panel B**). Closer inspection of the ancestral surnames revealed among the test subject's genetic relatives reveals that they are dominated by Scottish Plantation surnames in Antrim and a mix of Gaelic Irish and Plantation surnames within Donegal.*

Linking an Ancestral surname with an Autosomal DNA identified location

The challenge of autosomal DNA analysis is linking a location revealed in those results with one of the test subject's ancestral surnames. That can be very challenging when one's ancestral surnames are common. However, for less common surnames, which are far more limited in their distribution, one can easily link an ancestral surname to an emerging autosomal location.

Although a previous Y-DNA at Scottish Origenes identified a paternal connection with the Muirs of the Isle of Bute, family lore links the test subject's most Muir ancestors with the Plantation of Ulster in the early 17th Century, see **Figure 3**. Many Scottish surnames change over both time and distance, particularly within Ireland where for example Scottish 'McCrindle' became 'McReynolds,' 'Moubray' became 'Mayberry' and 'McWhirter' became 'Merryweather,' a similar process has seen Scottish 'Muir' become Irish 'Moore.' Since farmers with each Plantation surname still concentrate in the area where one's ancestor first settled, one can examine early census data to determine where the Planter Scots 'Muirs' settled. Early census data reveals 9 distinct clusters of Protestant Moore farmers within Ulster in Northern Ireland, see **Figure 4**. If there is a link with the Scots-Irish Moores, then there may be clues among the detail revealed by the test subject's autosomal genetic relatives. An examination of the test subject's autosomal DNA results revealed strongest links to Antrim where one finds 2 groups of Plantation Moores, see **Figure 2** and **4**. A closer inspection of the ancestral surnames and locations revealed among his genetic relatives failed to conclusively connect his ancestry with the Scots Irish Moores of Antrim, see **Figure 5**. However, many of the Plantation Scots left together and settled together within Ireland, and hence the surnames of the Plantation community that surrounds each of the 9 groups of Scots Irish Moores should reveal clues as to their Scottish (or English) origin, and mirror many of the surnames that surround the Muirs of the Isle of Bute, see **Figure 6**. An examination of the surnames that surround the Plantation Moore community of Southeast Antrim failed to identify any surnames associated with the Isle of Bute, see **Figure 7**. In contrast, an examination of the Moores of Ballymoney in North Antrim reveals almost all of the Scottish surnames that dominate the Isle of Bute, see **Figure 8.** These results indicate that some of the Muirs of Bute took part in the Plantation of Ulster and settled in the farmland that surrounds the town of Ballymoney.

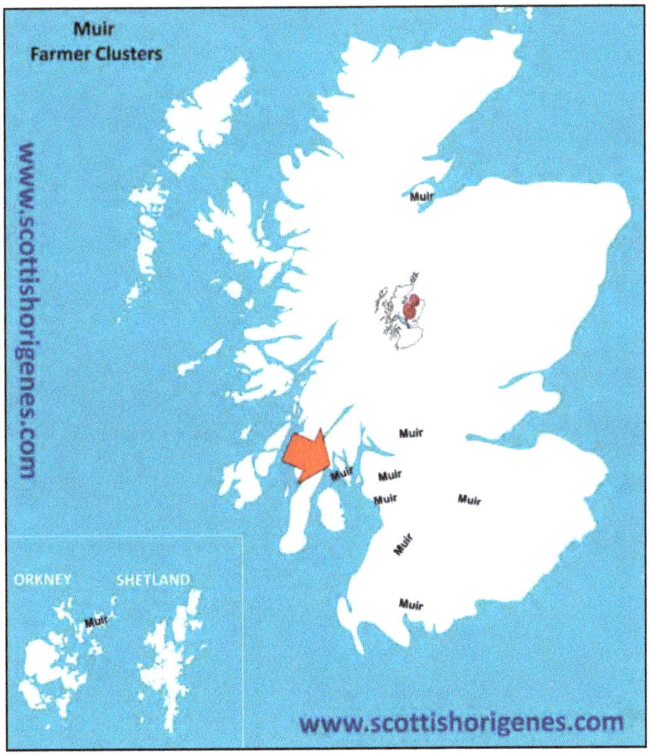

***Figure 3**: The Scottish Muir farming community. An examination of the distribution of farmers named Muir in early Scottish census data reveals 9 distinct groups, and hence potentially 9 genetically distinct Scottish Muir Clans. Y-DNA testing has confirmed a paternal ancestral link with the Muirs of the Isle of Bute (red arrow). Each surname has been placed on the map in the area where farmers with that surname concentrate in early census data. The most common spelling is detailed in each location.*

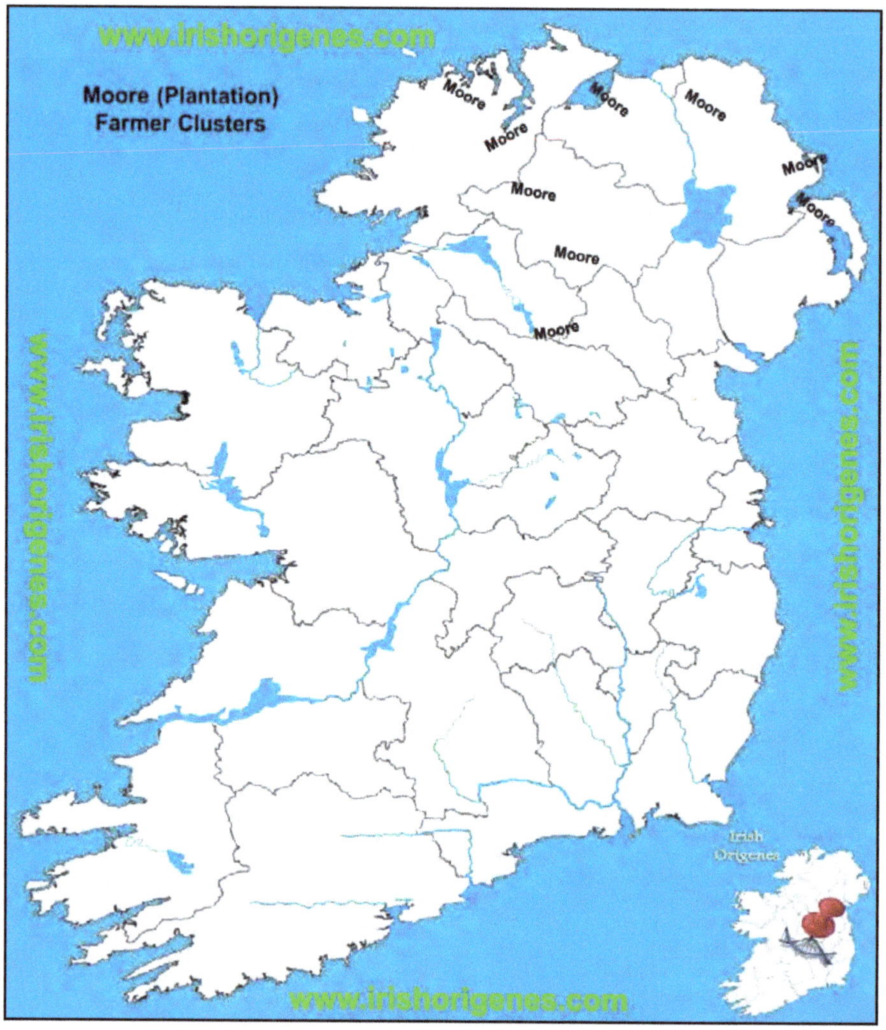

Figure 4: *The Scots-Irish Moores. An examination of the distribution of Protestant farmers named Moore in early Irish census data reveals 9 distinct groups. Each surname has been placed on the map in the area where farmers with that surname concentrate in early census data. The most common spelling is detailed in each location*

Autosomal Match Detail		
Ancestral Surname	**Frequency**	**Locations**
Moore	54	1 x UK 6 x USA (New Hampshire / Hartford, CT / Province of New Jersey / Newfoundland / KY) 3 x Ireland (Kilkeel, Co. Down / Londonderry)
Muir	4	1 x Scotland
Moir	2	1 x Ireland

Figure 5: *Moore autosomal matches. An examination of the test subject's autosomal matches revealed many genetic relatives with Moores in their ancestral tree, some of whom record ancestral detail. A disproportionate number reveal connections with Ireland, although no clear area within Ireland emerged.*

Figure 6: *The Surnames of the Isle of Bute. An examination of the surnames associated with the Isle of Bute reveals many (blue arrows) which are common among the Plantation community of Northern Ireland. Some, like Muir and MacFie, change within Ireland, becoming Moore and McAfee. Each surname is positioned in the location where farmers with that surname concentrate in early census data. The most common spelling is detailed. Surnames in* ***red font*** *(like* ***MacFie****) are associated exclusively with a single location within Scotland.*

***Figure 7**: The Plantation surnames of Belfast Lough. Antrim dominates among the ancestral detail revealed by the test subject's autosomal genetic relatives. The land surrounding Belfast Lough was an area heavily colonised by the Scots and English in the early 1600s, and an examination of that area reveals 2 communities of Moore farmers (red arrows). However, few of the surnames associated with the Isle of Bute can be found among the surrounding plantation farming community (blue arrow). The Moores of Southeast Antrim and Northeast Down did not originate from the Isle of Bute. Each surname is positioned in the location where farmers with that surname concentrate in early census data. The most common spelling is detailed.*

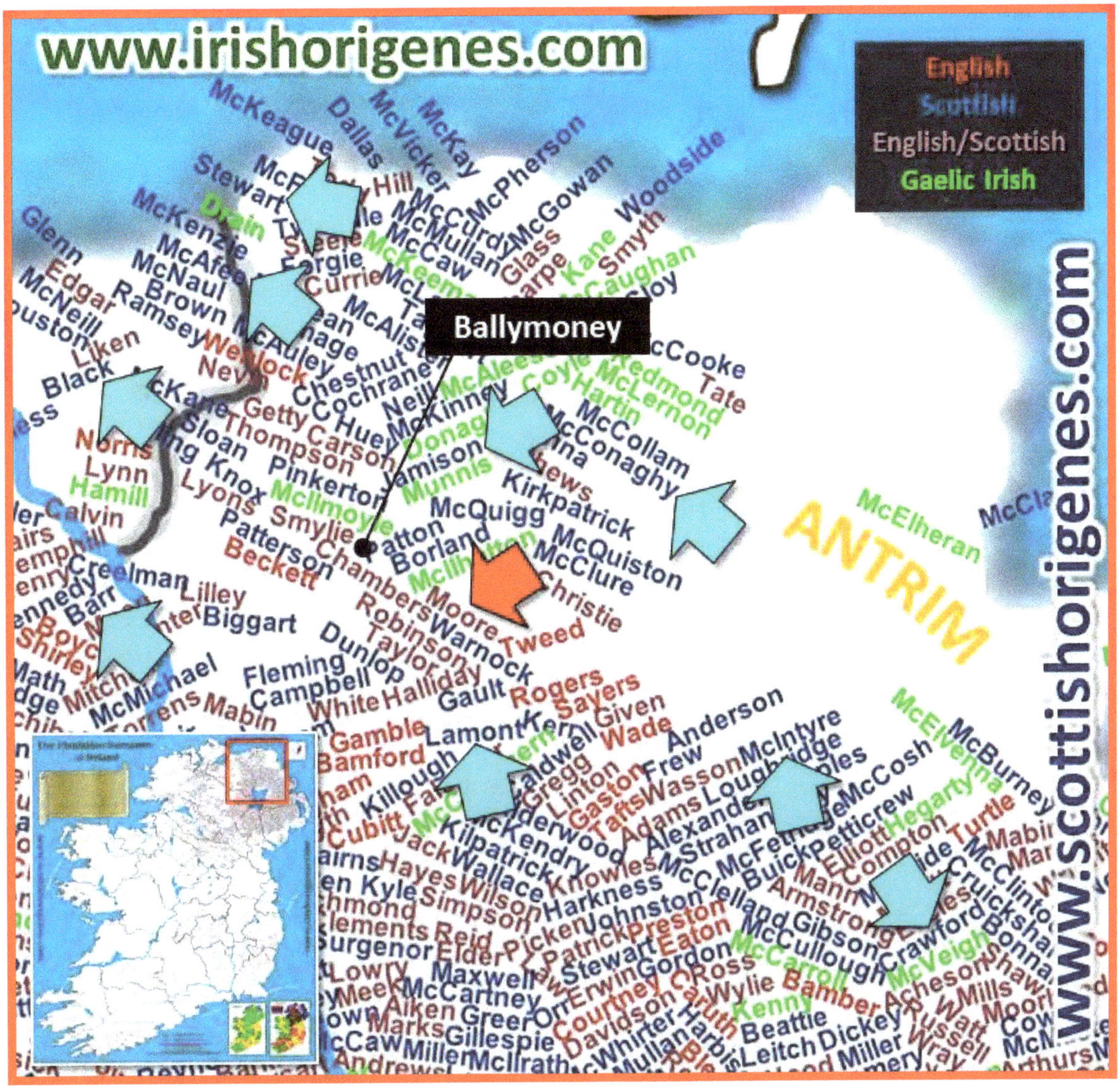

Figure 8: The Plantation surnames of Ballymoney. Antrim dominates among the ancestral detail revealed by the test subject's autosomal genetic relatives. North Antrim was an area heavily colonized by the Scots and English in the early 1600s, and an examination of the area surrounding Ballymoney town reveals Moore farmers (red arrow) surrounded by almost all of the surnames that are associated with the Isle of Bute (blue arrows). The results indicate that the Moores of Ballymoney originated from the Isle of Bute. Each surname is positioned in the location where farmers with that surname concentrate in early census data. The most common spelling is detailed.

Summary

The test subject's autosomal DNA results indicate a strong Scots Irish ancestral connection, and reveal that that link is most likely via the Plantation Moores of Ballymoney in North Antrim. Commercial ancestral DNA testing of Protestant Moores that farm in the area surrounding Ballymoney would conclusively confirm the ancestral link with that area.

APPENDIX 5

1630 Ulster Muster

1630 Ulster Muster

Vicky Jacobs Thu, Feb 25, 2021 at 12:32 PM
To: enquiry@uhf.org.uk

Dear Ulster Historical Foundation,

I am seeking a knowledgeable answer from people of authority. Do you think it may have been pssible for a man of the age of 74-76 years, along with two sons ages 52-56, to have been listed in the 1630 Ulster Muster Rolls? This family would have been living in Dunluce County on the Earl of Antrim's Estates PRE-PLANTATION and so would have been an older family than the average planters.
I am looking forward to hearing from you and thank you in advance for your assistance.

Kind regards,
Vicky Jacobs

Kathryn McKelvey <kathryn.mckelvey@uhf.org.uk> Wed, Mar 3, 2021 at 2:53 AM
To: Vicky Jacobs

Hi Vicky,

Thank you for your email. I have checked with our research Director who has advised me that in his opinion it is *possible* for a man in his mid 70's to appear in the muster roll, assuming he was in reasonable health, and that he may well have had two sons listed who were in their 50's.

When he checked further in the Muster Rolls, he found the following:
-The men who mustered should have been able-bodied and aged 16-60.
-However, there are instances of older men appearing.
-The older men identified for certain were leading tenants who appeared without arms, though this need not necessarily be the case in every instance.
-Settlers in North Antrim and County Down appear to have been about 5-10 years older than those in other Ulster Counties.
-It is also possible that the original settler and one of his grandsons had the same forename.
-Therefore, rather than the original settler and his sons, it could be the son, a grandson, and either another son or a second grandson.

I hope this answers your query.

Many thanks,

Kathryn McKelvey
kathryn@uhf.org.uk
Accounts Manager
Ulster Historical Foundation
Bradley Thallon House
44D Kiltonga House
Newtownards
Co. Down BT23 4TJ

www.ancestryireland.com

APPENDIX 6

Reconstructing the Moore Ancient Paternal Ancestral Journey

by Dr. Tyrone Bowes,

9 Jun 2017

The Moore Ancient Paternal Ancestral Journey

Reconstructing the Moore Ancient Paternal Ancestral Journey

www.irishorigenes.com
www.scottishorigenes.com
www.englishorigenes.com
www.welshorigenes.com

Dr Tyrone Bowes
19/06/2017

Dr Tyrone Bowes (tyronebowes@gmail.com)

The Moore Ancient Paternal Ancestral Journey

INTRODUCTION

The more Y-DNA genetic markers (STRs) or mutations (SNPs) that two people share the more recent their common male ancestor once lived. In this manner, the genetic surname matches that appear at the 67 and 37 Y-DNA STR marker levels in one's commercial ancestral Y-DNA test results will typically reflect ones ancestral neighbours from the time when paternally inherited surnames became common (which was approximately 1,000 years ago in the Britain and Ireland). But the Y-DNA test results also reveals many more people who share less Y-DNA STR genetic markers, which reflect shared paternal ancestry prior to the appearance of surnames, and it is those genetic relatives that can reveal clues as to one's *ancient* paternal ancestral journey.

To reconstruct Mr Moore's ancient paternal ancestral journey his FTDNA Y-DNA STR results were uploaded to the Ysearch.org database and the match criteria lowered to reveal additional genetically matching individuals. Many of these new matches reveal details of the geographical origin of their earliest known paternal ancestor, see **Figure 1**. By plotting those ancestral locations, and sorting the test subject's ysearch genetic matches according to the *estimated* number of shared genetic markers, one can begin to reconstruct Mr Moore's ancient (pre-surname) paternal ancestral journey, see **Figure 2**.

Mr Moore's Ancient Eastern European origin

The test subject's Ysearch.org genetic relatives are *NOT RANDOM*; the paternal ancestral locations revealed by his Ysearch.org genetic relatives are limited almost exclusively to Great Britain, Scandinavia, Central and Eastern Europe, see **Figure 2**. It is within the Steppes of Western Russia where the test subject's most distant genetic relatives record their earliest paternal ancestors, and it was there that his paternal ancestral journey as recorded by his commercial ancestral Y-DNA test results began, see **Figure 2**. It was there, almost certainly along the banks of the Voronezh River, that the R1a1a mutation first appeared in the test subject's direct male ancestor approximately 5,800 years ago, see **Figure 2** and **3**. His paternal ancestors spread westward, most likely in waves, some taking a route that led to Bohemia in the modern Czech Republic in Central Europe, while others took a northerly route into Pomerania in modern Poland, see **Figure 2** and **3**.

Dr Tyrone Bowes (tyronebowes@gmail.com)

Ysearch.org Matches							
Surname	**User ID**	**Origin**	**Haplogroup**	**Tested With**	**Markers Compared**	**Genetic Distance**	**Estimated shared markers**
Newton	JXQ74	Bury St. Mary, Suffolk County, England	Unknown	Family Tree DNA	44	6	38
MacEachern	VWQPW	Argyllshire, Scotland	R1a1*	GeneTree	50	4	36
MACDONALD	79QAJ	Western Isles, Scotland	Unknown	Family Tree DNA	25	2	23
MacDonald	MRNBR	Skye, Uist, Western Isles, Scotland	Unknown	Family Tree DNA	27	4	23
Howell	AKE7P	[illegible], Wales	Unknown	Family Tree DNA	25	3	22
McArthur	6QXRU	Isle of Mull, Argyllshire, Scotland	Unknown	Other - Genebase	27	5	22
Hawthorne	B943D	Greenagh, Drumsnatt, Monaghan, Ireland	R1a1a (tested)	Family Tree DNA	27	5	22
Kalbac	NF5ET	Blatna, Bohemia, Austro-Hungarian Empire	Unknown	Family Tree DNA	25	4	21
MacNeil	DJN8K	Barra, Scotland	Unknown	Family Tree DNA	25	4	21
Kielec	YB5M2	Padew, Poland	R1a1a1 (tested)	Family Tree DNA	25	4	21
Jamieson	W8VK6	Sandness, Shetland Isles, Scotland	R1a1 (tested)	Family Tree DNA	25	4	21
Blance	923CK	[illegible], Shetland Isles, Scotland	Unknown	Family Tree DNA	25	5	20
David	HTR8N	Velechvin, Böhmen/Bohemia, Austria	Unknown	Family Tree DNA	25	5	20
Konczak	8PGU6	MORZEWO, Poland	Unknown	Family Tree DNA	25	5	20
Parker	KADA3	Waddington, Yorkshire, England	Unknown	Ancestry.com	26	6	20
Ramberg	J6K28	[illegible], Nord-Trøndelag, Norway	Unknown	Family Tree DNA	25	5	20
Ruhrdanz	ZWMYD	Friedland, Germany	Unknown	Family Tree DNA	25	5	20
Norum	JA6J3	Nord-Trøndelag, Norway	R1b1a (tested)	Family Tree DNA	25	5	20
O'Connor	R3U94	Hastings, East Sussex, England	R1a1a (tested)	Family Tree DNA	25	5	20
SZOZDA	F58DH	plesnikow, Galicia/Galizien/Halychyna, Austria	R1a1a (tested)	Family Tree DNA	25	5	20
Caine	U4865	ISLE OF MAN, Isle of Man, United Kingdom	R1a1 (tested)	Family Tree DNA	25	5	20
Panzer	WGGR7	Pomerania/Pommern, Germany	R (tested)	Family Tree DNA	25	5	20
Bonsiden	VQJ96	Buckeburg, Germany	Unknown	Family Tree DNA	25	6	19
Boric	5PGHN	Balan Potok, Austro-Hungarian Empire	Unknown	Family Tree DNA	25	6	19
Greer	PXRZX	Isle of Man, England	Unknown	Family Tree DNA	25	6	19
Cinkovic	CFSU7	Gorski Kotar, Croatia	Unknown	Family Tree DNA	25	6	19
Eagen	XKFX2	Moymore, Clare, Ireland	Unknown	Family Tree DNA	25	6	19
Faber	HECZC	Bialystok, Poland	Unknown	Family Tree DNA	25	6	19
Gryszkiewicz	8RPC4	Hrodno, Belarus	Unknown	Family Tree DNA	25	6	19
Johansen	4X5NH	Gildeskål, Nordland, Norway	Unknown	Family Tree DNA	25	6	19
Knizhik	HPFSW	Gornostopol, Ukraine	Unknown	Family Tree DNA	25	6	19
⋮	⋮	⋮	⋮	⋮	⋮	⋮	⋮
Tschantz	PWKGA	Langnau im Emmental, Switzerland	R1a1 (tested)	Family Tree DNA	12	2	10
Udovich	QJPFZ	[illegible], Slovenia	R1a1 (tested)	Family Tree DNA	12	2	10
Dragan Stefan	F77G4	Beograd, Serbia	R1a*	Family Tree DNA	15	5	10
Gasparik	NDA2U	[illegible], Slovakia	R1a*	Other - DNAtest.sk	16	6	10
Guild	2WQ7D	[illegible], Scotland	R1a*	…r - DNA Solutions Pt…	12	2	10
Kaufer	WQ422	[illegible], Czech Republic	R1a*	Other	16	6	10
Holen	E3NN6	[illegible], Czechoslovakia	R1a*	…er - Forenzni DNA se…	16	6	10
Jakubcin	VX5BX	[illegible], Slovakia	R1a*	Other - DNAtest s.r.o	16	6	10
Kucerka	HFRXM	[illegible], Romania	R1a*	Other - Genomia	12	2	10
Nekipelyy	J79BU	Karlovka, Ukraine	R1a*	Other	16	6	10
Polak	5WTKW	[illegible], Slovakia	R1a*	Other	16	6	10
Vodochodsky	WGHEQ	[illegible], Czechoslovakia	R1a*	- Geneticka laborat…	16	6	10
Vrsnik	UDUJ2	Prag, Czech Republic	R1a*	Other - Genebase	16	6	10
Zamecnik	YCH6B	[illegible], Czechoslovakia	R1a*	Other - Dr. Vanek	16	6	10
Matic	N2B8P	[illegible], Bosnia and Herzegovina	R1a (tested)	Family Tree DNA	12	2	10
Kibirov	TQHM4	Kashgar, China	R1*	Family Tree DNA	12	2	10
VENDRUSCOLO	QTVJ7	Rivarotta di Pasiano, Italy	R (tested)	Family Tree DNA	12	2	10
Berka	8297A	[illegible], Slovakia	Unknown	Family Tree DNA	12	3	9
Dovcik	X5YBP	[illegible], Slovakia	Unknown	…er - http://genebase	15	6	9
Felli	FABUQ	Scandriglia, Perugia, Italy	Unknown	Other - SMGF	13	4	9
KuchaÅ™	V8UJ3	[illegible], Czech Republic	Unknown	GenetickÃ¡ laborato…	15	6	9
Leda	9FKHA	[illegible], Poland	Unknown	Other	15	6	9
Zheng	F5845	Taiwan, Province of China	Unknown	…her - Fudan Univers…	14	5	9
Fetisov	RMTJ7	Bryansk, Russia	R1a1a*	Other - Gentis	15	6	9
Leone	8RNKM	Sicily	R1a1a (tested)	Family Tree DNA	12	3	9
Meisser	8KR85	Sachsen-Altenburg/Saxe-Altenburg, Germany	R1a1a (tested)	Family Tree DNA	12	3	9
Borstad	4TFKX	Fortun, Sogn og Fjordane, Norway	R1b1*	…) - University of Leice…	15	6	9
Bednar	K8UAP	[illegible], Czechoslovakia	R1a*	Other - DNAtest s.r.o	15	6	9
Godin	54QBY	[illegible], France	R1a*	Other - dna.com	15	6	9
KLUDT	R9ZTH	Almaty, Kazakhstan	R1a*	Other	15	6	9
Seps	JE5NG	[illegible], Czech Republic	R1a*	…ther - genetic biotech…	15	6	9
Zinsheimer-Ivanovic	989F2	[illegible], Croatia	R1a (tested)	Family Tree DNA	12	3	9
Chronister	N3K5B	Wolfsassing, Lower Austria/Niederösterreich, Austria	Unknown	Other - sgmf.org	14	6	8
TkÃ¡Ä	KJ5Z3	[illegible]	Unknown	Family Tree DNA	14	6	8

Scotland
England
Wales
Ireland
Northern Europe
Central Europe
Eastern Europe
Western Europe

***Figure 1**: Snapshot of Mr Moore's genetic matches as revealed in the Ysearch.org database. By uploading the test subject's Y-DNA results to the Ysearch database and dropping the match criteria it revealed over 300 genetic relatives who reveal details (village, town or county plus Country) of their earliest known paternal ancestral origins; which can be sorted according to the number of estimated shared genetic markers (**far right panel**). Individuals with recorded ancestors within the Americas, within early 19th Century cities, or with Plantation-settlement in Northern Ireland are excluded from analysis; as they are the result of recent migration. The test subject's closest genetic relatives in the ysearch database are dominated by individuals with recorded ancestral links with Scotland, while more distant genetic relatives record ancestral links with mainland Europe.*

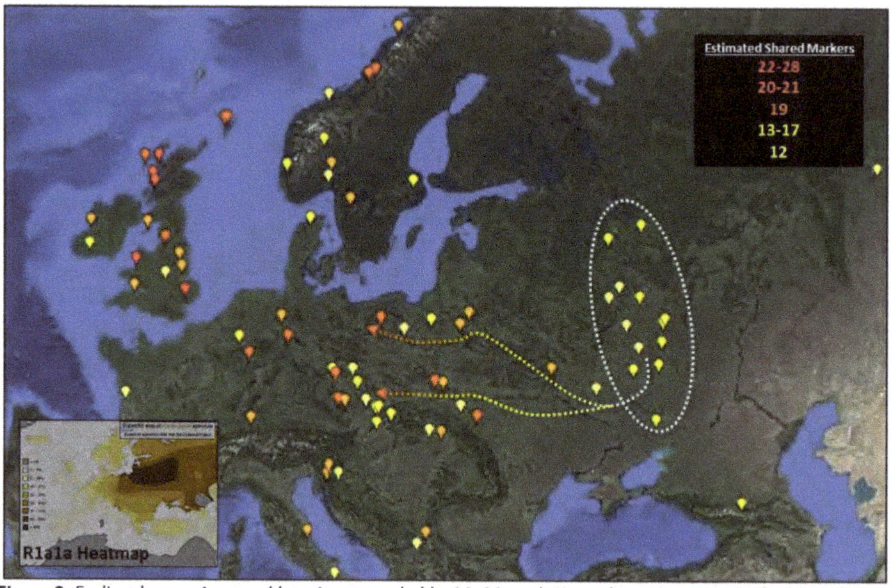

***Figure 2**: Earliest known Ancestral locations revealed by Mr Moore's Ysearch.org genetic matches. Distribution mapping of Mr Moore's Ysearch matches reveals that his most distant genetic relatives record ancestral links within the Steppes of Western Russia (white broken circle) where his R1a1a Haplogroup is believed to have appeared in a single male approximately 5,800 years ago. His ancient paternal ancestors spread west into Central Europe.*

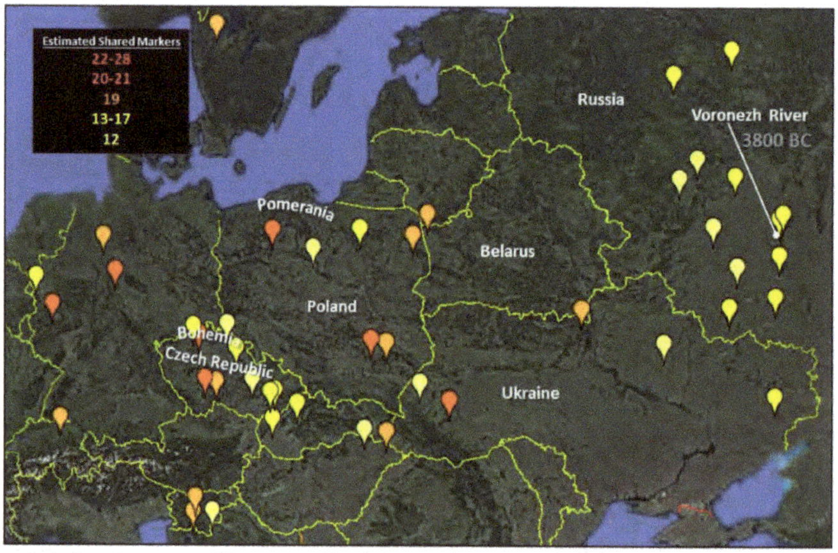

***Figure 3**: A closer inspection of the ancestral locations revealed by the test subject ysearch.org genetic matches reveals his most distant relatives with recorded ancestral links along the River Voronezh. More recent relatives reveal links with Pomerania in modern Northern Poland and Bohemia in the modern Czech Republic. This indicates that R1a1a males spread in at least two separate waves into Central Europe; north into Pomerania, and south into Bohemia.*

Mr Moore's Viking Origin

The test subject's paternal ancestors took the northern route into Pomerania and spread along the coast of modern Poland and Germany into Denmark, before making the short crossing into the modern borderlands of Norway and Sweden, where a small cluster of genetic relatives record their earliest paternal ancestral locations, see **Figure 4**. His paternal ancestors spread north along the Norwegian coast, and by the beginning of Europe's Viking Age in 793AD, they were living on the banks of River Namsen, see **Figure 4**. His paternal ancestor left the Namsen River valley area of Central Norway to participate in the Norse conquest of Great Britain and Ireland, and by the dawn of the appearance of surnames in 1000AD his paternal ancestor had settled on the Isle of Bute where he had aquired the 'Muir' surname.

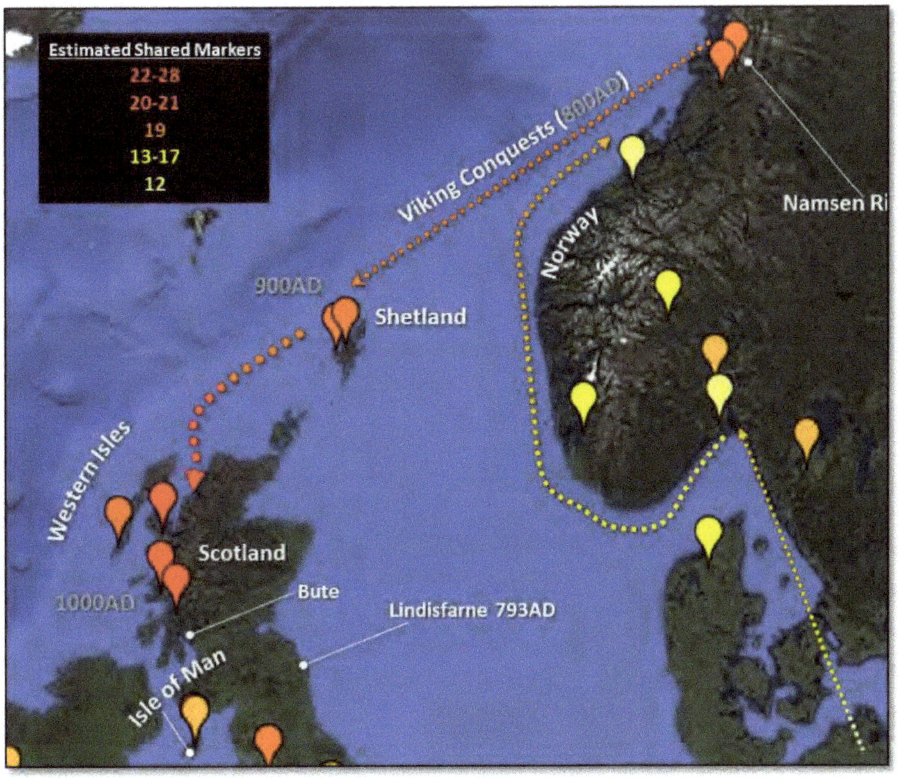

Figure 4: *Viking Conquests. The test subject's paternal ancestors spread from Pomerania into Southern Norway before spreading along the Norwegian coast, eventually settling in the Namsen River valley. At the dawn of Europe's Viking era, his paternal ancestor left Norway and eventually settled on the Isle of Bute where he acquired the 'Muir' surname.*

SUMMARY OF MR MOORE'S PATERNAL ANCESTRAL JOURNEY

Mr Moore's Y-DNA results indicate that his paternal ancestral journey as recorded by his Y-DNA results began on the banks of the River Voronezh in modern Russia approximately 5,800years ago. His paternal ancestors gradually spread west into Central Europe. While some of his paternal genetic relatives spread south into what would become Bohemia, his paternal ancestors spread north into what is today known as Pomerania, before spreading up along the cost into Scandinavia. By the dawn of the Viking Age (790AD) his paternal ancestors were living along the banks of the Namsen River in Central Norway before venturing west and settling in Shetland. From Shetland, they spread southwest conquering and settling along Scotland's west coast. By 1000AD his paternal ancestor had settled permanently on the Isle of Bute where he acquired the 'Muir' surname.

APPENDIX 7

Kings and Queens of Scotland and England

(Britannica 2018)

Reign	Name
843-858	Kenneth I MacAlpin
858-862	Donald I
862-877	Constantine I
877-878	Aed (Aodh)
878-889	Eochaid (Eocha) and Giric (Ciric)
889-900	Donald II
900-943	Constantine II
943-954	Malcolm I
954-962	Indulf
962-966	Dub
966-971	Culen
971-995	Kenneth II
955-997	Constantine III
997-1005	Kenneth III
1005-1034	Malcolm II
1034-1040	Duncan I
1040-1057	Macbeth
1057-1058	Lulach
1058-1093	Malcolm III Canmore
1093-1094	Donald Bane (Donalbane)
1093-1094	Duncan II
1094-1097	Donald Bane (restored)
1097-1107	Edgar
1107-1124	Alexander I
1124-1153	David I
1153-1165	Malcolm IV
1165-1214	William I the Lion
1214-1249	Alexander II
1249-1286	Alexander III
1286-1290	Margaret, Maid of Norway

Reign	Name
1306-1329	Robert I the Bruce
1329-1371	David II

The House of Stewart (Stuart)

1371-1290	Robert II
1390-1406	Robert III
1406-1437	James I
1437-1460	James II
1460-1488	James III
1488-1513	James IV
1513-1542	James V
1542-1567	Mary, Queen of Scots

King of Scotland, England and Ireland

1567-1625	James VI & I
1625-1649	Charles I

The Commonwealth

1653-1658	*Oliver Cromwell*
1658-1659	*Richard Cromwell*

The King restored

1660-1685	Charles II
1685-1688	James II
1688-1702	William III (of Orange)
1688-1694	& Queen Mary

Kings of Norway

(Wikipedia Contributors 2021)

Reign	Name
~872-932	*Harald Fairhair*
~932-934	*Eric Bloodaxe*
~934-960	*Haakon the Good*
~961-970	*Harald Greycloak*
970-995	Haakon Sigurdsson
995-1000	Olaf I Tryggvason
1000-1015	Eric Haakonsson
1015-1028	Olaf II Haraldsson
1028-1035	Cnut the Great
1035-1047	*Magnus the Good*
1046-1066	*Harald Hardrada*
1066-1069	Magnus II Haraldsson
1067-1093	Olaf III Haraldsson
1093-1095	*Haakon Toresfostre*
1093-1103	*Magnus Barefoot*
1103-1115	Olaf IV Magnusson
1103-1123	Eystein I Magnusson
1103-1130	*Sigurd the Crusader*
The Civil War Era 1130-1240	
Several Fought for Power	
1130-1135	*Magnus the Blind*

Reign	Name
1130-1136	Harald IV Magnusson
1136-1155	Sigurd II Haraldsson
1136-1161	Inge I Haraldsson
1142-1157	Eystein II Haraldsson
1142-1145	Magnus V Haraldsson
1157-1162	Haakon II Sigurdsson
1161-1184	Magnus V Erlingsson
1184-1202	Sverre Sigurdsson
1202-1204	Haakon III Sverresson
1204	Guttorm Sigurdsson
1204-1217	Inge II Bardsson
1217-1263	Haakon IV Haakonsson *Haakon the Old*
1240-1257	Haakon V Haakonsson
1257-1280	Magnus VI Haakonsson
1273-1299	Eric II Magnusson
1299-1319	Haakon V Magnusson
1319-1343	Magnus VII Eriksson
1343-1380	Haakon VI Magnusson
1380-1387	Olaf IV Haakonsson

Lords [Kings] of the Isles

(Wikipedia Contributors 2021)

Rulers of the Hebrides and Man

Reign	Name
1098-1102	Magnus Barelegs
1102-1103	Sigurd Magnusson
1103-1110	Lagmann Godredsson
1111-1112	Domnall mac Taidc Ui Briain
1112-1152	Olave the Red
1154-1156	Godred the Black
1156-1158	Somerled's sons & Godred the Black
1158-1164	Somerled *His dominion covered 25,000 square miles and more than 500 islands.*

Kings of Man and the North Isles

Reign	Name
1164	Reginald
1164-1187	Godred the Black
1188-1226	Ragnvald
1226-1237	Olaf the Black
1230	Ospakr-Hakon
1230	Gofraid Donn
1237-1248	Harald Olafsson
1249	Ragnvald Olafsson
1249-1250	Harald Godredsson
1252-1265	Magnus Olafsson

Kings of the South Isles (Sudreys); titles of various islands were shared by the family of Somerled

Reign	Name
1164-*c.*1175	Dugald, son of Somerled
1164-1207	Ranald, son of Somerled
?-*c.*1244	Duncan, son of Dugald
?	Dugald Screech, son of Dugald
?-1230	Somerled, son of Dugald

Reign	Name
1207?-1247?	Ruari (Ruaidhri), son of Ranald
1248-1263	Ewen of Argyll, son of Duncan
1249-1266	Dugald MacRuaidhri

APPENDIX 8

List of Some Gunners of Dover Castle, Archcliffe Fort and Moate's Bulwark

In an effort to honor Edward Moore and the gunners of Dover Castle in the 17th century, I have compiled a list of the gunners' names along with their known dates.

This list of gunners was extracted from BritishHistory.ac.uk Calendar of State Papers which are preserved in the State Paper Department of Her Majesty's Public Record Office, Great Britain.

Calendars are chronological lists of documents or manuscripts. The calendars themselves are often full enough to serve as good substitutes for the complete manuscripts. At present, most all important original archives have been consolidated and are held at the National Archives at Kew in Richmond, near London, since 1996. An example of a good Calendar excerpt is that of 5 October 1623 listed below:

> *Oct. 5. Dover Castle. 21. Wm., Eldred, Master Gunner of Dover Castle, to the same. The room adjoining Arthur's Hall, the wall above the well tower, and the kitchen chimneys of the castle are blown down. The church steeple has partly fallen, and if his Lordship had not, at his own cost, put in a new beam, and repaired the roof, it would all have been down this winter. A small cost now would prevent much mischief that is likely to happen. (British History Online 1859)*

In the early 1600's, the gunners were chosen from amongst local men by the castle warden. Lord Zouch, in 1618, made official order to gunners that they must "reside at their posts" (British History Online 1858) Lord Zouch was Lord Warden of the Cinque Ports from 1615–1624; then the post was taken over by the Duke of York.

During the Commonwealth, 1649–1660, gunners were mentioned being used for war ships, but never by name. In general, no mentions were made of gunners at castles or forts.

After the Restoration of Charles II in 1660, decisions for the position of gunners were made in London at Whitehall, Windsor, by the Ordnance Board or by the King himself.

Gunner	Date	Source	#	Notes Mentioned in State Papers
Allison, Thomas	1687-89	JII, Gen. Index A		late gunner in Archcliffe Fort [d. before 19 Nov 1687]
Barker, James	2 Nov 1615	JI, vol. 83, 1611-18		for captaincy of the Bulwark's at Dover, for life
Beeching, John	30 June 1673	ChII, vol. -, 1673		in place of Wm. Burneley, deceased. Order: Whitehall
Brand, John	Jul-Sep 1683	ChII, Gen. Index B		deceased
Brown, John	11 Dec 1615	JI, vol. 84, 1611-18		
Burnell, James	Jul-Sep 1683	ChII, Gen. Index B		deceased
Chesterman, Rog	27 Dec 1625	ChI, vol. 12 Dec 17-31	Dom.	in place of John Chesman
Cook, James	Dec 1618	JI, vol. 104, 1611-18	#115	of Dover. Pet. Lord Zouch for pos. in DC or bulwark
Copper, Thomas	Dec 1618	JI, vol. 104, 1611-18	#117	of Dover. Pet. Lord Zouch for pos. in DC or bulwark
Crowde, David	1687-89	JII, Gen. Index C		late gunner in Dover Castle
Crumpe, John	Dec 1618	JI, vol. 104, 1611-18	#118	of Dover. Pet. Lord Zouch for position in Dover Castle
Deacon, James	1687-89	JII, Gen. Index D		late gunner in Dover Castle [d. before 25 Mar 1688]
Eldred, William	5 Oct 1624	JI, vol. 173, 1623-5		for DC repairs after big storm. Master Gunner, est. 1613
Ford, John	Jul-Sep 1683	ChII, Gen. Index F		
Frank, William	1683-84	ChII, Gen. Index F		gunner at Archcliffe Fort
Fryer, John	1683-84	ChII, Gen. Index F		gunner at Dover Castle
Gillet, Nicholas	1687-89	JII, Gen. Index G		late gunner in Dover Castle [d. bef. 19 Nov 1687]
Ginings, Joseph	21 Dec 1631	ChI, vol. 203, 1631-3	#1261	
Graunt, Edward	Dec 1618	JI, vol. 104, 1611-18	#123	petition to Lord Zouch for a position in Dover Castle
Hales, Robert	Dec 1618	JI, vol. 104, 1611-18	#124	petition to Lord Zouch for a position in Dover Castle
Hamond, Thomas	19 Nov 1687	JII, vol. 3, 1687-9	#534	in the place of Nicholas Gillet
Harris, William	Dec 1618	JI, vol. 104, 1611-18	#125	petition to Lord Zouch for a position in Dover Castle
Harvery, Thomas	Dec 1617	JI, vol. 94, 1611-18	#118/9	to share lodging at DC with gunner, William Hales
Harvey, Thomas	Oct 1615	JI, vol. 82, 1611-18	#10	of Ilthorne, pet. for gunner's place, is willing to become res.

Gunner	Date	Source	#	Notes Mentioned in State Papers
Hobday, Robert	13 Nov 1615	JI, vol. 83, 1611-18		now deceased, gunner
Hogbeane,Wm	Dec 1618	JI, vol. 104, 1611-18	#118	of Folkestone. Pet. Lord Zouch for pos. in Dover Castle
Hopkins, Thomas	25 Mar 1688	JII, vol. 3, 1687-9	#939	in place of James Deacon
Hugett, John	6 Feb 1690	Wm & Mary 1689-90		in the room of John Crayden. Order from Whitehall.
Hunt, Nicholas	19 Sep 1686	JII, vol. 2, 1686-7		gunner DC in place of Edw. Moore, dcd. [d. bef. 1687-9]
Knott, Nicholas	27 Jan 1617	JI, vol. 90, 1611-18		
Lambe, James	29 Aug 1689	Wm & Mary 1689-90		in the room of Thomas Hamond, Dover Castle
Lambe, John	26 Mar 1686	JII, vol. 2, 1686-7	#343	for gunner in Archcliffe Fort. Order from King.
Marsh, Richard	2 Dec 1689	Wm & Mary 1689-90		in the room of Thomas Hopkins
Moore, Edward	1686-87	JII, Gen. Index M		late gunner in Dover Castle [d. bef. 19 Sep 1686]
Nipe, John	1 Apr 1687	JII, vol. 2, 1686-7	#1635	for gunner in Archcliffe Fort in place of John Lambe
Norwood, John	26 Mar 1686	JII, vol. 2, 1686-7	#343	in place of Peter Theobould, dcd. Order from King.
Oldfield, David	9 Jan 1690	Wm & Mary 1689-90		in room of James Deane. Order from Whitehall.
Owen, Robert	Oct 1615	JI, vol. 82, 1611-18	#11	of Dover, in place of brother Rich. Austen, non-res.
Partridge, Rand.	Dec 1618	JI, vol. 104, 1611-18	#134	succeeded David Fidge
Partridge, Tho.	5 Oct 1624	JI, vol. 173, 1623-5	#143	
Poker, Mathew	27 Jan 1617	JI, vol. 90, 1611-18		[& 1620]
Powell, John	21 Dec 1686	JII, vol. 2, 1686-7	#1261	in place of Richard Theobald
Rawlines, Tho.	1 Apr 1687	JII, vol. 2, 1686-7	#1634	in the room of Richard Theobald and John Norwood
Raymond, Tho.	11 Dec 1615	JI, vol. 84, 1611-18		
Saunders, Anth.	29 Nov 1631	ChI, vol. 203, 1631-3		gunner of Dover Castle for 30 years
Scott, John	29 Aug 1689	Wm & Mary 1689-90		[d. before 21 Aug 1690]
Scott, John	19 Nov 1687	JII, vol. 3, 1687-89	#533	to Archcliffe Fort in the place of Thomas Allison
Scott, Richard	21 Aug 1690	Wm & Mary 1690-01		DC, in room of John Scott, dcd. Orders from Whitehall
Seymer, Samuel	Jul-Sep 1683	ChII, Gen. Index S		deceased

Gunner	Date	Source	#	Notes Mentioned in State Papers
Slater, William	1687-89	JII, Gen. Index S		gunner in Moate's Bulwark
Smith, Benjamin	1687-89	JII, Gen. Index S		gunner in Dover Castle
Smith, Peter	Dec 1618	JI, vol. 104, 1611-18	#138	petition to Lord Zouch for a position in Dover Castle
Smith, Thomas	21 Jul 1623-5	JI, vol. 149, 7/18-31		
Stewart, Alex.	8 Jan 1686	JII, vol. 3 1687-9	#16	
Stringer, Robert	Jul-Sep 1683	ChII, Gen. Index S		deceased
Sudell, Edward	4 Nov 1684	ChII, vol.-, 1684-5		in the place of William Wooley, deceased
Sutton, Stephen	12 Oct 1689	Wm & Mary 1689-90		in the room of John Tooth
Sweeting, John	Oct 1615	JI, vol. 82, 1611-18	#12	to Archcliffe in place of John Jagger, Lond. non-res.
Taylor, Robert	Dec 1618	JI, vol. 104, 1611-18	#139	petition to Lord Zouch for a position in Dover Castle
Theobould, Peter	Jul-Sep 1683	ChII, Gen. Index T		admitted as gunner for Dover Castle
Tooth, John	17 Sep 1688	JII, vol. 13, 1687-89	#1511	as gunner in room of Nich. Hunt, dcd. Windsor
Turpin, Isaac	Dec 1618	JI, vol. 104, 1611-18	#140	petition to Lord Zouch for a position in Dover Castle
Watson, Nicholas	1683-84	ChII, Gen. Index W		warrant admitting him gunner Archcliffe Fort
Weele, Samuel	1683-84	ChII, Gen. Index W		late gunner in Moate's Bulwark
White, Alex	11 Dec 1615	JI, vol. 84, 1611-18		of Dover
Winter, Henry	1683-84	ChII, Gen. Index W		late gunner in Moate's Bulwark
Wooley, William	1684-85	ChII, Gen. Index W		gunner in Dover Castle [d. bef. 4 Nov 1684]
Woolve, Christop.	29 Aug 1689	Wm & Mary 1689-90		Archcliffe Fort
Worley, William	1683-84	ChII, Gen. Index W		late gunner in Dover Castle
Young, Thomas	11 Dec 1615	JI, vol. 84, 1611-18		of Dover, in place of Charles Crimble, in Ireland

Source: BHO | BRITISH HISTORY ONLINE https://www.british-history.ac.uk/cal-state-papers/domestic

GLOSSARY

Adventurers • Men who would advance money to meet the cost of the war in order to be repaid by the confiscated rebel estates.

Ballybetagh • A territorial unit controlled by an Irish sept (ruling family) usually containing around sixteen townlands. It was considered capable of supporting 300 cows and it contained 960 acres.

Balliboes • Roughly synonymous with Townland, Balliboes were economic units based on the amount of food the land would provide.

Board of Ordnance • A civilian body of great antiquity which was responsible for artillery and engineer services, commissariat duties and the provision of weapons and ammunition for both Army and Navy.

Card Money • Faced with a shortage of coins, the authorities of New France devised a novel system for payment. Card Money was used from 1685 to 1759. At first, the notes were made from playing cards; a denomination was written on the back of the card and it was signed by the Intendant and the Governor. These cards were redeemed for actual money when the king's ship arrived with the annual funds from France.

Clan • A family with political and legal functions descended from a single ancestor.

Creach • A cattle raid which included burning homes and taking portable goods.

Creaghts • A herd of cattle with its keepers. Irish moved their cattle into the mountains during the summer where they built temporary shelters.

Demesne • All the land retained and managed by a lord of the manor under the feudal system for his own use, occupation, or support.

Denization • A certificate one had to apply for and purchase through the English government which gave a person semi-equal footing as that of an English subject in Ireland.

Escheated lands • Confiscated lands.

Exchequer • The former government office responsible for collecting revenue and making payments on behalf of the sovereign, auditing official accounts, and trying legal cases relating to revenue.

Fief • An estate of land, especially one held on condition of feudal service.

Fosterage • A Gaelic custom whereby nobles committed the upbringing of their children to others with the aim of establishing a political connection.

Freeholders • Lease holders with subletting rights.

Gallowglass • A professional foot soldier, armed with double headed axe, originally from Scotland.

Garrison • The collective term for a body of troops stationed in a particular location, originally to guard it. A fortified military headquarters.

Gentleman of the Ordnance • A man who was described as something more than an ordinary soldier, had a little more pay, and does not stand guard; not an officer but was senior to a Master Gunner.

Glebe Lands • An area of cultivable lands belonging to a parish or Ecclesiastical benefice.

Kern • Irish Gaelic warriors who were from a poorer class than the galloglass and not as heavily armed and wore no helmets or chain mail.

Landwaiter • A customs officer in England who takes account of imports for purposes of taxation and watches over and certifies to the observance of the prescribed form in the shipping of exports.

Lordship • Territory ruled by a Gaelic lord; the mode of Gaelic rule; the duration of a Gaelic lord's rule.

Marshal of the Army • Head of the military establishment and commander of government forces in the absence of the lord deputy or provincial president.

Mattross- Soldier in the Train of Artillery, next in rank below the gunners; their duty is to assist the gunners in traversing, sponging, loading and firing of guns. They carry firelocks and march along with the store wagons, both as a guard and to help in case a wagon should break down.

Old English • Original Catholic Englishmen who settled in Ireland in the 1190's.

Privateering • Privately owned commissioned vessels which were armed to attack enemy ships, usually vessels of commerce. Governments used this method as their Navy. Privateering was carried on by all nations from the earliest times until the 19th century. Crews were not paid by the commissioning government but were entitled to cruise for their own profit, with crew members receiving portions of the value of any cargo or shipping that they could wrest from the original owners. From 1690, French privateers were particularly active against English commerce.

Reivers • Scottish Border occupants who raided English towns over the border and stole their cattle, burned the homes and carried off portable goods. They consisted of loyal yet smaller clans from the same districts who banded together to perform the creach.

Servitors • Men who had served the King in Ireland as soldiers or government officials; mostly veterans of the Nine Year's War. They received tracts of land in lieu of being paid throughout their service. Altogether the servitors received nearly 55,000 acres in lieu of back-pay owed in the Plantation counties. They were also allowed to buy up grants of Ulster land very cheaply. Most of them were granted estates of 1,000 –2,000 acres, although there were also settlers who only received as little as 200 acres. They could also buy land cheaply in order to fund war efforts.

Surrender and Regrant • A Gaelic Lord would surrender his Lordship to the king and then he would be given his lands back as a feudal fief and given a title. He had to promise to bring the people on his land under English rules and promise to send men from his estate to fight for the king.

Tanaiste • Designated successor in a Gaelic lordship.

Tates • Secular (non- religious) townlands.

Tuath - Tribal or Clan territory (anglicized as Tuogh).

Undertakers • Men who agreed to undertake the "planting" of British settlers on the estates they were given. They received the largest allocation of land in the Plantation Scheme.

Voyagers • The name given to men who had experience in the fur trade among the Indians.

Wood Kern • An armed peasant that lived in the woods.

REFERENCES

1868. *The National Gazetteer of Great Britain & Ireland.* Vol. 12. London: Virtue & Co.

Andra-Warner, Elle. 2009. *Hudson's Bay Company Adventures.* Toronto: Heritage House Publishing Company Ltd.

Arthur, Dorothy. 2008. *Ballymoney Old Church Graveyard.* Ballycastle: Impact Printing.

—. 2012. *Derrykeighan Old Church Graveyard.* Ballycastle: Impact Printing.

—. 2014. *Kilraughts Old Church Graveyard.* Ballycastle: Impact Printing.

Ascoli, David. 1983. *A Companion to the British Army 1660-1983.* London: Harrap Ltd.

Atherton, G. M. 2003. *Soldiers of the Castle, Dover Castle Garrisoned.* Dover: Triangle Publications.

Barker, Nigel. 1993. "The Building Practice of the English Board of Ordnance, 1680-1720." Chap. 15 in *English Architecture Public and Private; Essays for Kerry Downes*, edited by John Bold and Edward Chaney, 199-214. London: Hambledon Press.

Bassett, George Henry. 1888. *The Book of Antrim.* reprint: Books Ulster, 2002.

Bates, Zachary A. 2014. "James I and Britsh Identity: The Development of a British Identity from 1542-1689." *DISCOVERY: Georgia State Honors College Undergraduate Research Journal* 2. Accessed December 13, 2021. https://www.scholarworks.gsu.edu/discovery/vol2/iss1/2.

Baxter, Angus. 4th Edition 1999. *In Search of Your British & Irish Roots.* Genealogical Publishing Co,. Inc.

Beaty, Kristine G. 2009. *Finding the "Scot" in the Scottish-American: An Investigation of Scottish Identity through Mitochondrial DNA and Y-chromosome Markers.* Master's Thesis, University of Kansas: Academia.edu.

Bell, Robert. 2021. *The Book of Ulster Surnames.* Belfast: Ulster Historical Foundation.

Bennett, Thomas James Gilliland. 1974. *North Antrim Families.* Volturna Press.

Birch, ed. 1742. "A Collection of the State Papers of John Thurloe, Vol. 7, March 1658-May 1660." *British History Online.* Edited by Thomas Birch. Accessed April 29, 2020. http://www.british-history.ac.uk/thurloe-papers/vol7/pp204-211.

Biron, Herve. 1969, revised 1982. "Guillaume Gaillard." *Dictionary of Canadian Biography, vol. 2.* Toronto: University of Toronto/Universite Laval.

Borins, E. H. 1969, revised 1982. "Claude de Bermen de La Martiniere." *Dictionary of Canadian Biography, vol. 2.* Toronto: University of Toronto/Universite Laval. Accessed August 28, 2020. http://www.biographi.ca/en/bio/bermen_de_la_martiniere_claude_de_2E.html.

Borins, Edward Harold. 1968. *La Compagnie du Nord: 1682-1700.* Master's Thesis, Montreal: McGill University Press.

Bowes, Dr. Tyrone. 2019. *Eric Moore; An Autosomal DNA Case Study.* DNA Case Study, London: Dr. Tyrone Bowes.

Bowes, Dr. Tyrone. 2017. *Pinpointing the Moore Scottish Paternal Ancestral Genetic Homeland.* DNA Case Study, London: Dr. Tyrone Bowes.

Bowes, Dr. Tyrone. 2017. *Reconstructing the Moore Ancient Paternal Ancestral Journey.* DNA Case Study, London: Dr. Tyrone Bowes.

Bown, Stephen R. 2020. *The Company: The Rise and Fall of the Hudson's Bay Empire.* Toronto: Doubleday Canada.

Britannica, T. Editors of Encyclopaedia. 2018. "Kings and Queens of Scotland." *Encyclopedia Britannica.* October 2018. Accessed August 26, 2021. https://www.britannica.com/topic/Kings-and-Queens-of-Scotland-1856934.

British History Online. 1861. "Charles II - volume 62: November 1-15, 1662." *Calendar of State Papers Domestic: Charles II, 1661-2.* Edited by Mary Anne Everett Green. London: Her Majesty's Stationery Office. 538-59. Accessed April 11, 2020. http://www.british-history.ac.uk/cal-state-papers/domestic/chas2/1661-2/pp538-559.

—. 1913. "Entry Book: July 1679, 1-10." *Calendar of Treasury Books, Volume 6, 1679-1680.* Edited by William A. Shaw. London: His Majesty's Stationery Office. 116-126. Accessed August 17, 2020. http://www/british-history.ac.uk/cal-treasury-books/vol6/pp116-126.

British History Online. 1802. "House of Commons Journal Vol 7: 27 July 1659." *Journal of the House of Commons* (His Majesty's Stationery Office) (1651-1660): 734-36. Accessed April 11, 2020. http://www.british-history.ac.uk/commons-jml/vol7/pp734-736.

British History Online. 1802. "House of Commons Journal Vol 8: 29 June 1660." *Journal of the House of Commons* (His Majesty's Stationary Office) (1660-1667): 77-78. Accessed April 11, 2020. http://www.british-history.ac.uk/commons-jrnl/vol8/pp77-78.

—. 1858. "James I - volume 104: December 1618." *Calendar of State Papers Domestic: James I, 1611-18.* Edited by Mary Anne Everett Green. London: Her Majesty's Stationery Office. 599-614. Accessed August 13, 2020. http://www.british-history.ac.uk/cal-state-papers/domestic/jas1/1611-18/pp599-614.

—. 1859. "James I - volume 173: October 1624." *Calendar of State Papers Domestic: James I, 1623-25.* Edited by Mary Anne Everett Green. London: Her Majesty's Stationery Office. 347-369. Accessed August 7, 2020. http://www.british-history.ac.uk/cal-state-papers/domestic/jas1/1623-5/pp347-369.

—. 1972. "James II - volume 3: September 1688." *Calendar of State Papers Domestic: James II, 1687-9.* Edited by E. K. Timings. London: Her Majesty's Stationery Office. 261-291. Accessed January 19, 2021. http://www.british-history.ac.uk/cal-state-papers/domestic/jas2/1687-9/pp261-291.

—. 1911. "January 1648: An Ordinance for Constituting a Committee of Militia within the Hamblets of the Tower of London." *Acts and Ordinances of the Interregnum, 1642-1660.* Edited by C.H. Firth and R.S. Rait. London: His Majesty's Stationery Office. 1057-58. Accessed August 6, 2020. http://www.british-history.ac.uk/no-series/acts-ordinances-interregnum/pp1057-1058.

—. 1998. "Stepney: Early Stepney." *A History of the County of Middlesex: Volume 11, Stepney, Bethnal Green.* London: Victoria County History. Accessed June 13, 2021.

C. H. Firth, LL.D. 1902. "Royalist and Cromwellian Armies in Flanders, 1657-1662." *Transactions of the Royal Historical Society.* London: Offices of the Society. 67-110.

Case on behalf of the Right Honourable Edith Maud, Countess of Loudoun...and Hastings, in the Peerage of England. 1870. 21851 c 41 (House of Lords, 25, Abingdon Street, Westminster, S.W.).

Cavendish, Richard. 2007. "The Flight of the Earls." *History Today*, Spetember 9: 7. https://www.historytoday.com/archive/fight-earls.

1637-47. *Census Substitutes for Co. Derry.* Accessed Nov 21, 2018. http://rootsireland.ie/derry.

Champion, Justin. 1993. "Epidemics and the Built Environment in 1665; The annual Bill of Mortality for London and its environs, 1665." *Epidemic Disease in London*, 35-52. Accessed April 12, 2020. http://www.archives.history.ac.uk/history-in-focus/medical/epichamp.html.

Champion, Justin. 1993. *Epidemics and the Built Environment in 1665.* Online Working Paper Series, London: Centre for Metropolitan History, No. 1, pp.35-52.

Charles Dalton, F.R.G.S., ed. 1892. *English Army Lists and Commission Registers, 1661-1714.* Vol. 1. London: Eyre & Spottiswoode.

Charles Harding Firth, M.A. 1909. *The Last Years of the Protectorate, Vol. 1 1656-1657.* London: Longmans, Green & Co.

n.d. *Clan Muir.* Accessed August 21, 2019. http://www.1066.co.nz/Mosaic%20DVD/whoswho/text/Clan_Muir%5B1%5D.htm.

1999. *Clan Muir Society.* Accessed November 8, 2019. http://www.clanmuirsociety.org.

Clowes, Markham, Mahan, Wilson, Roosevelt and Laughton. 1898. *The Royal Navy: A History from the Earliest Times to the Present, Vol. 2.* London: S. Low, Marston and Company, Limited.

Colonel C. Field, R.M. 1935. "The Soldiers of Cromwell's "New Model" at the Battle of Dunkirk, 1658." *Journal of the Society for Army Historical Research* (Society for Army Historical Research) 14 (54): 102-108.

Cournoyer, Jean. 2021 edition. *La Memoire du Quebec online.* Accessed August 6, 2021. https://www.memoireduquebec.com/wiki/index.php?title=Beaumont_(municipalite).

Cuarta, Brian Mac. 2007. "Religious Violence Against Settlers in South Ulster, 1641-2." Chap. 7 in *Age of Atrocity; Violence and Political Conflict in Early Modern Ireland*, edited by Padraig Lenihan & Clodagh Tait David Edwards, 154-175. Dublin: Four Courts Press LTD.

Dalton, Charles, ed. 1892. *English Army Lists and Commission Registers, 1661-1714.* Vols. 1, 1661-1685. London: Eyre & Spottiswoode.

Davies, J. D. 2017. *Kings of the Sea.* Barnsley: Seaforth Publishing.

Denissen, The Rev. Fr. Christian. 1987. *Genealogy of the French Families of the Detroit River Region.* Revision 1701-1936. Edited by PhD Harold Frederic Powell. Vol. II. Detroit: Detroit Society for Genealogical Research.

Duane, William. 1810. *A Military Dictionary; An Explanation of the Several Systems of Discipline of Different Kinds of Troops, Infantry, Artillery and Cavalry.* Philadelphia: William Duane.

Duffy, Sean. 1991. *The 'Continuation' of Nicholas Trevet: A New Source for the Bruce Invasion.* Dublin Institute, School of Celtic Studies report, Dublin: Proceedings of the Royal Irish Academy, Vol. 91c, 303-315.

Duncan, Major Francis. 1879. *History of the Royal Regiment of Artillery; Compiled from the Original Records* . Third. Vol. I. II vols. London: John Murray.

Edwards, Nancy. 1999. *The Archaeology of Early Medieval Ireland.* New York: Routledge.

Erck, John Caillard, ed. 1851. *A Repertory of the Inrolments on the Patent Rolls of Chancery in Ireland, Commencing with the Reign of King James I.* . Vol. 1. Dublin: J. M'Glashan. http://catalog.hathitrust.org/Record/008403135.

Estes, Roberta. 2019. "2019: The Year and Decade of Change." *DNAeXplained - Genetic Genealogy.* December 31. Accessed January 2, 2022. https://www.dna-explained.com.

—. 2021. "Clock is Ticking : In 28 days, Ancestry can do anthing they want with Every Image in your Tree." *DNAeXplained - Genetic Genealogy.* August 4. Accessed January 2, 2022. https://www.dna-explained.com.

Eupedia contributors. 2015. "The Genetic Map of Europe." *Brilliant Maps.* April 21. Accessed October 9, 2021. https://www.brilliantmaps.com/the-genetic-map-of-Europe.

Find My Past. n.d. *Record Transcription: England Deaths & Burials 1538-1991.* Accessed April 14, 2020. https://www. findmypast.com/transcript?id=R_270475983.

Firth, Charles Harding, M.A. 1964. *The Last Years of the Protectorate, 1656-1658: Vol. II 1657-1658.* Reissued. New York: Russell & Russell, Inc.

Ford, Alan. n.d. "Force & Fear of Punishment: Protestants & Religious Coercion in Ireland, 1603-33 Chapter Four." *Academia.edu* . Accessed March 20, 2020.

1901. *Forebears.io.* Accessed Aug 2019. https://www.forebear.io/northern-ireland/ulster/antrim/ballymoney.

Forkan, Kevin. 2005. "Army List of the Ulster British Forces, 1642-1646." *Archivium Hibernicum* (Catholic Historical Society of Ireland) 59: 51-65. http://www.jstor.org/stable/402852202.

Forrest, Bob. 2008. "The Maiden City: The Inhabitants of the City of Derry/Londonderry Before the Siege (c.1600-1688)." Vers. Part Three. *CoTyroneIreland.com.* Accessed November 23, 2018.

Fraser, Antonia. 1979. *King Charles II.* London: Weidenfeld & Nicolson.

Gamble, Ronnie. 2016. *The Killowen Series 2: Militias & Rebellions* . Coleraine: Ronnie Gamble.

Gentles, Ian. 1997. "The New Model Officer Corps in 1647: A Collective Portrait." *Social History* (Taylor & Francis, Ltd.) 22 (No. 2): 127-44. Accessed April 26, 2020. https://www.jstor.org/stable/4286412.

Giguere, Georges-Emile. 1966, revised 2014. "Charles Albanel." *Dictionary of Canadian Biography, vol. 1.* Toronto: University of Toronto/Universite Laval. Accessed September 23, 2020. http://www.biographi.ca/en/bio/albanel_charles_1E.html.

Godkin, James. n.d. "The Rebellion of 1641: Extract from the Land-War in Ireland (1870), A History for the Times." *County Tyrone Ireland Genealogy Research.* Accessed August 16, 2019. https://cotyroneireland.com/muster/reb1641.html.

Grant, James. 1897. *British Battles on Land and Sea.* London: Cassell & Co., Ltd.

Great Britain, Public Record Office. 1878. *Calendar of State Papers, Domestic Series, 1652-1653; preserved in her Majesty's Public Recod Office.* Edited by Mary Anne Everett Green. London: Longman & CO.

—. 1964. *Calendar of State Papers, Domestic Series, James II; Preserved in the Public Record Office.* Vols. II, Jan 1686-May 1687. London: Her Majesty's Stationary Office.

—. 1860. *Calendar of State Papers, Domestic Series, of the Reign of Charles II; 1660-1661.* Edited by Mary Ann Everett Green. London: Longman, Green, Longman & Roberts.

Great Britain, Public Records Office. 1861. *Calendar of State Papers Domestic series of the Reign of Charles II: 1660-1662.* Edited by Mary Ann Everett Green. London: Longman, Green, Longman & Roberts.

Grenier, F. 1966, revised 2014. "Pierre Allemand." *Dictionary of Canadian Biography, vol. 1.* Toronto: University of Toronto/Universite Laval. Accessed September 11, 2020. http://www.biographi.a/en/bio/allemand_pierre_1E.html.

Gwynne, John. 1822. *Military Memoirs of the Great Civil War; Being the Military Memoirs of John Gwynne.* Edinburgh: printed by James Ballantyne & Co.

Hamilton, Sir F. W., K.C.B., Lieut.-Gen. 1874. *The Origin and History of the First of Grenadier Guards Vol. 1.* 3 vols. London: John Murray.

Hamilton, Sir James. 1867. *The Hamilton Manuscripts.* Edited by T.K. Lowry. Belfast: Archer & sons.

Harris, Jason. May 2007. "Ireland in Europe: Paolo Giovio's 'Descriptio', 1548." *Irish Historical Studies* XXXV (No. 139): 265-288.

Havranek, Rachael Hayden. 2014. "A Weed in the Corn: Surrender and Regrant in the 16th Century." *Academia.edu Web site.* May 15. Accessed 10 25, 2019. http://www.academia.edu.

Hay, Maciamo. 2021. "Haplogroup R1a (Y-DNA)." *Eupedia.com.* January. Accessed October 12, 2021. https://www.eupedia.com/europe/haplogroup_R1a_Y-DNA.shtml.

Helene Bourque, Donald Dion, Brigitte Ostiguy. 1999. *Island of Orleans: Enchanted Isle.* Quebec: Les Editions du Chien Rouge.

Henning, Basil Duke. 1983. "Strode, John II (1627-86), of Dover Castle, Kent." *History of Parliament Online.* Accessed July 24, 2018. http://www.historyofparliamentonline.org/volume/1660-1690/member/strode-john-ii-1627-86/of-dover-castle/kent.

Hill, Christopher. 1961. *The Century of Revolution; 1603-1714.* London: Routledge Classics.

Hill, J. Michael. 1993. "The Origins of the Scottish Plantations in Ulster to 1625: A Reinterpretation." *Journal of British Studies* (Campridge University Press on behalf of The North American Conference on British Studies) 32 (1): 24-43. Accessed March 13, 2018. http://www.jstor.org/stable/176018.

Hill, Rev. George. 1873. *An Historical Account of the MacDonnells of Antrim: Including Notices of Some Other Septs, Irish and Scottish.* Belfast: Archer & Sons.

—. 1877. *An Historical Account of the Plantation of Ulster at the Commencement of the 17th Century, 1608-1620.* Belfast: M'Caw, Stevenson & Orr.

—. 1865. *The Stewarts of Ballintoy.* Coleraine: John M'Combie.

Historical Manuscripts Commission. 1899. *Report on the Manuscripts of the Marquis of Ormonde, Preserved at the Castle, Kilkenny. Vol. II.* Manuscript, London: Eyre and Spottiswoode.

Historical Manuscripts Commission. 1895. *The Manuscripts of The Marquis of Ormonde, Preserved at The Castle, Kilkenny Vol.1.* Manuscripts, London: Eyre and Spottiswoode.

Hunter, R. J. 2012. *'Men and arms' The Ulster settlers, c. 1630.* Belfast: Ulster Historical Foundation.

—. 2018. *Plantations in Ulster, 1600-41.* Edited by Ian Montgomery & William Roulston. Belfast: Public Record Office of Northern Ireland & Ulster Historical Foundation.

n.d. *Irelands Eye.* Accessed May 11, 2019. http://www.irelandseye.com/aarticles/history/events/dates/earls.shtm.

n.d. *Irish Identity.* Accessed May 23, 2019. http://www.irishidentity.com/stories/normans.htm.

Irish Record Commissioner. 1830. "Calendar of Patent Rolls in Ireland of James I." Dublin.

Jette, Rene. 1983. *Dictionnaire Genealogique des Familles du Quebec.* Montreal: Les Presses de l'Universite de Montreal.

Johnson, Alice M. 1966. "Charles Bayly." *Dictionary of Canadian Biography, vol. I.* University of Toronto/ Universite Laval. Accessed July 20, 2020. http://www.biographi.ca/en/bio/bayly_charles_IE.html.

—. 1966, revised 1979. "John Abraham." *Dictionary of Canadian Biography, vol. 1.* Toronto: University of Toronto/Universite Laval.

—. 1966, revised 1979. "William Bond." *Dictionary of Canadian Biography, vol. 1.* Toronto: University of Toronto/Universite Laval.

Johnston, John. 1978. "The Scotch Settlement of County Fermanagh, 1610-1630." *Clogher Record* (Clogher Historical Society) vol. 9 (No. 3): pp. 367-373.

—. 2018. "Ulster Muster Rolls." *Plantations Family Conference.* Belfast: PRONIonline.

Jones, Clifford. 2015. *The Sea and the Sky; The History of the Royal Mathematial School of Christ's Hospital.* Horsham, West Sussex: Clifford Jones.

Jordan, Don. 2018. *The King's City.* New York: Pegasus Books, Ltd.

Khatchadourian, Raffi. 2021. "How Your Family Tree Could Catch a Killer." *The New Yorker*, November 15. https://www.newyorker.com/magazine/2021/11/22/how-your-family-tree-could-catch-a-killer.

Kirkland, Rev Trevor. 2018. "The Reformation in Ireland after 1536." *The Bulwark* 10-15.

L' Hotel Dieu de Quebec. 1662-1757. "Registre des Abjurations." Register , Quebec.

Laforest, Thomas J. 1999. *Our French-Canadian Ancestors.* Vol. XXVIII. Palm Harbor: The LISI Press.

Lamontagne, Leopold. 1966, revised 1979. "Pierre de Troyes." *Dictionary of Canadian Biography, vol. 1.* Toronto: University of Toronto/ Universite Laval. Accessed August 28, 2020.

Langlois, Michel. 1998. *Dictionnaire Biographique des Ancetres Quebecois (1608-1700).* Vols. 3, Lettre J. a M. Quebec: Archives Nationales du Quebec.

Lenihan, Padraig. 2001. *Confederate Catholics at War, 1641-49.* Cork: Cork University Press.

—. 2008. *Consolidating Conquest - Ireland 1603-1727.* Harlow, Essex: Pearson Education Limited.

Lewis, Samuel. 1840. *A Topographical Dictionary of Ireland Vol., 1.* London: S. Lewis & Co.

—. 1837. "Omagh: A Topographical Dictionary of Ireland." *Library Ireland.* Accessed November 2, 2019. https://www.libraryireland.com/topog/O/Omagh-Omagh-Tyrone.php.

Lieut.-Gen. Sir F. W. Hamilton, K.C.B. 1874. *The Origin and History of the First of Grenadier Guards.* Vol. 1. 3 vols. London: John Murray.

Lionel Jean, reviewer. updated 2019. "Hudson's Bay, The North Sea, 1682-1713." *New France.* June 6. Accessed September 12, 2020. http://www.axl.cefan.ulaval.ca/francophonie/Nlle-France-Baie_d'Hudson.html#7_La_Compagnie_de_la_Baie_du_Nord.

Lisle, Leanda de. 2017. *The White King; Charles I, Traitor, Murderer, Martyr.* New York: Public Affairs.

London Metropolitan Archives. 2010. "London, England, Church of England Baptisms, Marriages and Burials, 1538-1812." *Ancestry.com.* Ancestry.com Operations, Inc. Accessed August 2, 2020. http://www.ancestry.com/imageviewer/collections/1624/images/31280_194860-00078.

Longueville, Thomas. 1907. *Marshal Turenne.* London: Longmans, Green & Co.

Mac Giolla-Domhnaigh, Padraig. 1923. *Library Ireland.* Accessed May 2019. https://www.libraryireland.com/Anglicised Surnames/Moore-Mure-Muir.php.

Macafee, Bill. 2018. *Databases compiled from Seventeenth-Century Census Substitutes.* Accessed 2019. http://www.billmacafee.com.

Macauley, Iain. n.d. "The 1641 Rising & The English Civil War." *Fermanagh District Council.* Accessed March 20, 2020.

MacKay, Douglas. 1936. *The Honorable Company: A History of the Hudson's Bay Company.* Indianapolis & New York: The Bobbs-Merrill Company.

Mancke, Elizabeth. 1988. *A Company of Businessmen: The Hudson's Bay Company and Long-Distance Trade, 1670-1730.* Winnipeg: Rupert's Land Research Center.

Manuscript of Flatey, 1229. 1784. "Norwegian account of Olave, the Black King of Man, composed in the Islandic language by Thordr, a writer of the 13th century." In *Chronicon Manniae, or a Chronicle of the Kings of Man, Supposed to be Written, by the Monks of the Abbey of Russin*, 123. Perth: John Gillies.

Markus, Gilbert. 2012. *Place-Names of Bute.* Glasgow: Paul Watkins Publishing.

Marsh, Simon. 2016. "The Arming of the London Auxiliary Regiments to the Trained Bands During the Civil War." *Arquebusier* XXXXIV/VI: 19.

Martin, Dr. Daniel. 1999. *Carluke St. Andrew's Church.* Accessed May 2019. http://carluke-standrewschurch.org/history/.

McCavitt, John. 2002. *The Flight of the Earls.* Dublin: Gill & Macmillan.

McDermott, Marc. 2021. "Best DNA Test Kits." *Smarter Hobby.* November 17. Accessed January 2, 2022. http://smarterhobby.com.

McDonnell, Hector. 2004. *A History of Dunluce.* Environment & Heritage Service.

McGarry, Tim. 2015. "Minding Our Language - Ulster-Scots (Part 1)." *Forged in Ulster.* YouTube, December 22. https://www.youtube.com/warch?v=AMNRKeOVF9s.

McGurk, John. 2002. "The Kinsale Campaign Siege, Battle and Rout." *Seanchas Ardmgach: Journal of the Armagh Diocesan Historical Society* 19 (1): 59-69. Accessed Mar 3, 2020.

McShane, Angela. 2011. "Recruiting Citizens for Soldiers in Seventeenth-Century English Ballads." *Journal of Early Modern History* 105-137.

Mervyn, Sir Audley. 1642. *An Exact Relation of All Such Occurrences as Have Hapned in the Severall Counties of Donegall, London-Derry, Tyrone, and Fermanagh in the North of Ireland Since the Beginning of This Horrid, Bloody, and Unparaleld Rebellion There.* Report to the House of Commons, London: Printed Norton and Field, for Ralph Rounthwait, Bookseller.

Mesa, Eduardo de. 2014. *The Irish in the Spanish Armies in the Seventeenth Century.* Woodbridge, Suffolk: The Boydell Press.

Montgomery, William of Rosemount, Esq. 1869. *The Montgomery Manuscripts: 1603-1706.* Edited by Reverend George Hill. Belfast: Archer & Sons.

Moore, Kurt. 2010. *Electric Scotland.* Accessed May 17, 2017. http://www.electricscotland.com/escgi/print.pl.

Moore, Maurice. 2016. *Thomas Moore: Collection of Family Archives.* Quebec: self.

Morgan, Hiram. 1999. *Tyrone's Rebellion: The Outbreak of the Nine Years War in Tudor Ireland.* London: The Boydell Press.

Moriarty, G. Andrews. 1966, revised 1979. "Zachariah Gillam." *Dictionary of Canadian Biography, vol.1.* Toronto: University of Toronato/Universite Laval. Accessed July 20, 2020. http://www.biographi.ca/en/bio/gillam_zachariah_1E.html.

Munn, Alfred Moore. first published 1925, reprinted by Ballinascreen Historical Society 1985. *Notes on the Place Names of the Parish and Townlands of the County of Londonderry.* Cookstown / Draperstown.

Murdoch, Steve. 2008. "Anglo-Scottish Cultrue Clash? Scottish Identiries and Britishness, c. 1520-1750." *Cycnos* 25 (2): 245-266.

Mure, Sir William, Knight of Rowallan. 1825. *The Historie and Descent of the House of Rowallane.* Glasgow: Chalmers and Collins.

n.d. *Museum of London.* Accessed Sep 19, 2020. http://www.museumoflondon.org.uk/discover/great-fire-london-1666.

Nagel, Laswon Chase. 1982. *The Militia of London, 1641-1649.* PhD Thesis, London: no publisher.

Nute, Grace Lee. 2004 reprint of 1978 edition. *Caesars of the Wilderness; Medard Chouart, Sieur Des Groseilliers and Pierre Esprit Radisson, 1628-1710.* St. Paul: Minnesota Historical Society Press.

—. 1966, revised 2016. "Medard Chouart Des Groseilliers." *Dictionary of Canadian Biography, vol. 1.* Toronto: University of Toronto/Universite Laval. Accessed September 11, 2020. http://www.biographi.ca/en/bio/chouart_des_groseilliers_medard_1E.html.

—. 1969, revised 1982. "Pierre-Esprit Radisson." *Dictionary of Canadian Biography, vol.2.* Toronto: University of Toronto/Universite Laval. Accessed September 22, 2020. http:/www.biographi.ca/en/bio/radisson_pierre_esprit_2E.html.

O'Donovan, John. 1861. "The Maguires of Fermanagh." *Duffy's Hibernian Magazine*, April.

O'Neill, Dr. Eoin. 2009. "Elizabeth I and the Nine Years' War." Presentation at the 'Elizabeth I and Ireland' Conference, 12-14 Nov 2009, Storrs, University of Conneticut.

O'Neill, Eoin. 2009. "Towards a new interpretation of the Nine Year's War." *The Irish Sword* XXVI (no. 105): 241.

O'Neill, Margaret. 2014. *Lost Dunluce Town Reveals Plantation Secrets.* News Article, BBC News NI.

O'Sullivan, Harold. 2000. *John Bellew, a Seventeenth-Century Man of Many Parts; 1605-1679.* Dublin: Irish Academic Prss.

Ottawa River Heritage Designation Committee. 2005. "The Fur Trade along the Ottawa River." Vers. 2.5.7. *Canadian Heritage Rivers System.* QLF Canada. Accessed Jan 5, 2021. http://www.ottawariver.org/pdf/07-ch2-5.pdf.

Patterson, James. 1852. *History of the County of Ayr: with a Genealogical Account of the Families of Ayrshire.* Vols. Vol, II. Einburgh: Thomas George Stevenson.

Perceval-Maxwell, M. 1990. *The Scottish Migration to Ulster in the Reign of James I.* Belfast: Ulster Historical Foundation.

Plant, David. 2011. "Biography of Michael Jones." *BCW Project Biographies.* Accessed Apr 17, 2020. http://www.bcw-project.org/biography/michael-jones.

—. 2007. "Biography of Richard Cromwell." *BCW Project Biographies.* March 22. Accessed Feb 10, 2020. http://bcw-project.org/biography/richard-cromwell.

—. 2012. "Biography of Sir Thomas Fairfax." *BCW Project Biographies.* October 19. Accessed Feb 11, 2020. http://bcw-project.org/biography/sir-thomas-fairfax.

—. n.d. "Colonel John Moore's Regiment of Foot." *BCW Project.* Accessed Mar 1, 2018. http://wiki.bcw-project.org./commonwealth/foot-regiments/john-moore.

—. 2011. "Military Units of the Civil Wars, Commonwealth & Protectorate." *BCW Project.* Accessed April 4, 2020. http://bcw-project.org/military/units.

—. 2013. "The First Anglo-Dutch War: Military Overview." *BCW Project.* April 19. Accessed April 2, 2020. http://bcw-project.org/military/first-anglo-dutch-war/.

—. 2007. "The New Model Army." *BCW Project.* April 26. Accessed March 1, 2018. http://bcw-project.org/military/new-model-army.

Pothier, Bernard. 1969, revised 1982. "Pierre Le Moyne D'Iberville et D'Ardillieres." *Dictionary of Canadian Biography, vol. 2.* Toronto: University of Toronto/Universite Laval. Accessed August 25, 2020.

Pouliot, J. Camille. 1927. *Historical Reminder: Quebec and the Isle of Orleans.* Quebec: L'Action Sociale Ltee, Quebec.

Prendergast, John P., Esq. 1874. "Some Account of Sir Audley Mervyn, His Majesty's Prime Sergeant and Speaker in the House of Commons in Ireland, from 1661 till 1666." *Transactions of the Royal Historical Society* 3: 421-454.

Radisson, Pierre Esprit. 1885. *Voyages of Peter Esprit Radisson; transcribed from original manuscripts in the Bodleian Library and the British Museum with an introduction by Gideon D. Scull, London, England.* Cover design by Alex Struik, Coppell, TX, 21 July 2020. Boston: John Wilson and Son for the Prince Society.

Reid, John Eaton. 1864. *The History of the County of Bute and Certain Families Connected Therewith.* Glasgow: Thomas Murray and Son.

Ricardi Rawlinson, J. C. D. 1862. *Catalogi Codicum Manuscriptorum, Partis Quintae.* Codices, Bibliothecae Bodeianae , Oxford: Gulielmus D. Macray, A. M.

Ronald, Susan. 2007. *The Pirate Queen.* New York: HarperCollins Publishers.

Roots Ireland. n.d. *Derry/Londonderry Ancestry records online.* Accessed November 21, 2018. http://www.rootsireland.ie/derry.

Roy, Leon. 1978. *Les Terres de L'Ile d'Orleans.* Montreal: Bergeron & Fils.

Roy, Pierre Georges. 1928. *The Isle of Orleans.* Quebec: Historic Monuments Commission of the Province of Quebec.

Ruggles, Richard I. 1991. *A Country So Interesting: The Hudson's Bay Company and Two Centuries of Mapping 1670-1870.* Montreal & Kingston, London, Ithaca: McGill-Queen's University Press.

Salter, Mike. 2000. *The Castles of Kent.* Malvern: Folly Publications.

Simmons, Deidre. 2007. *Keepers of the Record: The History of the Hudson's Bay Company Archives.* Montreal & Kingston, London and Ithaca: Mc-Gill-Queen's University Press.

Smith, William J. 2013. "Towards a Cultural Geography of the 1641 Rising/Rebellion." In *Ireland: 1641-Contexts and Reactions*, edited by Micheal O' Siochru & Jane Ohlmeyer, 286. Manchester: Manchester University Press.

Snow, Dean R. 2001. "Scotland's Irish Origins." *Archaeology Magazine*, July/August: 2. https://www.archaeology.org.

Spencer, Dan. 2015. "The Provision of Artillery of the 1428 Expedition to France." *Journal of Medieval Military History, Vol. 13*, 179-192.

Statham, Samuel Percy. 1899. *The History of the Castle Town and Port of Dover.* Dover: Longmans, Green and Company.

Still, Gary. last updated 2018. *Red River Ancestry.* Accessed 2021. http://www.redriverancestry.ca.

Sweeting, Spike. 2014. *Capitalism, The State and Things: The Port of London, circa 1730-1800.* PhD Thesis, Warwick: University of Warwick, Department of History. http://www.go.warwick.ac.uk/wrap/67658.

Talbot, Eloi-Gerard. 1971-1978. *Genealogie des Familles Originaires des Comtes de Montmagny, L'Eslet, Bellechasse.* Vol. 11. Chateau-Richer, St. Charles: Chateau-Richer, Que., E.-G. Talbot.

The British Academy. 2002. *Provincial Towns in Early Modern England and Ireland: Change, Convergence and Divergence.* Edited by Peter Borsay & Lindsay Proudfoot. New York: Oxford University Press Inc.

The National Gazetteer. 1868. *The National Gazetteer of Great Britain & Ireland.* London: Virtue & Co.

n.d. "The Plantation of Ulster." *UlsterNationalist.freservers.* Accessed December 6, 2021. https://www.ulsternationalist.freeserves.com/custom2.html.

Thorman, G. E. 1966, revised 1979. "John Outlaw." *Dictionary of Canadian Biography, vol. 1.* Toronto: University of Toronto/Universite Laval. Accessed August 28, 2020. http://www.biographi.ca/en/bio/outlaw_john_1E.html.

—. 1969, revised 1982. "Thomas Moore." *Dictionary of Canadian Biography, vol. 2.* Toronto: University of Toronto/Universite Laval. Accessed August 21, 2020. http://www.biographi.ca/en/bio/moore_thomas_2E.html.

Tour, Henri de la. 1735. *The History of Henri de la Tour D'Aubergne, Viscount de Turenne, Marshal-General of France.* Vol. II. 3 vols. London: James Bettenbam.

Trinitiy College Library Dublin. n.d. "1641 Depositions." *http://1641.tcd.ie/depositions.* Accessed February 26, 2018.

Turcotte, L. P. 1867. *Histoire de L'Ile D'Orleans.* Quebec: Atelier Typographique du Canadien.

Ulster Ancestry. n.d. *The Story of the Army of the Laggan.* Accessed July 24, 2018. http://www.ulsterancestry.com/newsletter-content.php?id=509.

Ulster-Scots Agency. 2006. "The Dawn of the Ulster-Scots Heritage Trail." Belfast, NI: Ulster-Scots Agency. http://www.HamiltonMontgomery1606.com.

—. 2007. "The Story of the Presbyterians in Ulster; Pocket History and Heritage Trail." Belfast, NI: Ulster-Scots Agency.

Walsh, Dennis. 2003. *Ireland's History in Maps; The Baronies of Ireland (Ulster).* Accessed September 29, 2020. https://www.sites.rootsweb.com/~irlkik/ihm/barony-map-ulster.htm.

Walter, John. 2013. "Performative Violence and the Politics of Violence in the 1641 Depositions." In *Ireland: 1641 - Context and Reactions*, by edited by Micheal O' Siochru' & Jane Ohlmeyer, 286. Manchester: Manchester University Press.

Wanklyn, Malcolm. 2016. *Reconstructing the New Model Army, Vol 2: Regimental Lists 1649-1663.* Solihull: Helion & Co. Ltd.

—. 2015. *Reconstructing the New Model Army, Vol. 1: Regimental Lists April 1645 to May 1649.* Solihull: Helion & Company Ltd.

Watkins, Sarah-Beth. 2019. "The Tragic Daughters of Charles I." 165. Alresford, Hampshire, UK: John Hunt Publishing Ltd.

Wikipedia contributers. 2021. "Charles d'Albert d'Ailly." *Wikipedia, The Free Encyclopedia.* June 23. Accessed May 12, 2022. https://en.wikipedia.org/w/index.php?title=Charles_d%27Albert_d%27Ailly&oldid=1030110169.

Wikipedia Contributors. 2021. "List of Norwegian Monarchs." *Wikipedia, The Free Encyclopedia.* August 22. Accessed September 4, 2021. https://en.wikipedia.org/w/index.php?title=List_of_Norwegian_Monarchs&oldid=1040058730.

—. 2021. "List of Rulers of the Kingdom of the Isles." *Wikipedia, the Free Encyclopedia.* August 30. Accessed September 16, 2021. https://en.wikipedia.org/w/index.php?title=List_of_rulers_of_the_Kindom_of_the_Isles&oldid=1041352948.

Wilson, Clifford P. 1966, revised 1979. "John Bridgar." *Dictionary of Canadian Biography, vol. 1.* Toronto: University of Toronto/Universite Laval. Accessed September 22, 2020. http://www.biographi.ca/en/bio/bridgar_john_1E.html.

Woodcock, George. 1970. *The Hudson's Bay Company.* New York: Crowell-Coller Press.

Yirka, Bob. 2019. *Genetic study shows deep Norwegian lineage in people of northern Scotland.* Press Release, Medical Xpress. Accessed September 28, 2021. https://medicalxpress.com/news/2019-09-genetic-deep-norwegian-lineage-people.html.

Zoltvany, Yves F. 1969, revised 1982. "Charles Aubert de la Chesnaye." *Dictionary of Canadian Biography, vol. 2.* Toronto: University of Toronto/Universite Laval. Accessed May 12, 2022. http://www.biographi.ca/en/bio/aubert_de_la_chesnaye_charles_2E.html.

INDEX

E

F

G

H

I

J

K

L

M

N

O

CPSIA information can be obtained
at www.ICGtesting.com
Printed in the USA
BVHW022045251122
652771BV00031B/549

9 781737 643654